Demokratie, Sicherheit, Frieden
Democracy, Security, Peace

herausgegeben von Hans-Joachim Gießmann
Series Editor Hans-Joachim Gießmann

begründet von Dieter S. Lutz †
founded by Dieter S. Lutz †

DSF   Band 174
DSP   Volume 174

Eine Veröffentlichung aus dem Institut für
Friedensforschung und Sicherheitspolitik
an der Universität Hamburg

A publication of the Institute for Peace Research and
Security Policy at the University of Hamburg

Andrea Berg/Anna Kreikemeyer (eds.)

Realities of Transformation

Democratization Policies in Central Asia Revisited

Nomos

Die Deutsche Bibliothek – CIP-Einheitsaufnahme

Die Deutsche Bibliothek verzeichnet diese Publikation in
der Deutschen Nationalbibliografie; detaillierte bibliografische
Daten sind im Internet über http://dnb.ddb.de abrufbar.

Bibliographic information published by Die Deutsche Bibliothek

Die Deutsche Bibliothek lists this publication in the Deutsche
Nationalbibliografie; detailed bibliographic data is available
in the Internet at http://dnb.ddb.de.

ISBN 3-8329-1637-7

1. Auflage 2006
© Nomos Verlagsgesellschaft, Baden-Baden 2006. Printed in Germany. Alle Rechte,
auch die des Nachdrucks von Auszügen, der photomechanischen Wiedergabe und der
Übersetzung, vorbehalten. Gedruckt auf alterungsbeständigem Papier.

This work is subject to copyright. All rights are reserved, whether the whole or part of
the material is concerned, specifically those of translation, reprinting, re-use of illustrations, broadcasting, reproduction by photocopying machine or similar means, and
storage in data banks. Under § 54 of the German Copyright Law where copies are made
for other than private use a fee is payable to »Verwertungsgesellschaft Wort«, Munich.

Contents

Acknowledgements   7

Andrea Berg/Anna Kreikemeyer
Introduction: Democratization Policies in Central Asia Revisited   9

Part I: Democratization of Power Structures?

Paul Georg Geiss
State and Regime Change in Central Asia   23

Judith Beyer
Rhetoric of 'Transformation'. The Case of the Kyrgyz
Constitutional Reform   43

Farkhod Tolipov
Power, Nation-Building and Legacy – A Comparative
Analysis of Central Asian Leadership   63

Atyrkul Alisheva
Kyrgyzstan: The Public and the Authorities   81

Part II: Democratization through External Actors?

Anna Kreikemeyer
Balancing Between Commitments and Co-operation.
The OSCE in Central Asia   101

Andrea Berg/Anna Kreikemeyer
The ODIHR Human Rights Monitoring and Reporting
Training. A Cross-National Analysis   117

Andrea Berg
Who's Afraid of George Soros? The Conflict Between
Authoritarian Rulers and International Actors in Central Asia   127

Part III: Democratization of the Judicial Sector?

Marina Pikulina
Power Structures and Problems of Law Implementation
in Uzbekistan   143

Sofiya Issenova
Reform of the Judicial System in Kazakhstan:
Review of the Effectiveness of OSCE Efforts   157

Dosym Satpayev
Creating Mechanisms for Social Lobbying in Kazakhstan   179

Sofiya Issenova
Quasi-Judicial Institutions. The Ombudsman in Kazakhstan   191

Part IV: Security through Democratization?

Andrea Berg
All Eyes on Central Asia. Disintegration in Kyrgyzstan
and Uzbekistan   211

Anna Kreikemeyer
Instability in the Ferghana Valley: International Reactions   227

Appendix: Relations Between Central Asian States and
Multilateral Organizations. A Chronology
(compiled by John Myraunet and Fausta Šimaitytė)   249

Contributors   265

Acknowledgements

In the era of globalization, democratization has become a universal trend, and this does not exclude Central Asia. However, there is some evidence that many international organizations lack tailor-made democratization strategies as well as in-depth knowledge of the Central Asian states. Furthermore, scholars and practitioners are trying to get to the bottom of the correlation between democratization and security.

The drafting for the project *"Security through democratization? A theoretically based analysis of security-related democratization efforts made by the OSCE"* was initiated in 2001 at the Centre for OSCE Research (CORE) in Hamburg. In January 2003, the research project focusing on developments in Kazakhstan, Kyrgyzstan and Uzbekistan was started. Throughout the project, the aim was to produce useful comparative analyses that might shed light on individual issues or states, and on regional similarities or differences.

This book is the outcome of the collaborative work by a core team led by Andrea Berg and Anna Kreikemeyer (Centre for OSCE Research in Hamburg, Germany). The team is comprised of the following persons: Atyrkul Alisheva (Institute for Regional Studies in Bishkek, Kyrgyzstan), Sofia Issenova (Global Internet Policy Initiative in Almaty, Kazakhstan), Marina Pikulina (S-Monitor Group in Tashkent, Uzbekistan), Dosym Satpaev (Assessment Risks Group in Almaty, Kazakhstan), and Farkhod Tolipov (University of World Economy and Diplomacy in Tashkent, Uzbekistan). Judith Beyer (Max-Planck-Institute for Social Anthropology in Halle, Germany) and Paul Georg Geiss (Department of Political Science at the University of Vienna, Austria) provided additional articles. John Myraunet and Fausta Šimaitytė compiled the chronology of OSCE activities in Central Asia.

Many people and institutions have been involved in making this study possible and in enabling the publication of this book. We are particularly grateful to the Volkswagen Foundation for providing generous financial support for the whole research project.

The authors also received organizational support and helpful advice in the form of interviews with representatives of the delegations of the Central Asian states to the OSCE in Vienna, with officers in the OSCE Centres in Almaty, Bishkek and Tashkent, and with the ODIHR in Warsaw, who helped with collecting data on the Human Rights Monitoring and Reporting Training and offered to organize a side event at the Human Dimension Seminar in May 2004. Last but not least, we also received help from the German Delegation at the OSCE and the Conflict Prevention Centre of the OSCE as well as other OSCE units.

We wish to thank Dr. Wolfgang Zellner, Acting Head of CORE, who provided encouragement, time and energy to the research group. We gratefully acknowledge the assistance of Burkhard Conrad and Fausta Šimaitytė. Further, we are indebted to Veronica Trespalacios and Elizabeth Hormann for their skilful technical assistance with the editing process and proofreading of the manuscript. Special thanks go to Jacob Holm Jorgensen who edited the English texts provided by our Central Asian partners, combining in-depth knowledge on the region with great sensitivity for translations issues.

This project has engaged a good deal of professional energy from the research team over the last three years. For all of us, the project and exchange of opinions has been very enriching. We hope that the readers of this book share the same experience.

Hamburg, November 2005

Andrea Berg/Anna Kreikemeyer

Introduction: Democratization Policies in Central Asia Revisited

Many arguments have been made to prove or confute the view that democracy is a universal value. Regardless of the pros and cons, the international community decided to make democracy-building one of the key elements of foreign policy in the early 1990s. "Fostering democracy actively – be it in the form of democratization support or democratization pressure – is at the top of Western foreign political agendas today ... In addition to normative reasons the external effect of initiating peace and order is seen as the most important legitimation. [This is in line with a certain] self confidence about one's own systemic superiority that has begun to characterize the external behaviour of democratic states especially in the field of ‚humanitarian intervention'."[1]

This attitude is rooted in the high expectations of democratization after the political events in Eastern Europe in the late 1980s and the dissolution of the Soviet Union in 1991 to the effect that democracy is approached as merely a matter of time.[2] Assuming the expansion of the "third wave of democratization",[3] the optimistic view "that despite unfavourable economic and social context conditions democracies could be 'made'",[4] was nourished. The euphoria initiated by the fall of the Iron Curtain washed away more sceptical approaches toward transition. As early as the mid 1980s, O'Donnell and Schmitter drew the conclusion from analysing political change in Latin America and Southern Europe that transition is an open process that leads "from certain authoritarian regimes toward an uncertain 'something else'. That 'something else' can be the establishment of a political democracy or the restoration of a new, and possibly more severe, form of authoritarian rule. The outcome can also be simply confusion, that is, the rotation in power of successive governments, which fail to provide any enduring or predictable solution to the problem of institutionalizing political power. Transitions can also develop into widespread, violent confrontations, eventually giving way to revolutionary regimes which promote changes going far beyond the political realm."[5]

Analysing the implementation of aid policies in Eastern Europe, Wedel wrote at the beginning of the new century: "Thus, in the early days of independ-

---

1   Müller 2002: 47.
2   Wedel called the period in the early 1990s "triumphalism" followed by a phase of "disillusionment" and a phase of "adjustment". Cf. Wedel 2001: 7.
3   The "third wave of democratization" refers to the transitions to democracy in Southern Europe and Latin America in the 1970s and 1980s. Cf. Huntington 1991.
4   Croissant 2002: 10.
5   O'Donnell/Schmitter 1986: 3.

ence, Central and Eastern Europe and the West were in agreement: the West would help the East, and the East would show its gratitude through loyalty and quick reform."[6] After a decade of independence, analysts were faced with the fact that, although the newly independent states started the process of transition from the same point of origin, as a non-democratic type of regime, neither the courses nor the aims of the transition processes were uniform or standardized as a result. Post-Soviet transition can at best be described in most cases as "transitions from something that is not democracy to something that is or tries to be or at least pretends to be democracy".[7]

Research on political developments in post-Soviet Central Asia still too often revolves around the questions of why democracy has not taken root and what the obstacles to democracy-building are. The five newly independent states are characterized as democracies with adjectives such as "illiberal democracies", "authoritarian democracies", "neo-patrimonial democracies," "pseudo democracies" or "proto democracies".[8] All these representations of democracy have one common feature: they conceptualize the current regimes by comparing them to consolidated liberal democracies. In consequence, the situation in the region is evaluated as a failure of democratization; yet, the abandonment of this ideological bias and the recognition of political realities in the region are often lacking. However, such an approach is not only typical for the analysis of (non)-democratization in Central Asia. In their detailed and fascinating article on regime change without democratization in the Middle East, Albrecht and Schlumberger argue, "what we should investigate from a comparative politics perspective is not the 'failure' of democracy or democratization, but rather the 'success' of authoritarianism in the Middle East and North Africa".[9] In fact, doubt should be cast on whether we are actually getting closer to understanding political change in Central Asia, or to creating solutions to political problems by talking about "failed democratization". Would it not be more fruitful to act on the assumption that the results of political change are open, and to analyse their dynamics instead?

In this book, we argue that the three Central Asian countries – Kazakhstan, Kyrgyzstan and Uzbekistan – do not belong to a third wave of democratization, but to "a fourth wave of regime change – to democracy and dictatorship".[10] Yet, we also maintain that democracy – or the "rhetoric of democracy" – is, nevertheless, a main source of legitimacy for the rulers as well as for civil society activists. Our main focus is on providing insights into the wide range of transformation realities encountered by the various institutions and actors.

---

6 Wedel 2001: 22.
7 Nodia 1996: 17.
8 See Zakharia 1997.
9 Albrecht/Schlumberger 2003: 6.
10 McFaul 2002: 213.

Democratization versus maintaining power?

According to the thesis of democratic peace, which has been under discussion for almost 20 years, democracy, institutional co-operation and security reinforce each other.[11] Thus, in general, democratization by external actors appears as an instrument of conflict prevention.[12] However, several authors question this linear correlation. Mansfield and Snyder point to the fact that under the conditions of institutional weakness, democratization from the outside could generate conflicts. Especially in the early stages of democratization, liberalization seems to be conflict-prone. An incomplete democratization continuously carries heightened risks. The introduction of new instruments such as elections, election campaigns and competition into the political process could produce a state of opposition between persons, ideas or interests.[13] In fact, these arguments confirm our research results especially with regard to the Kyrgyzstan parliamentary elections of spring 2005.

In Central Asia, the claim of fostering security through democratization has to be viewed against the background of a complex political situation. Several values and norms exist parallel to one another: the Soviet heritage, regionalism, clientelism and tribal affiliation among others. Formal and informal institutions mix steadily with the effect of control deficits. A kind of "institutionalized informalism"[14] characterizes the economic structures and decision-making processes of rent-seeking, exclusive distribution coalitions and corruption. Of utmost importance is power maintenance in such a context.[15] Political leaders act within an area of tension between different internal client groups on whom the president is dependent to varying degrees. In order to maintain power, influential positions are used as a resource by the respective leader and are distributed among relatives, loyal allies or representatives of different client groups.[16] This manner of "recruitment" prevents institutional autonomy as well as economic reform.

The fact that economic and political power are interlinked and remain mostly in the hands of a few persons as well as the fact that economic reforms have not led to economic wealth for the majority of the population are very problematic. The distribution of resources among the traditional business elites, in combination with declining living standards, leads to the socio-economic exclusion of certain societal groups. In addition, ethnic, religious and economic fragmentation aggravates such trends.

Our findings underline that it is highly contentious to analyse these developments as a temporary phenomena that will fade away in the foreseeable fu-

---

11 For further information on democratic peace see Sandschneider 2003; Hasenclever 2002; Kahl/Teusch 1998 and earlier Rittberger 1987; Czempiel 1986.
12 See Lund 1998, 1996; Matthies 1997.
13 See Mansfield/Snyder 1995; Schlotter 2002; Kahl/Teusch 1999, 1998.
14 Rüb 2002: 111.
15 Cummings et. al. 2002 gives a detailed overview on the careers of the five Central Asian presidents.
16 See Khegai 2004; Cohen 2003; Gullette 2002; Collins 2000; Vaisman 1995.

ture. In the current situation, it seems much more likely that the political regimes of some of these countries have acquired serious political persistence without having fulfilled the criteria of democratic consolidation. According to McFaul, in many cases, these regimes are just as consolidated as the liberal democracies. In his view, power is the decisive factor for the development of a transformation regime. A dictatorial autocracy of ruling from above is only stable as long as power relations are clear.[17]

The evaluations of international organizations stress the limits of their co-operation with authoritarian regimes in Central Asia in a self-critical manner. The conditioning of aid (i.e. the fulfilment of commitments to human rights norms) by several external actors is foiled by the wholehearted support of the regimes by other external actors.[18] Thus, all external actors must pay attention to the question of how they can uphold the dialogue with the current leaders and contribute to further reform without strengthening elite networks by providing them with financial resources.

While many scholars cover the democratization policies of the UN[19] and of the US[20], the EU[21] and the OSCE still need considerable research, especially with respect to the CIS states. The OSCE has a programmatic goal of integrating human rights and democracy in its concept of comprehensive security. From this, it draws its legitimization to interfere in a limited and co-operative manner in the internal affairs of its participating States in cases of grave violations of human rights, democracy and rule of law in order to re-establish security and stability. In this way, it connects the norms of the security dimension to those of the human dimension in a unique way. The democratization policy of the OSCE is thus legitimized not only by the goal of fostering democracy, but also indirectly by aiming at averting dangers to stability and security. Therefore, it is assumed to have a conflict prevention role.[22] Yet, we scarcely have empirical evidence for this role, especially with respect toward its field activities in non-democratic regimes.[23] Many articles in this book cover certain activities or policies of the OSCE and thus contribute to a better understanding of its role in Central Asia.

---

17 See Crossant 2002, Mc Faul 2003. A comparable continuation of a political transitory situation, prolongued transitions or continuous transitional conditions that develop into a regime character can be observed for Africa. Here Müller talks about a peripherisation comparable to Africa. Cf. Müller 2002: 17, see also Erdmann 2002.
18 See Berg/Kreikemeyer/Rahmonova-Schwarz 2004.
19 See Joyner 1997.
20 See Robinson 1996.
21 See List 1997.
22 See Siekman 1994.
23 "It can not be ruled out that, in the long term, regular monitoring with respect to human rights standards that regularly leads to negative assessments as well as the work of field missions contribute to a democratization of political systems by heightening domestic pressure. However, they can as well lead to a de facto retreat of these states from the OSCE in a kind of 'sulky self-isolation'. Due to the brief experience here we cannot yet draw concrete conclusions about the effects of the OSCE and its activites on these countries." Schlotter 2000: 19-20; see also Flynn/Farrell 1999; on Bosnia-Herzegovina see du Pont 2000, 1999.

Structure of the book

Part I: Democratization of Power Structures?

In his article, *Geiss* introduces state and regime change in Central Asia as an example for social change in non-European societies. He criticizes the normative character of the concept of transition and relates the political changes in Central Asia to those in non-European societies such as Africa, the Middle East or Latin America, where concepts like personal rule, patrimonialism, or neo-patrimonialism can better explain "the dominance of highly personalized and privatized post-colonial state structures, which, only in formal terms, established 'modern' bureaucratic polities".[24] In Geiss' view, the model of the "bureaucratic developmental state" is especially apt for explaining political change in Central Asia. Here "the development problem [...] appears to be fundamentally a political one and is, as such, linked to the question of how bureaucratic developmental state structures can be strengthened in order to overcome patrimonialism and the established primacy of politics in legal and administrative processes."[25]

In the second article, *Beyer* shows the effects of the Western concept of "transformation" and the respective rhetoric on the Kyrgyz constitutional reform in 2003 and contrasts this with an anthropological approach. She criticizes the frequent equation of the term "transformation" with real-life social change occurring today. She also points out that one is also dealing with a powerful rhetoric that has found its way out of Western scientific discourses into public discourses in the Central Asian states.[26] According to Beyer, these roots can be traced back to the Soviet era. This is one of the reasons why she prefers an anthropological account of "transformation", which is characterized by long-term field research and an actor-centred approach and supports a pluralistic concept of culture.

Tolipov provides a comparative analysis of Central Asian leadership with a special focus on power, nation-building and the legacy of authoritarian rulers. The article deals with their roles, images, status and personal characteristics, their accession to and retaining of power, how they rule their respective countries and the expected effects of their soon-to-be ending presidencies. Tolipov poses questions such as: "What are the power resources of presidents and their political regimes? What types of leadership exist? Who are those leaders who share a common background that dates back to the Soviet period? Do they shape the common future of Central Asia?"[27] One of his main arguments is that all five leaders are authoritarian rulers, whose apparatus often plays the

---

24   Geiss in this volume, p. 23.
25   Ibid., p. 36.
26   Cf. Beyer in this volume, p. 41.
27   Tolipov in this volume, p. 61.

role of real, albeit informal, state power and keeps control of the other power branches.

In the last article of Part I, *Alisheva* focuses on the relationship between the public and the authorities in Kyrgyzstan before the turmoil in March 2005. Since Alisheva is the director of a local NGO in Kyrgyzstan, she was able to provide many interesting insights into the role of civil society – namely political parties, non-governmental organizations and the local self-government. In her view, all political parties lack clear programmes and fail to involve the public. This is why their impact in the political system has been quite insignificant. Civil society does not have any influence on economic, social, nor political reforms in the country either, because policy-making is almost exclusively reserved for governmental institutions. She very much appreciates a first public dialogue with the participation of officials of the highest level, which was initiated by civil society with the active support of the OSCE. Finally, she sees an important factor in the democratization of both political life and political institutions in human rights education and demands a nation-wide training programme for democracy in order to strengthen the political culture especially that of the younger generation.

Part II: Democratization through External Actors?

The second part of the book focuses on problems of democratization through external actors. *Kreikemeyer* analyses the relationship between the OSCE and its Central Asian participating States. She recapitulates four different stages in the development of this relationship. With a special emphasis on the implementation of the concept of comprehensive security, she sheds light on specific, political, strategic and instrumental challenges. In her view, the OSCE will only be able to make contributions to the reform processes when the governments accept it. The attitude of the different regimes depends to a great extent on the balance of OSCE security dimensions at the project level on the ground. Given the still authoritarian character of the regimes in Central Asia, however, an important issue for the Organization is the compatibility of anti-terrorist activities with human rights. Concerning work in the field, the knowledge base of informal institutions, typical of the region's institutional landscape, needs to be improved. Furthermore, field missions should try to integrate this political context constructively without lowering its normative standards. In comparison to other institutions, the core strength of the OSCE lies in its political capabilities to work both with the authorities and with civil society on the ground and, at the same time, on an international level in the areas of promoting dialogue, conflict prevention and conflict management.

In the following cross-national analysis, *Berg* and *Kreikemeyer* analyse the effects of a concrete activity by the OSCE as an external actor on a certain target group. The authors chose an OSCE project that took place in all of the three countries included in the research project, the ODIHR Human Rights

Monitoring and Reporting Training. Questions focused on organizational aspects of the seminar as well as on content. Two questions were designed to find out about the link between the participants and the respective OSCE Centres. Several questions were dedicated to the influence of the seminar on the participant's successive work. While the evaluations of the exchange of experience between trainer and participants differed to a great extent, most respondents agreed that the training was successful with respect to adaptability, impact, cost effectiveness and visibility. The competency of the OSCE in human rights issues was judged positively.

In the third article in this part of the book, *Berg* analyses the tensions between authoritarian rulers and international actors in Central Asia. Berg identifies policy patterns used by the presidents in Central Asia with respect to their relations with international actors in order to maintain power. "This process of maintaining power is interrupted when international organizations keep adhering to standards for elections, and prior to elections, hold seminars on elections, election observation and similar topics."[28] Furthermore, she discusses dynastic potentials in Kazakhstan, Kyrgyzstan and Uzbekistan. Regarding pre-emptive strategies focusing on arguments and measures employed by the present rulers against international actors, Berg carefully studies their behaviour both towards George Soros' Open Society Institute (OSI) and the OSCE. The author notes that, as the fear of a potential spread of "coloured revolutions" seems to be growing, since the events in Uzbekistan in May 2005, Kazakhstan has also begun to restrict the activities of external non-governmental and international organizations.

Part III: Democratization of the Judicial Sector?

The third part of the book includes four articles on the democratization of the judicial sector. In her article, *Pikulina* outlines the existing "non-separation of powers" and discusses the issue of drafting and adopting laws, on the one hand, and the (non)-implementation of these laws, on the other. Finally, she analyses the effect of legal reforms on economic activities and provides insight into the role of the OSCE in the reform process. She argues that, in Uzbekistan, reforms take place mainly on paper while there is a huge gap with respect to implementation. The main factor hindering the development of the rule of law is the "administrative structure, the lack of separation of powers and the dominance of particular interests".[29] Permanent changes in the legislation and in sub-normative acts have led to disorientation, especially for farmers, traders and small businesses, who are not always familiar with the current legislation. The OSCE has tried to help reform the judicial and legal systems of Uzbekistan, but the structure of both the government and society hinder changes. What is needed, according to Pikulina, is a reform of

---

28   Berg in this volume, p. 129.
29   Pikulina in this volume, p. 141.

the executive branch and educational programmes focusing on the culture of pluralism and democracy.

Issenova discusses the judicial system of Kazakhstan. Her article features an analysis of major achievements and challenges related to the implementation of the reform. Its main components are the re-organization of courts and law enforcement bodies, the introduction of the life-long appointment of judges and the staffing of the judiciary, the implementation of measures aimed at raising judges' status and the level of welfare and the establishment of special institutions to ensure the effective implementation of justice and judicature. The independence of judges and the rules of appointment are especially challenging in a political system in which the executive power is hardly counterbalanced by the legislative power. Issenova draws the conclusion that in many instances, the judicial reform, as such, has failed to ensure the true independence of judges from political influence. Regarding the contributions of the OSCE to the judicial reform in Kazakhstan, she provides a review of the events organized by the Supreme Court and the OSCE Centre in Almaty within the framework of methodological and consulting assistance. In her final recommendations on prospective sectors of OSCE assistance in future judicial reform, Issenova stresses the need for training and an increased transparency of appointments and trials.

In the third article of this chapter, *Satpaev* describes the current state of lobbyism in Kazakhstan as a still corporative model of lobbyism in contrast to the pluralist model, which prevails in democracies. He analyses current legal efforts as well as preconditions both in the political system and in society for improving the basis for social lobbying. In his view, it is not yet possible to talk about the existence of a third sector, "as it is still impossible to try to uncover and express social interests without having mechanisms for their defense against the authority".[30] For this purpose, the third sector has to improve its vague notions of the decision-making procedure as well as of the legal sphere. In Satpaev's view, the OSCE must play an important role in supporting the evolution of a republican political system toward openness of dialogue with civil society. This could contribute to both local and national efforts to establish mechanisms for social lobbying by organizing respective training activities for representatives of NGOs and for state employees.

In the fourth article, *Issenova* analyses the efficiency of the ombudsman as a new democratic institution in the political system of Kazakhstan. After introducing various ombudsman functions and models, she discusses the limitations of the human rights commission under the president, which led to the establishment of an ombudsman. Special emphasis is again given to the critical aspects of the appointment procedure, independence, confidentiality and pluralism. In the development of the draft law, the main stumbling block was the procedure for the ombudsman's appointment. According to experts from the administration, it would be difficult to avoid non-transparency and to rely

---

30   Satpaev in this voulme, p. 181.

on the appointed person's independence, since the ombudsman has to be appointed by the president in the last analysis. A comparative analysis of the range of powers and the competence of the ombudsman in other countries of the Central Asian region (Kyrgyzstan, Uzbekistan) leads to the conclusion that the authority this institution has in Kazakhstan is limited. Issenova argues that the administrative reforms in Kazakhstan have peaked and therefore have now entered a stagnation period.

Part IV: Security through Democratization?

While the security situation in Central Asia seemed rather stable at the beginning of the research project in 2003, this changed in late 2004 and early 2005. The two articles in the fourth and last part of this book have a special focus on these developments.
Berg discusses the turmoil in Kyrgyzstan in March 2005 and the Andijan massacre in Uzbekistan in May 2005. She provides information on the course of both events as well as on the political and socio-economic background. She argues that, after the March events and the presidential elections on 10 July 2005, the situation in Kyrgyzstan has been characterized by destabilization and a fragile security situation. Furthermore, the so-called "Tulip Revolution" was not a regime change, but a power change. It did not fundamentally alter the patrimonial networks in Kyrgyzstan, but did destabilize the central authority's ability to allocate resources. As regards the events in Andijan, Berg highlights the reality of insufficient information and an ongoing "information war". She compares several reports of international institutions and international non-governmental organizations. Looking toward the future, she underscores the importance of the rule of law for the internal and external security of both countries and reminds readers of the importance of legal security.
In the second article, *Kreikemeyer* surveys international reactions to the above-mentioned events. Her key question tackles the following issues: "What are the reactions of neighbouring states, hegemonic powers, multilateral and donor organizations as well as non-governmental organizations? What can we learn from their behaviour in this Central Asian crisis? What will be the consequences for future stability in this region?"[31] While she discusses the behaviour of the neighbouring Central Asian states in the first part of the article, in the second part she analyses the responses of the three hegemonic powers, China, Russia and the United States, which are competing for influence in Central Asia, especially in the energy sector. The third part deals with the state of multilateralism in terms of the stability crisis. Here Kreikemeyer examines the development of a post-Soviet multilateralism into a multi-vector one and the co-operation and integration of it into the framework of the Commonwealth of Independent States (CIS), the Shanghai Co-

---

31 Kreikemeyer in this volume, pp. 221-222.

operation Organization (SCO) and the OSCE. She also reflects on the mostly Western international organizations such as the European Union (EU) and international financial institutions such as the European Bank for Reconstruction and Development (EBRD). Finally, and in contrast, she discusses the reactions of international human rights organizations.

Bibliography

Albrecht, Holger/Oliver Schlumberger. 2003. ‚Waiting for Godot'. Regime change without democratization in the Middle East. Paper prepared for the Fourth Mediterranean Social and Political Research Meeting, Florence, 19-23 March.
Berg, Andrea/Anna Kreikemeyer/Delia Rahmonova-Schwarz. 2004. Wie sicher ist die Seidenstraße? Stabilitätsgefährdungen in Zentralasien. In: Christoph Weller/Ulrich Ratsch/Reinhard Mutz/Bruno Schoch/Corinna Hauswedell (Eds), *Friedensgutachten 2004*, Münster 2004, pp. 98-106.
Cohen, Abraham. 2003. Are Central Asia's Weak States Getting Weaker? In: *Central Asia – Caucasus Analyst*, February 12.
Collins, Kathleen A. 2000. *Clans, Pacts, and Politics: Understanding Regime Transition in Central Asia*. Stanford, pp. 93-141.
Croissant, Aurel. 2002. Demokratische Grauzonen – Konturen und Konzepte eines Forschungszweigs. In: Bendel, Petra/Aurel Croissant/Friedbert W. Rüb (Eds) *Zwischen Demokratie und Diktatur. Zur Konzeption und Empirie demokratischer Grauzonen*. Opladen, pp. 9-53.
Cummings, Sally N. (ed.). 2002. *Power and change in Central Asia*. London, 2002.
Czempiel, Ernst-Otto. 1986. *Friedensstrategien: Systemwandel durch internationale Organisationen, Demokratisierung und Wirtschaft*. Paderborn.
Erdmann, Gero. 2002. Neopatrimoniale Herrschaft – oder: Warum es in Afrika so viele Hybridregime gibt. In: Bendel, Petra/Aurel Croissant/Friedbert W. Rüb (Eds), *Zwischen Demokratie und Diktatur. Zur Konzeption und Empirie demokratischer Grauzonen*. Opladen 2002, pp. 323-43.
Flynn, Gregory/Henry Farrell. 1999. Piecing Together the Democratic Peace: The CSCE, Norms, and the "Construction" of Security in Post-Cold War Europe. In: *International Organization*, (53) 3, pp. 505-535.
Gullette, David. 2002. Tribalism in Kyrgyzstan examined. In: *Central Asia and the Caucasus*, (14) 2, pp. 31-37.
Hasenclever, Andreas. 2002. The democratic Peace meets International Institutions. In: *Zeitschrift für Internationale Beziehungen*, 1, pp. 75-111.
Huntington, Samuel. 1991. *The Third Wave. Democratisation in the Late Twentieth Century*. University of Oklahoma Press.
Joyner, Christopher. 1997. The United Nations and Democracy. In: *Global Governance*, (5) 3, pp. 333-358
Kahl, Martin/Ulrich Teusch. 1998. Zur Bedeutung interner Verfasstheit für das auswärtige Verhalten von Staaten. In: Carlo Masala/Ralf Roloff (Eds), *Herausforderungen der Realpolitik*, Köln.
Lauth, Hans-Joachim/Liebert, Ulrike (Eds). 1999. *Im Schatten demokratischer Legitimität. Informelle Institutionen und politische Partizipation im interkulturellen Demokratievergleich*. Opladen /Wiesbaden.
List, Martin. 1997. Demokratisierungspolitik – vergleichend und kritisch betrachtet. In: *Politische Vierteljahresschrift* (38) 2, pp. 338-343.
Lund, Michael S. 1996. *Preventing Violent Conflicts: A Strategy for Preventive Diplomacy*. Washington.
Lund, Michael S. 1998. Preventing Violent Conflicts. Progress and Shortfall. In: Peter Cross (ed.), *Contributing to Preventing Action*. CPN-Yearbook 1997/98, Baden-Baden, pp.15-59.

Mansfield, Edward/Jack Snyder. 2002. Democratic Transitions, Institutional Strength, and War. In: *International Organization*, (56) 2, pp. 297-337.
Mansfield, Edward D./Jack Snyder. 1995. Democratisation and War. In: *Foreign Affairs* (74) 3, , pp. 79-97.
Matthies, Volker. 1997. *Der gelungene Friede. Beispiele und Bedingungen erfolgreicher friedlicher Konfliktbearbeitung*. Bonn.
McFaul, Michael. 2002. The Fourth Wave of Democracy *And* Dictatorship. Noncooperative Transitions in the Postcommunist World. In: *World Politics*, (54) 2.
Müller, Harald. 2002. Antinomien des demokratischen Friedens. In: *Politische Vierteljahresschrift*, (43) 1, pp. 46-81.
Nodia, Ghia. 1996. How Different Are Postcommunist Transitions? In: *Journal of Democracy*, (4) 7.
O'Donnell, Guillermo/Schmitter, Philippe C. 1986. *Transitions from Authoritarian Rule. Tentative Conclusions about Uncertain Democracies*. Baltimore and London: The Johns Hopkins University Press.
Pont, Yannick du. 1999. Der Chancengleichheit den Boden bereiten: Demokratisierung durch Förderung eines pluralistischen und gemäßigten Parteiensystems in Bosnien und Herzegowina. In: Institut für Friedensforschung und Sicherheitspolitik an der Universität Hamburg/IFSH (Ed.): *OSZE- Jahrbuch 1999*. Baden-Baden, pp. 345-364.
Pont, Yannick du. 2000. *Bringing Civil Society to Bosnia & Herzegovina. OSCE measures to develop Civil Society*. Amsterdam.
Rittberger, Volker. 1987. Zur Friedensfähigkeit von Demokratien. In: *Apuz* (B 44), pp. 3-12.
Robinson, William I. 1996. *Promoting Polyarchy: Globalization, US Intervention, and Hegemony*. Cambridge.
Rüb, Friedbert W. 2002. Zwischen Demokratie und Diktatur. Zur Konzeption und Empirie demokratischer Grauzonen. Opladen, pp. 23-118.
Sandschneider, Eberhard. 2003. *Externe Einflüsse auf Institutionenbildung in Transformationsprozessen*. In: http://www.angoy.de/hw/projekte/sfb/d2.htm [10.10.2005.]
Schlotter, Peter. 2000. Die OSZE. Leistungsfähigkeit einer internationalen Organisation. In: *Die Friedens-Warte. Journal for International Peace and Oganisation*, (75) 1, pp. 11-30.
Siekmann, Rob. 1994. The Linkage between Peace and Security and Human Rights in the CSCE Process. In: *Helsinki-Monitor* (5) 1, pp. 43-51.
Vaisman, Demian. 1995. Regionalism and Clan Loyality in the Political Life of Uzbekistan. In: Ro'i, Yaacov (Ed.) 1995: *Muslim Eurasia, Conflicting Legacy*, Ilford, pp. 105-122.
Wedel, Janine R. 2001. *Collision and Collusion. The Strange Case of Western Aid to Eastern Europe*. New York: Palgrave.
Zakaria, Fareed. 1997. The Rise of Illiberal Democracy. In: *Foreign Affairs*, (76) 6.

Part I:
Democratization
of Power Structures?

Paul Georg Geiss

State and Regime Change in Central Asia

Although most political scientists agree that the dominance of regionalism and political clientelism makes Central Asian politics different from politics in Western democracies,[1] this empirical fact has not led to alternative conceptual frameworks in the study of regime change. Political change continues to be conceptualized as a transition process from totalitarian Soviet regimes to some kind of democratic political order. This is the case, although most scholars agree that this kind of transformation was not successful and that the more promising democratic reform countries, such as Kazakhstan and Kyrgyzstan, also ended up becoming "authoritarian" regimes during the 1990s. This view is partly convergent with local accounts of political change, which also presume a transition period, but disagree about the nature of the current regimes.[2]

Western analysts hold the contrasting view that a Central Asian country like Kazakhstan "could have developed a pluralistic or quasi-pluralistic political system and a transparent market economy if its leaders had only shown the will to discipline themselves."[3] According to this view, Central Asian elites failed to truly liberalize political participation, hindered the emergence of independent mass media and fell short of organizing free and fair elections, strengthening parliamentarism, decentralizing state structures, combating corruption, and establishing the rule of law. In a nutshell, they failed to overcome their democratic deficits and deficiencies in the transitional process.

As many African, Asian and Latin American regimes of the Third Wave of democratization, those of Kyrgyzstan and Kazakhstan did not move towards the Western model and still do not seem able to overcome the problem of "democratic consolidation". Therefore, transitologists started conceptualizing these relatively stable pseudo-democracies as a distinct regime type which they called "delegative",[4] "illiberal",[5] "obstructed",[6] or "defective democracies",[7] or which they identified as "hybrid regimes" consisting of a mixture of both "authoritarian" *and* "democratic" regime properties.[8]

The current conceptualization of political change as a process from totalitarian and authoritarian to democratic regimes is misleading and grasps only shallow features of political system change and continuity in the newly inde-

---

1 See Collins 2003; Cummings 2002; Luong 2002.
2 See Geiss 2000.
3 Brill Olcott 2002: 2.
4 See O'Donnell 1994.
5 See Zakaria 1997.
6 See Schubert/Tetzlaff 1998.
7 See Merkel 1999.
8 See Rüb 2002.

pendent states. This is true for two main and related reasons: one is linked to the fact that Central Asian societies established quite different societal constraints in politics, which makes it difficult to apply accumulative knowledge gained from the systems change in European societies. The other is connected with the highly influential triad of democratic, authoritarian and totalitarian systems, which Juan Linz authored in his research article in the Handbook of Political Science.[9] This is problematic, although it became a credo in the field of comparative politics and seemed to fit the research needs of more than one generation of political scientists studying democratic and non-democratic regime change. Nevertheless, Linz's influential definition of authoritarianism was not based on a theory of state or society. It only provided an analytical elaboration of a rather political perception of regime types in Europe and Latin America and extended it to non-European societies. In this way, authoritarian regimes were defined as non-democratic "systems with limited, not responsible, political pluralism" and as non-totalitarian due to their lack of an "elaborate and guiding ideology" and of "intensive political mobilization".[10] Both theories of democracy and totalitarianism, however, only delivered normative, i.e. essentialist arguments on why this analytical differentiation qualified to guide empirical research. Scholarly debate was rather focused on the exact properties, which differentiate these political systems, and the distinguishable subtypes, which enable the measuring of the exact status of real regimes on their way toward a liberal democracy.

Whereas the Euro-centric perspective (containing the goal of establishing democratic constitutional states) might be proper to analyse regime and system change in Southern and Eastern Europe – where political elites made or still make tremendous efforts to be eligible to join the European Union and align(ed) state institutions and processes of political exchange to Western legal and administrative standards – this perspective has already raised serious concerns in Latin America. Although state structures seem to be based on political community structures only to a limited extent, in Latin America – where the constitutional state with its rationale bureaucracy has only been established in a few countries like Brazil and to a certain extent Chile – this perspective seems inadequate. The analysis of the African "democratic experiment" of all 29 former single-party states, where contested elections were held at the beginning of the 1990s, heralded more doubts about the validity of this approach. Even the most optimistic analyst could not interpret this new wave of African democratic transition as a move towards liberal democracy. This is largely due to state decay and highly personalized and privatized state structures.[11] In Asia, the impact of different cultural dimensions of authority and community structures define societal parameters for democratization that

---

9 See Linz 1975.
10 Linz 1964; Linz 1975: 264.
11 See Bratton/Van de Walle 1997.

would only appear deficient when measured against Western standards, which are unsuitable for comparison in this context.[12]

Lacking a theory of societal change in European and non-European countries and being mainly concerned with the horizons of action of political elites and institutional arrangements, transitology did not pay much attention to the cultural dimension of authority and to the political community structures which shape formal and informal institutions and the socio-cultural embedment of law and constitutions.[13] Given that it was committed to a political systematization of regime types, it also did not grasp the need to base a theory of regime change on a theory of societal change and to relate contemporary regime types to the state structures involved. It is the state type and its communal and socio-cultural embedment in societies that define constraints on institutions, regime change and liberalization in the sphere of political change. For this reason, we will have to sketch different state types in non-European societies in order to be able to conclude on their applicability in a Central Asian context.

States in non-European societies

The debates and scholarly endeavours to discuss and differentiate state structures in Middle Eastern, African, Asian and Latin American studies are relatively isolated. Since the 1980s, Africanists have introduced concepts like personal rule, patrimonialism or neo-patrimonialism in order to explain the dominance of highly personalized and privatized post-colonial state structures, which, only in formal terms, established "modern" bureaucratic polities. Current democratization and transition research still attribute high heuristic value to this concept – which aimed at specifying Max Weber's archetype of patrimonial state authority – even though Africanists disagree to which extent (neo-)patrimonialism relies on legal-rational bureaucratic elements and whether it can be institutionalized, as well as whether it represents a transitional or an independent hybrid system type; and whether all African states based on democratic and non-democratic regimes can be described as neo-patrimonial.[14] However, scholars less familiar with this Weberian tradition developed their own concepts to describe African state structures and their decay.

In Middle East Studies, the (neo-)patrimonial state and the concept of *rentier* states are the two established state models of political studies. Both secular regimes and traditional monarchies with "modernized" bureaucracies work in a similar way, and the debate about the hyphenated "neo-" in front of the term "patrimonialism" is not as rigorous as it is among Africanists. Neverthe-

---

12 See for example Pye 1985; Geiss 2004 b.
13 See Geiss 2002 a.
14 See e.g. Erdmann 2002.

less, numerous studies on Middle Eastern *rentier* states seem to suggest that *rentier* states and patrimonial states are different state types.

Although Latin American studies provided the base for authoritarianism and democratization research, a quick overview of the literature reveals that the applied analytical frameworks to the study of state structures remain diffuse. Despite O'Donnell's influential work on Brazil and Argentina being new types of bureaucratic-authoritarian states, which accentuate the dominance of technocratic-bureaucratic roles and the constraints put on the "popular sector",[15] countries like Brazil continue to be described as patrimonial states whose privatization of offices keep performance capacities low.

When scholars of Asian studies describe political regimes as bureaucratic-military, patrimonial or sultanistic, it is often unclear whether similar or different types of state structures are involved – although there is agreement that the state plays a decisive role in promoting economic growth. Thus, the apparently arbitrary use of state and regime types in area studies seems to only represent the arbitrary conceptualizations and approaches to comparative politics, which do not sufficiently differentiate between political systems and regime types. In state-centric societies, political systems do not only comprise administrative structures, but also the spheres of political exchange (regime), law and constitution which emerge from the interpenetration of the administrative system with the economic, communal and socio-cultural subsystems of a society. For this reason, the Anglo-American opposition of state and (civil) society more often than not has hindered the analysis of political change in non-European societies.

Since a comparative analysis of the often isolated debates in area studies has not yet been undertaken from the perspective of historical sociology, we, for the time being, hold the neo-patrimonial state and the bureaucratic developmental state as representing two basic political systems or state types in non-European societies to which various schools of thought and state concepts can be referred and to which the transitological agenda of regime change has to be related.[16]

The (neo-)patrimonial state

The concept of the "patrimonial state" goes back to Max Weber's political sociology and his ideal type of traditional authority.[17] Patrimonial authority – such as gerontocracy, patriarchalism and feudalism – is a form of traditional authority based on the "sanctity of age-old rules and powers"[18] and established by relations of loyalty between the ruler and the ruled. In contrast to

---

15 See O'Donnell 1973, 1978; Collier 1979.
16 See Wimmer 2000; Hartmann 1997;
17 See Weber (1921-1925) 1972: 130-40, 580-653
18 Weber 1978: 226.

other forms of traditional authority, political obedience is no longer rooted in a legal community of companions, but based on relations of piety and faithfulness between master and the submissive dependents (e.g. bondmen and servants) who care for their master's needs within the domain (Greek: *oikos*) and whose interests are only considered according to usage and local customs. Due to the political extension of this form of state authority to extra-patrimonial[19] territories and people and the establishment of an administrative staff, patrimonial states emerged, which did not acknowledge a division of public and private spheres and which were quite common as ruling organizations in European and extra-European history. This kind of political administration continued to be regarded as a personal affair of the ruler, who would levy taxes as a useful supplement to his own property. The patrimonial offices do not have clearly defined jurisdictions and responsibilities; their holders can be patrimonially recruited servants, freely recruited "favourites of all kind"[20] and independent officials who enter the service of the ruler. Thus, the ideal type of the patrimonial state is conceptually opposed to the rational bureaucratic state which is based on expert officialdom, rationalized bureaucratic hierarchies, prescribed career tracks and contracted salary and pension rights and which Weber analysed with reference to the emergence of the modern Prussian state.

It was Guenter Roth who introduced the concept of patrimonialism to comparative politics at the end of the 1960s,[21] and this spread an understanding of patrimonialism in terms of patron-client relations and political clientelism. This became a major research concept in the 1970s and 1980s.[22] A second track of reception of this Weberian concept was established by Shmuel N. Eisenstadt, who observed that many regimes in decolonized Asian and African societies maintained many features of patrimonialism and personal rule, although "modern" bureaucratic administrations had been established. Due to this merging of "traditional" and "modern" features, he called these regimes (neo-)patrimonial.[23] This concept of patrimonialism as a regime type also found supporters among comparativists.[24] Even though patrimonialism as a regime type may be able to explain short-term electoral changes, it still seems unfit for the analysis of the problem of political change, since regime change does not involve administrative and legal structures.[25] It is rather proposed here that patrimonialism be conceptualized as specific state or political system type in which the constitutional, legal and political exchange spheres (regimes) are little developed and undifferentiated.

---

19 The Roman *patrimonium* (patrimony) was the paternal household in which the *pater familias* (father of the family) ruled over all members.
20 Weber 1978: 228.
21 See Roth 1968.
22 See Gellner 1982.
23 See Eisenstadt 1973.
24 See Snyder, 1992; Bratton/Van de Walle 1994, 1997.
25 See Engel/Erdmann 2002..

In order to analyse political system change in Egypt, Peter Pawelka introduced a model of (neo-)patrimonial state, where the ruler directs "all political decisions through a network of personal relationships" and in which "neither state officials nor institutions ... can maintain any independence."[26] Power is concentrated within society by a centralized apparatus (bureaucracy) and within this apparatus through the personal traits of the political leader. In this power structure, administrative elites compete for attention from the ruler and his close circle, and for consideration of their ideas, programmes and interests in the administrative decision-making process. Performance and malfunctions of these political systems depend highly on the political skills and abilities of the ruler. "The permanent disputes and rivalries within the elite impede the emergence and development of long-term goals and the efficient employment of capacities to solve problems. Due to the balancing of competing groups, patrimonialism turned out to be remarkably stable."[27]

On analysing state structures in pre-Soviet, Soviet and independent Central Asia, I used a similar concept of patrimonial state, based on action theory and made use of the voluntaristic interpenetration theory of Richard Münch.[28] The persistence of (neo-)patrimonial rule in the region became visible by way of personal loyalty relations between members of the personal and bureaucratic administration; and their head continued to ensure state unity and relative political stability.

In the Muslim patrimonial states *amlokdors* (tax inspectors) and *begs* (wealthy persons) were obedient to the *khan* (ruler) or *emir* (commander) and openly demonstrated submissiveness with gifts and flatteries. This is similar to the way first secretaries of the *oblast'* (region) and *rayon* (district) committees showed loyalty to the first secretary of the republic. These types of loyalty relations and clientelism shaped all spheres of the Soviet party and state structures –and emphasized the Secretary General as its ultimate and highest point of reference. National independence did not change these types of authority relations. Since the 1990s, the unity of the state has been secured by the loyalty of *hakims* (mayors), governors and governmental elites to the president, who had become much stronger and who, because of the dissolution of Soviet Union mechanisms of control, had usurped the power to appoint all officials and were no longer controlled by any superiors. Due to the state control of resources, the ruling elites control the means to secure loyalty and trust and to give patronage and render clientelism a material base.[29] The earlier Soviet destruction of local legal cultures established the dominance of politics in the area and erased legal constraints, which could regulate political succession, as was the case in the pre-Soviet patrimonial states where Is-

---

26   See Pawelka 1985.
27   Pawelka 1985: 25f.
28   See Geiss 2003: 86-96, 126-237.
29   See Geiss 2004 a; Geiss 2002 b: 10-15.

lamic, Mongol and other customary traditions both shaped dynastic and electoral forms of political succession.[30]

Bureaucratic developmental state

During the last 40 years, only a few non-European societies have successfully undergone sustainable processes of industrialization and achieved economic growth rates averaging above four per cent annually. States like South Korea, Taiwan and China in East Asia, Singapore and Malaysia in South East Asia and Botswana in Africa belong to this group. As not all of them had authoritarian regimes, this economic success cannot be linked to a particular regime type, exclusively. Instead, Adrian Leftwich proposed to explain this enormous economic success with reference to a particular state type, which he called the developmental state.[31] It was Chalmers Johnson who introduced this concept of the state to development studies at the beginning of the 1980s by analysing the successful Japanese and Taiwanese development models. In doing so, he made apparent the shortcomings of earlier schools which proclaimed state dependency on class structures and on the system of world economy, and which tended to interpret non-European states in economic terms.[32]

In his comparative study of political and economic change, Leftwich identified six main features of the developmental state, which he regarded as necessary for a successful industrialization of society:

1. The existence of a nationally minded political-military elite aimed at industrializing their society to secure its statehood and to defend it against external threats.
2. The relative autonomy of state institutions and elites from particularistic demands of private, class, regional or sectoral interest groups and the capacity to pursue national developmental goals. This autonomy, however, was embedded in a dense network of both governmental and non-governmental actors.
3. A powerful, competent and insulated economic bureaucracy concentrated in key state agencies like the Ministry of International Trade and Industry in Japan, the Economic Planning Board in South Korea and the Council of Economic Planning in Taiwan and, which promoted – in contrast to neo-liberal economic orthodoxies – the establishment of their own competitive export-oriented industries with a policy mix of economic reforms, protectionism, strategic investments and financial control.

---

30 See Geiss 2001.
31 See Leftwich 1995.
32 See Johnson 1982.

4. Weakness of social classes and of private interest groups.
5. Effective management of non-state economic interests by promoting a "corporatist economy" and private economic institutions.
6. Legitimating the developmental state by economic success and the establishment of a social infrastructure (education, health, roads, public housing programmes etc.).

This list of the developmental state's properties is by no means exhaustive, but shows similarities with the bureaucratic-authoritarian state which Latin Americanists observed in countries like Argentina and Brazil of the 1960s and 1970s and which are also analysed as "authoritarian corporatism" in comparative politics.[33] Although O'Donnell's analysis of authoritarian state structures has been criticized for its socio-economic bias and most Latin American authoritarian regimes were not, or were only based on weak developmental state structures, some of the analysed features of the bureaucratic authoritarian state (e.g. its controlling and regulatory capacity, its capacity to penetrate society, dominance of technocratic and formal-bureaucratic roles and techniques of ruling, the state as strategic promoter of economic growth and of export-led national economies) were acknowledged in scholarly debates.[34] Bruce Cumings called authoritarian Asian developmental states "bureaucratic-authoritarian industrialising regimes" and identified similar features of statehood as causal factors for the dramatic economic performance of East Asia.[35]

We prefer to use the concept of developmental state over other terms with a similar empirical reference subject, due to its sounder use as a basic concept for its democratic and authoritarian subtypes. The latter is contrasted with concepts like the bureaucratic-authoritarian state, which identifies this state type with the specific type of regime. Also, the bureaucratic developmental state is not to be mistaken with the state in the so-called "developing countries", as some scholars argued in the 1980s,[36] but instead refers to a state type, which empowers reform-oriented and reform-skilled elites to formulate and achieve economic and social developmental goals. On differentiating regime and state types, political continuity can also be better analysed in many non-European neo-patrimonial societies where autocratic and democratic regime types frequently change.

Various approaches in the field of the comparative study of state structures can be referred to two basic types of statehood: Gunnar Myrdal's concept of the "soft state",[37] and Joel S. Migdals "state capacity approach", which differentiates weak and strong states,[38] or more recent endeavours to establish

---

33 See Schmitter 1979.
34 See Collier 1979; Wimmer 1996.
35 See Cumings 1987.
36 See Simonis 1985.
37 See Myrdal 1970.
38 See Migdal 1988.

typologies of states with regard to the efficiency of the rule of law and the degree of democratic legitimacy,[39] or with regard to the state's relative autonomy and implementation capacity.[40] From the perspective of sociology of development, the bureaucratic developmental state appears to overcome patrimonial statehood by advancing public and state interests over the private and particularistic interests of officials and politicians, by protecting property rights and by promoting legal regulation of the economy and of politics.[41]

Even if the problems of statehood and the malfunctions of (neo-)patrimonial administrations can be compared with European absolutist states in the 17th and 18th centuries due to the importance of and dependence on the ruler's personal traits and skills, these similarities do not imply that the differentiation of the political system in non-European societies promotes a convergence of state structures. This is true because statehood is always embedded in societies in a historical-specific way and emerges from the interpenetration of other societal spheres; structures or action orientations within the sphere of political exchange emerge from the interpenetration of the administrative and the economic system. Legal systems materialize from the interpenetration of administrative and communal action orientations, whereas regulating constitutional orders originate from the interpenetration of administrative and socio-cultural subsystems of a society. The latter is based on the value discourse of a society and enables the socially binding construction of symbols.[42] For this reason, particular state structures will also be shaped by communal commitments and cultural orientations of specific societies after political community structures and normative order have been formed.

Still of necessity is a comparative, systematic and sociologically guided analysis of non-European political systems which relates the constitutional, legal, administrative and regime structures of a political system to the economic, communal and socio-cultural subsystems of a society, and which is aimed at constructing a sociologically-based typology of political systems by comparing states and societies and linking the state of the art in comparative law, administration and politics with political sociology. Such a research project could modify and refine the used differentiation of the basic state types which I have proposed in this study.

State structures and political change in independent Central Asia

Up until the 1980s, Sovietologists held the view that the Soviet Union established strong state structures and that its economic and political capacity of societal penetration relied on formal organizational roles. Party and adminis-

---

39 See Rüb 2003.
40 See Croissant 2003.
41 See Wimmer 2000.
42 See Münch 1992: 29-51, 303-530; Münch, 1987: 45-64, 76-123.

trative apparatuses were submitted to the party leadership in a hierarchical vertical power structure, which was much more able to establish an effective central government than Tsarist Russia was. More recent empirical studies challenged this view and described – even for the Stalinist period – everything but a tightly organized and centrally controlled party structure outside of Moscow.[43] Informal networks did not only put constraints on central state institutions,[44] but also appropriated a considerable share of economic and political resources controlled by the centre, and led to widespread forms of "economic corruption".[45] The significance and influence of these informal networks of the Soviet nomenklatura were exposed and became highly visible in post-Soviet Russia, when state assets were privatized.

In all Central Asian republics, national independence initially increased the patrimonialization of the state structures. The breakdown of the Soviet-planned economy and of the interregional division of labour, the abolishment of financial transfers and subsidized goods decreased available resources to maintain the Soviet welfare state and to fund health and education services. As a result, political elites also started to question the previous social responsibilities of the state. This increasingly led to a narrow perception of public interests in terms of political stability and interethnic peace. The dissolution of the Soviet Union also dried up the centrally controlled allocation channels of goods and services to the mass population and took away the central control mechanism to secure cheap supplies of basic commodities.

It was the more personal rule of former first party secretaries as elected presidents, which followed the balanced institutional net of external actors (the KGB, military-industrial complex, military, public prosecutor, centrally controlled plants, trade unions, etc.) and internal republican elites (regional party and administrative cadres) under the leadership of the Communist Party of the Soviet Union and its Secretary General. These newly elected presidents became powerful, as they started to become responsible for the cadre policy within the administrative and economic structures according to their own volition. Due to the lack of legal regulations on politics,[46] or strong military structures, it was the staff policy of the president, which increasingly helped secure the unity of the state.

In striving for international recognition and for domestic secular legitimacy, all Central Asian states enforced constitutions, which formally adopted many articles from Western constitutions, but actually provided only a legal framework for the dominant position of the president in relation to the executive, legislative and judicial branches of power.[47] Since the efficient monop-

---

43 See Getty 1986; Pethyridge 1990.
44 See Willerton 1992.
45 See Rutland 1993.
46 See Geiss 2001.
47 See Constitution of the Republic of Kyrgyzstan 1998, §§ 46-53; Constitution of the Republic of Uzbekistan 1992, § 92; Constitution of the Republic of Turkmenistan 1997, §§ 54-60.

oly of coercive force depends on personal relations of piety and loyalty between administrative staff members and their head, the strong position of the president seems to correspond to the demands of patrimonial politics. The head of state does not only symbolize the state's unity, but also appears as a de-facto guardian of political stability and of the order of the state. For this reason, criticism of the president and his office is perceived as calling into question the polity's order and, as such, is sanctioned by intimidation, rigorous tax inspections and actions of slander, even in the supposedly more liberal Central Asian republics like Kazakhstan and Kyrgyzstan.

Under these circumstances, completely free democratic elections pose considerable threats and challenges to the political stability of the state. If the supreme position of leadership becomes vacant, various networks of political groups and regional elites will compete for more political influence and try to marginalize or neutralize their opponents by forming new political alliances. On the one hand, if one candidate is able to win the power struggle and becomes the head of state, he will try to regain political balance and integrate regional and republican elites by transferring influential administrative offices to influential people of his choice. On the other hand, he will try to deprive his direct opponents of power. However, the re-establishment of the political balance is not always successful. Due to the low level of legal constraints, political succession is often problematic and fuels domestic unrest, which may sometimes lead to civil wars, as was the case in Tajikistan.

In view of the president's power position and the dependence of political stability on his person, it is not astonishing that the Central Asian presidents have tried to minimize the political risks of elections by controlling central and regional electoral commissions, the registration process of parties and candidates, and by influencing the coverage by the mass media. Up to now state elites have found political and legal ways to extend the limit of two constitutional terms in office for all acting Central Asian presidents, be it through the political instrument of referenda, through sophisticated constitutional expertise about the second term nature of the president's next period in office, or through constitutional amendments. Due to increasingly similar patrimonial state structures, the problem of political succession in Central Asia does not differ from those experienced in many states in Africa and the Middle East, nor has the ethnicization of state and society changed the cultural preferences of economic and political elites for informal arrangements. The latter has aimed at establishing the nation state as the normative political order after the fall of communism took over some of the public agenda.

The Tajik civil war also indicated the political dynamics that could emerge if the ruling elites are not ready to form informal political alliances with competing regional leaders and ignore the normative implications of their rule. Thus, the ruling elites from Khujand (Leninabad) tried to conserve communism as a normative base of authority even after the failed August-coup of 1991, and were thus not receptive for a new evaluation of the political role of

Islam and the titular nationality's cultural heritage. For this reason, elites from the marginalized southern regions like the Gharm valley and Qurghonteppa started to interpret and legitimize their political opposition in more Islamic terms and successfully mobilized their fellow countrymen against the ruling elites from Khujand and Kulob. This led to the civil war of 1992, which caused 50,000 deaths and hundreds of thousands of displaced persons.

The Tajik civil war also showed that personal rule, to a significant extent, depends on the political skills of the ruling elite. On the one hand, wrong perceptions of the domestic interrelations of forces could quickly drive the political situation out of control. On the other hand, personal predilections or the paranoia of ruling presidents could strongly shape public life and considerably hinder the proper functioning of state and economy. For example, the increasing seclusion of Uzbekistan from the Uzbek minorities in neighbouring border regions, the economic remoteness and the harsh and counter-productive policy toward Islam is explained by the amplified security needs of the president after the failed assassination attempts of 1999. This is especially true for Turkmenistan, where the completely unpredictable domestic and foreign policies are shaped by the sudden changes of mind, personal preferences and the paranoia of president Saparmurad Niyazov or *Turkmenbashy* the Great, as he is officially called now.

In the thirteen years of national independence, significant political, economic and cultural changes have occurred in all Central Asian republics and have led to processes of differentiation of the Soviet state structures, which, despite the initial trends of patrimonialization, show considerable differences now.

Tajikistan

In Tajikistan, the civil war of 1992 caused the decay of central state structures. Only after the UN-mediated peace agreement of 1997 did a long-drawn-out reconciliation process integrate the leading members of the United Tajik Opposition into the state apparatus and prevent Tajikistan from becoming a failed state. In the following ruling, president Rahmonov used his strong position to marginalize opposition parties in the presidential election of 1999 and the parliamentary elections of 2000 and 2005 by no longer granting 30 per cent of the senior governmental offices to members of the opposition, as had been agreed to before. Nevertheless, central governmental control remained low in regions like the Gharm valley or the Pamir, where local leaders – loosely allied with the Islamic opposition – continued to maintain control on state and security apparatuses. It was not only the civil war, but also the breakdown of the planned economy and the central resource allocation, which, in particular, hit Tajikistan. Tajikistan is one of the least economically developed Soviet republics. With the exception of the aluminium plant in Ghizar, it lacks industrial branches capable of bringing in hard currency. Due to the low state revenues and the augmenting control of state institutions by followers of the president from his home and power base in Kulob, the Tajik state can hardly serve – beyond the particularistic demands of its ruling elite – public interests which are now basically identified with peace and securing political stability. Western NGOs and the Ismailian Aga-Khan Development Network in Badakhshon increasingly provide the funding of welfare facilities. Legal and constitutional systems continue to play only minor roles in the political system.

Kyrgyzstan

Central state structures in Kyrgyzstan remain, but they are no longer able to perform all previous state functions. The Batken crisis of 1999 and 2000, caused by Uzbek Islamist groups occupying Southern Kyrgyz villages, indicated the weakness of the state in the domains of the underfunded military and security apparatus. Many facilities in the public health and education sector are only able to continue functioning with the help of NGOs supported by Western donor organizations. Due to the dominance of northern Kyrgyz clientele networks and the weakness of president Akaev to put through state interests against private interests of officials, patrimonial structures increasingly set the tone in the country, although the privatization of state assets (factories, sovkhozes, kolkhozes) limited the scope of available resources. Indicators of this development are the bureaucracy's low competence in economic policy, increasing foreign debt, rising dependency on Western aid, the irregular and delayed payment of state salaries, the short-term appointments of ministers, governors, *akims* and of the officials appointed by the latter. For this reason, the pressure has increased on officials to amortize "business allowances" and to grant gifts to superiors for having gained access to state resources during the period of office.

It is not yet clear whether the successful oppositional coup of March 2005[48] has only resulted in leadership change, or whether the new president Kurmanbek Bakiyev (from the south) and the designated prime minister Felix Kulov (from the north) want and will also be able to change state structures by promoting legal and administrative reforms. First reports on the recruitment of officials and the performance of the interim government have not spread optimistic prospects for such a change. The astonishingly high 89 per cent vote for Bakiyev in the presidential elections of July 2005, which allowed only political lightweights to contest against the incumbent, also increases doubts on the current view that the March coup promoted a regime change in Kyrgyzstan. The first six months of the new government's term has

---

48   For more details on this event see the article by Berg in the part IV of this volume.

only seen the replacement of governmental elites by a new political alliance, which might better politically represent both northern and southern Kyrgyzstan.

Uzbekistan

Uzbekistan is the Central Asian republic which has conserved the inherited Soviet state structures to the greatest extent. The state continued to control mature economic branches and to dispose of the revenues from the export of cotton, gold and other raw materials. The Kolkhoz system survived within newly founded peasant associations, which are still forced to accept state orders for the cultivation of land and to purchase exclusive rights on grain and cotton. This state control of resources and a slightly more effective tax system enabled the funding of the state's infrastructure and of social welfare transfers such as the payment of child benefits and public assistance for the poor. This was made possible through the newly established local administration, the *mahalla*-committee (neighbourhood-committee), even though it is only low-scale. Nevertheless, the high degree of state control opened up abundant opportunities to misappropriate economic resources to officials and their clientele. In comparison to Tajikistan and Kyrgyzstan, state structures more tightly control the population with the help of police and security apparatuses. Whereas the constitutional system remains undifferentiated, bodies of legal protection only represent – as in Soviet times – an extension of the administrative structure, a situation that remains highly politicized.

Turkmenistan

Turkmen national independence and statehood is highly shaped by the personality of the president. Niyazov, has had an accelerated elite circulation since the mid 1990s. It was during this time that he started making short-term appointments of ministers and governors and increasingly replaced Russophile "fellow combatants" and senior ministers with young inexperienced Turkmen. At the same time, his officials developed a cult of personality and a system of preceding obedience, which allows president Niyazov to now rule according to his own will and judgement without being bound to informal rules on how to use and share power. Thus, the current political system may be described as an extreme form of (neo-)patrimonial rule where the unity of the formal-bureaucratic state relies exclusively on the personal loyalty and obedience of the officials and the ability of the head of state to rule freely and unrestrained. In this extreme form of patrimonial rule, loyalty is no longer backed by patronage, protection and the good will of the ruler, but is instead extremely one-sided. Thus, the administrative staff is exposed to the arbitrariness of the ruler in a similar way to the population. This is why this form of neo-patrimonial rule is – as coined by Max Weber – also called neo-sultanism.

Kazakhstan

Kazakhstan is the only Central Asian country where political change can be partly interpreted – at least since the last five years – as a development toward a more bureaucratic developmental state structure. From the perspective of comparative regime study, the Kazakh and Kyrgyz cancellations of democratic-parliamentary reforms in the middle of the 1990s appear to be similar fallbacks to authoritarianism. From a sociological and developmental-theoretical point of view, both cases are to be evaluated in a more differentiated way. However, whereas, in Kyrgyzstan, the political marginalization of party pluralism was rather backed by a stronger patrimonialization of the state administration and strengthened political orientations toward the preservation of the *status quo* – due to the weak presidency – president Nazarbaev instrumentalized an "authoritarian" defusing of the state crisis, which emerged in the course of the political liberalization of 1994, and lead to more comprehensive administrative and legal reforms. As the only post-Soviet republic, Kazakhstan reduced the number of regional units from 20 to 16, abolished the corresponding regional administrations, reduced the number of ministries from 24 to 14 and rationalized ministerial commissions and committees in 1997. These reforms made one-third of the offices in the central administration redundant, and were followed by regulations establishing career tracks in civil service and a differentiation between political and administrative offices. At the same time, reforms were implemented in the sphere of property law and in the financial sector, and established a national system of registration of land ownership and more independent economic courts with more specialized and better-paid judges. The enhanced protection of property rights and the increased suability of contractual law also helped to strengthen private economic institutions and to promote the high economic growth rates of the last five years. The introduction of national pension funds and compulsory health insurance aimed at providing a new base for the former Soviet welfare state.

Conclusions

This very brief overview of the development of state structures shows that the analysis of political change from the perspective of comparative regime change is not only problematic for neglecting the societal embedment of politics, but also for restricting the research focus to processes of political exchange. From the perspective of the emergence of enduring political order, the problem of political change has less to do with the question of democratic regime transition, and is rather connected to the question of how the relatively sophisticated preconditions of statehood for more enduring forms of political liberalization can be established. The mainly Anglo-American type of state development through a pre-state organized and legally integrated civil society does not work in Central Asia, because the Sovietization of the region was linked with the destruction of the local legal cultures which regulate political structures. Western support for strengthening "civil society" in the area might successfully combat poverty, soften the state's retreat from its social responsibilities in the health and educational sector, and increase the level of economic autonomy and self-organization of single local groups. However, these endeavours do not promote civil society as a legally integrated societal entity, which is able to regulate and constrain the consolidation of state structures.

From the presented sociological perspective, the development problem of Central Asia appears to fundamentally be a political one and is, as such, linked to the question of how bureaucratic developmental state structures can be strengthened in order to overcome patrimonialism and the established primacy of politics in legal and administrative processes. Under the prevailing circumstances, this aim is unlikely to be achieved through premature forms of political liberalization, which undermine the state capacity for reforms and threaten political security. Reaching this aim is rather linked with the endeavours of the political elites to consolidate state structures. This developmental work can only be done by the political elites themselves and not by external actors, whose influence is bound to the support of reform endeavours.

If consolidated state structures belong to the necessary preconditions of successful institutionalization of political participation and pluralism, proper legal and administrative reforms will play a decisive role in overcoming the patrimonial state. Thus, considerations about reform strategies in the region have to take into account classical liberal rights agendas (protection of properties, *habeas corpus*, internal control mechanisms in the police and security apparatuses, etc.). Rather than just blaming the lapse of these states into patrimonialism on the deficiencies of legal regulations from the perspective of the Western constitutional state, and granting technical assistance for the improvement of formal legislation, which does not work under the existing societal conditions, a country-specific catalogue of measures to protect these rights should be established. Taking the prevailing forms of statehood into account, it seems premature to demand political rights for the *demos* (people) in societies where the state is not able to secure the property rights of its citizens. For this reason, it might be useful to analyse the Western human rights agenda with regard to their chances of realization under the prevailing forms of statehood and to specify the implementation of single rights with regard to corresponding necessary reform measures within the legal and administrative sphere. Such an approach will have to start from the local perception of reform problems.

As formal legal systems and the institutionalization of welfare committed bureaucracies emerge from the interpenetration of communal orientations of a society, the historical rift between state structures and local communities in Central Asia will only be overcome if Islamic and other forms of communal commitment are directed towards and linked to state institutions. Such processes can be catalysed if acknowledged informal instances of conflict regulation, for example, *aksakallar* (elders) in *mahallalar* (neighbourhoods), are integrated into the official legal system; if local administrations represent local communities; and if the state administration is opened up for the aggregation of communal interests. From this perspective, the mahallization of Uzbekistan may decrease the afore-mentioned rift – or if the official legal system also makes references to previously influential local legal traditions (like the *Sharia* or tribal customary law). Even if not all effective measures correspond to Western values, legislators will have to be responsive to the different socio-historical conditions for reforms in Central Asia and they will have to design agendas that take into account specific local traits if enduring forms of political order are to be achieved.

In contrast to impersonal authority relations in Western democracies, personal rule also implies different conditions for political stability and security policy. If the unity of the state is based on relations of political loyalty and is potentially threatened by political regionalism, concepts of security will have to pay more attention to the balance of powers between competing regions within a state and to the state type involved. From the perspective proposed here, it is also possible to analyse – in a more differentiated way – the abstract controversial debate on the conflicting aims of political stability and democratization in the newly independent republics.

Bibliography

Bratton, Michael/Walle, Nicolas van de. 1994. Neo-patrimonial Regimes and Political Transitions in Africa. In: *World Politics*, 46, July, pp. 453-489.
Bratton, Michael/Walle, Nicolas van de. 1997. *Democratic Experiments in Africa*. New York: Cambridge University Press.
Collier, David (ed.). 1979. *The New Authoritarianism in Latin America*. Princeton: Princeton University Press.
Collins, Kathleen A. 2003. The Political Role of Clans in Central Asia. In: *Comparative Politics*, 35 (2), pp. 171-90.
Croissant, Aurel. 2003. Staat, Staatlichkeit und demokratische Transformation. In: Bendel, Petra; et al (eds.). *Zwischen Demokratie und Diktatur. Zur Konzeption und Empirie demokratischer Grauzonen*. Opladen: Leske + Budrich, pp. 204-9.
Cummings, Sally (ed.). 2002. *Power and Change in Central Asia*. London/New York: Routledge.

Eisenstadt, Shmuel N. 1973. *Traditional Patrimonialism and Modern Neo-patrimonialism.* Beverly Hills: Sage.

Engel, Ulf/Erdmann, Gero. 2002. *Neo-patrimonialism Reconsidered – Critical Review and Elaboration of an Elusive Concept.* (Paper presented at the 45th African Studies Association meeting. Washington/DC, December 7) 20 p.

Erdmann, Gero. 2002. Neopatrimoniale Herrschaft – oder: Warum es in Afrika so viele Hybridregime gibt. In: Bendel, Petra; et al (eds.): *Zwischen Demokratie und Diktatur. Zur Konzeption und Empirie demokratischer Grauzonen.* Opladen: Leske + Budrich, pp. 323-43.

Geiss, Paul Georg. 2004. The Problem of Political Order in Contemporary Kazakhstan and Turkmenistan. In: Gammer, Moshe (ed). *The Caspian Region, Vol. I, A Re-emerging Region,* London: Routledge, pp. 203-27.

Geiss, Paul Georg. 2004. Political Community and State Structures: Europe and Japan in Comparative View. In: Gammer, Moshe (ed.): *Community, Identity and the State. Comparing Africa, Eurasia, Latin America and the Middle East,* London: Routledge, pp. 1-13.

Geiss, Paul Georg. 2003. *Pre-Tsarist and Tsarist Central Asia. Communal Commitment and Political Order in Change,* London/New York: Routledge Curzon.

Geiß, Paul Georg. 2002. *Die Gemeinschaftsgebundenheit formaler und informeller Politik. Über die Implikationen von Rechtsgemeinschaft und politischer Vergemeinschaftung für die Entstehung von Parteienpluralismus in der außereuropäischen Welt.* Hamburg: Deutsches Übersee-Institut.

Geiss, Paul Georg. 2002. Communal and Political Change in Central Asia. Some Preliminary Findings. In: *Central Eurasian Studies Review,* 1 (3), pp. 10-15.

Geiss, Paul Georg. 2001. Legal Culture and Political Reforms in Central Asia. In: *Central Asia and the Caucasus,* 6 (12), pp. 114-125.

Geiss, Paul Georg. 2000. Political Discourse on Authority Relations in Central Asia. A Sociological Elucidation. In: *Central Asia Monitor,* 6, pp. 1-6.

Gellner, Ernest. 1982. Patrons and Clients. In: Clapham, Christopher (ed.): *Private Patronage and Public Power: Political Clientelism in the Modern State.* New York: St. Martin's Press, pp. 1-6.

Getty, J. Arch. 1986. *Origin of the Great Purges,* Cambridge: Cambridge University Press.

Hartmann, Jürgen. 1997. Vergleichende Regierungslehre und Systemvergleich. In: Berg-Schlosser, Dirk/Müller-Rommel, Ferdinand (eds.): *Vergleichende Politikwissenschaft,* Opladen: Leske + Budrich, pp. 33-34.

Johnson, Chalmers. 1982. *MITI and the Japanese Miracle,* Stanford CA: Stanford University.

Leftwich, Adrian. 1995. Bringing Politics Back. Towards a Model of the Developmental State. In: *Journal of Development Studies,* 31 (3), pp. S. 401-427.

Linz, Juan L. 1975. Totalitarian and Authoritarian Regimes. In: Greenstein, Fred I./Polsby, Nelson W. (eds.): *Handbook of Political Science, Vol. 3 Macro Political Theory,* Reading, MA: Addison Wesley, pp. 175-412.

Linz, Juan L. 1964. An Authoritarian Regime: The Case of Spain. In: Allard, Erik; Littunen, Yrjo (eds.): *Cleavages, Ideologies and Party Systems,* Helsinki: Westmark Society, pp. 291-341.

Luong, Pauline Jones. 2002. *Institutional Change and Political Continuity in Post-Soviet Central Asia. Power, Perceptions, and Pacts,* Cambridge: Cambridge University Press.

Merkel, Wolfgang. 1999. Defekte Demokratie In: Merkel Wolfgang/Busch, Andreas (eds.): *Demokratie in Ost und West,* Frankfurt: Suhrkamp, pp. 361-81.

Migdal, Joel S. 1988. *Strong Societies and Weak States. State-Society Relations and State-Capability In the Third World,* Princeton, N.J.

Myrdal, Gunnar. 1970. The 'Soft State' in Underdeveloped Countries. In: P. Streeten, ed., *Unfashionable Economics. Essays in Honour of Lord Balogh,* London: Weidenfeld & Nicolson, pp. 226-243.

Münch, Richard. 1987. *Theory of Action. Towards a New Synthesis Going Beyond Parsons,* London: Routledge & Kegan Paul.

Münch, Richard. 1988. *Understanding Modernity. Towards a New Perspective Going Beyond Durkheim and Weber,* London: Routledge & Kegan Paul.

Münch, Richard. 1992 (1984). *Die Struktur der Moderne. Grundmuster und differentielle Gestaltung des institutionellen Aufbaus der modernen Gesellschaften*, Frankfurt.

O'Donnell, Guillermo. 1973. *Modernization and Bureaucratic-Authoritarianism. – Studies in South American Politics*, Berkeley: Institute of International Studies.

O'Donnell, Guillermo. 1978. Reflections on Patterns of Change in the Bureaucratic-Authoritarian State. In: *Latin American Research Review*, 13, pp. 3-39.

O'Donnell, Guillermo. 1994. Delegative Democracy. In: *Journal of Democracy*, 5 (1), pp. 55-69.

Olcott, Martha Brill. 2002. *Kazakhstan. Unfulfilled Promise*, Washington, DC: Carnegie Endowment.

Pawelka, Peter. 1985. *Herrschaft und Entwicklung im Nahen Osten: Ägypten*, Heidelberg: CF Müller Verlag.

Pethyridge, Roger. 1990. *One Step Backwards, Two Steps Forward*, Oxford: Clarendon Press.

Pye, Lucian W. 1985. *Asian Power and Politics. The Cultural Dimension of Authority*. Cambridge, MA: Harvard University Press.

Roth, Guenther. 1968. Personal Rulership, Patrimonialism, and Empire-Building in the New State. In: *World Politics*, 1, pp. 194-206.

Rutland, Peter. 1993. *The Politics of Economic Stagnation: The Role of Local Party Organs in Economic Management*, New York: Cambridge Univ. Press.

Rüb, Friedbert W. 2002. Hybride Regime – Politikwissenschaftliches Chamäleon oder neuer Regimetypus? Begriffliche und konzeptionelle Überlegungen zum neuen Pessimismus in der Transitologie. In: Bendel, Petra; et al (eds.): *Zwischen Demokratie und Diktatur. Zur Konzeption und Empirie demokratischer Grauzonen*. Opladen: Leske + Budrich, pp. 23-118.

Schmitter, Philippe C. 1979. Still the Century of Corporatism? In: Schmitter, Philippe C./ Lehmbruch, Gerhard (eds.), *Trends Towards Corporatist Intermediation*, London/Beverly Hills, pp. 7-52.

Schubert, Gunter/Tetzlaff Rainer (eds). 1998. *Blockierte Demokratien in der Dritten Welt*. Opladen: Leske + Budrich.

Simonis, Georg. 1985. Der Entwicklungsstaat in der Krise. In: Nuscheler, Franz (ed.), *Dritte Welt-Forschung. Entwicklungstheorie und Entwicklungspolitik* (PVS, Sonderheft 16) Opladen, Westdeutscher Verlag, pp. 157-183.

Snyder, Richard. 1992. Explaining Transitions from Neopatrimonial Dictatorships. In: *Comparative Politics*, 24 (4), pp. 379-400.

Weber, Max. (1921-1925) 1972. *Wirtschaft und Gesellschaft - Grundriss der verstehenden Soziologie*. In: Winckelmann, Johannes (ed.) Tübingen: JCB Mohr.

Weber, Max. 1978. *Economy and Society. An Outline of Interpretative Sociology*, ed. by G. Roth, C. Wittich, 2 vols., Berkeley/Los Angeles/London.

Willerton, John. 1992. *Patronage and Politics in the USSR*. Cambrigde: Cambridge Univ. Press.

Wimmer, Hannes. 2000. *Die Modernisierung politischer Systeme. Staat – Parteien – Öffentlichkeit*, Wien: Böhlau Verlag.

Wimmer, Hannes. 1996. Die Modernisierung des Staates als Entwicklungsproblem. In: Franz. Kolland et. al. (eds.), *Staat und zivile Gesellschaft. Beiträge zur Entwicklungspolitik in Afrika, Asia und Lateinamerika* (Historische Sozialkunde 8), Frankfurt/M: Brandes & Apsel/Südwind, pp. 17-38.

Zakaria, Fareed. 1997. The Rise of Illiberal Democracy. In: *Foreign Affairs*, 76, pp. 22-43.

Judith Beyer

Rhetoric of "Transformation": The Case of the Kyrgyz Constitutional Reform

In this article, the concept of *transformation*[1] is analysed from a new perspective that significantly differs from previous studies on the topic. In the case of the post-socialist republic of Kyrgyzstan, it is suggested that *transformation* should not always be equated with present-day real-life social change, but rather with the powerful rhetoric of Western scientific discourse, which has found its way into the public discourse of the Central Asian states. Moreover, the concept of *transformation* has not only been used in Kyrgyzstan since the country's independence; its roots can be traced back to the socialist era. In this paper, the changing attitude toward the concept of *transformation* within the discipline called transformation studies is reviewed first, after which an anthropological account of *transformation* is given in order to show that long-term field research, an actor-centred approach and a pluralistic conception of Soviet history all help to develop new ways of analysing social change in post-socialist countries. In the following, the local usage of the concept of *transformation* is investigated in the context of the Kyrgyz constitutional reform, which unfolded in 2003. An in-depth analysis of speeches given by the president, as well as newspaper articles from both governmental and oppositional newspapers show that *transformation* is used as a common rhetorical tool and is therefore a powerful instrument in current political debates in post-socialist Kyrgyzstan.

The development of the concept of transformation

The concept of *transformation* was developed in the context of worldwide political changes referred to as the "third wave of democracy".[2] These changes include the demise of authoritarianism in South-European states, the end of military dictatorships in Latin America in the 1980s, and the construction of new post-Soviet states following the break-up of the Soviet Union in the 1990s.[3] Due to the early and simplified assumption that social change occurs in a linear way, the concept of *transformation* was regarded as a promising analytical tool in the new branch of social science called transfor-

---

[1] In this article, the term "transformation" is viewed as encompassing other terms such as "transition" or "system change" (see also Merkel 1999: 76). The term "transformation" and its by-products has been used in italics throughout the whole article in order to stress the author's disagreement with the general assumptions behind this concept.
[2] Huntington 1991.
[3] See Schmitter and O'Donnell 1986; Merkel 1999.

mation studies. With it, it seemed possible to analyse and give a prognosis of the future in those parts of the world which had become subject to massive structural mutations.

Overall social change, however, was not only meant to be analysed, but also influenced. For the post-socialist republic of Kyrgyzstan, on which this article focuses, this resulted in a three-fold approach to change: from a planned to a market economy, from Soviet-ruled socialism to democracy and from an instrumentalist appropriation of law during the Soviet period to a de-facto rule of law. *Transformation* as well became quickly recognized and used by the Kyrgyz government itself in its attempts to not only create a national identity from scratch, but to also seek new forms of economic and political governance for the newborn state. Its first president, Askar Akaev, happily accepted international offers of transitologists to initiate and guide the country's process of *transformation*. Transitologists prescribed the treatment of "shock therapy", which included rapid economic stabilization, price liberalization, privatization, and an intense involvement of international organizations and external experts in local state affairs.[4] The country also relied on outside assistance when structuring the nation-state, privatizing state property and drafting laws.

The willingness of the "patient" to go on with the treatment prescribed by international organizations, such as the World Bank Group, brought Kyrgyzstan the reputation of a particularly reform-oriented country. At the outset of the therapies, the country seemed to be in stable condition, aiming high by claiming to be turning into the "Switzerland of Central Asia". In the years to follow, however, the "island of democracy" – as the country was called back then – also turned out to be just another authoritarian state. Its present problems (poverty, corruption, lack of legal certainty, unemployment and health care issues) are symptomatic of all countries that have been referred to as being "in transformation" and they are treated as such by the international community.

The above-mentioned problems of *transformation* states did not go unnoticed by transitologists. As a result, an enormous amount of literature has been written about why the *transformations* have failed. Reasons for the lack of success were sought in references to the "communist legacy" of those states[5] and the "passivity"[6] of its population. In recent years, however, transitologists have stopped looking for failures in the post-socialist states and have started questioning the adequacy of their own theories and models of *transformation*. A good example of a more critical approach toward *transformation* is Wolfgang Merkel's latest publication.[7] This book is the first volume of a new series called "Defective Democracy", which departs from the early assump-

---

4 See Sachs and Lipton 1990a, b.
5 King 2000: 165 f.
6 Bernhard 1996: 323.
7 Merkel et al. 2003.

tion that countries "in transformation" inevitably pass through the stages of liberalization and democratization in order to reach the final stage of consolidation in which newly established democratic institutions take root. In light of the fact that this consolidation has taken place in only a few countries, which have been ranked as being "in transformation", the new approach offered by Merkel et al. tries to adapt the model to the realities of post-socialist or post-authoritarian states. In doing so, however, the authors do not question the model itself, but only components of it.

Scholars from outside the branch of transformation studies, however, have different explanations for the incompatibility of the theories with the real-life situations with which the people in those countries are forced to deal. According to the political scientist Thomas Carothers, who has published extensively on the inadequacy of the "transition paradigm", as he calls it, the whole concept has to be discarded as dysfunctional:

> "The transition paradigm was a product of a certain time – the heady early days of the third wave – and that time has now passed. It is necessary for democracy activists to move on to new frameworks, new debates, and perhaps eventually a new paradigm of political change – one suited to the landscape of today, not the lingering hopes of an earlier era."[8]

The failure of many reforms, which were being carried out in the name of *transformation*, resulted in a severe loss of prestige of the sub-discipline transformation studies. Carothers' call to discard the paradigm altogether and move on to a new model of analysis of social change can be regarded as a most extreme reaction against transitology. As a result, the sub-discipline is now looking for new ways of dealing with the phenomenon of *transformation*. Within the past years, it has come closer to anthropological ways of analysing social change, for example, in arguing for more actor-centred approaches, or a more differentiated view on the impact of Soviet history on the post-Soviet successor states. This leads us to the question whether anthropology has something to offer to transitology.

Anthropological accounts of transformation

While scholars within the discipline of transformation studies regard countries such as Kyrgyzstan only to be "in transformation" because they are called post-Soviet or post-socialist (indicating that they had been stagnant up until then), anthropological studies hold a different view: change is not confined to a particular period, and history is regarded as inherently transitional. *Transformation*, therefore, can neither be viewed as a post-authoritarian or

---

8   Carothers 2002: 20.

post-socialist phenomenon alone, but should be seen as referring to any historical period of any state or any group. Thus, the need arises for contextualization. Also, the *transformation* of a given societal entity cannot be analysed without paying attention to what is empirically observable in the supposed *transformation* of that specific entity. Theoretical discussions, models and hypotheses need grounding in observations that are made in real-life situations.[9] Questions posed by anthropologists include: "What does change mean for the local population experiencing it?"; "What strategies do people develop in order to live in an environment that has been described as transitional by outsiders?" and "How do people react towards foreign models of *shock therapy* and *democratization*?"

A large number of case studies by anthropologists in post-socialist environments has provided answers to these questions, showing, for example, that aspects of market economy, which are being introduced to those countries, may be perceived negatively by the local population. Caroline Humphrey argues that, while production and manpower are aspects, which the local population can compare to components of the socialist economic model, consumption and trade are foreign to them. Trade is especially regarded as "speculative behaviour" since, according to the Marxist ideal, true value can only originate from manpower.[10] By investigating local economic perceptions, Humphrey was able to show why people do not accept the economic models that were intended for them by external experts. She also points out alternative strategies that people develop, such as savings strategies, or a return to subsistence economy, in order to withdraw from the mechanisms of the market.[11]

Ruth Mandel shows how international organizations unintentionally further increase the brain drain of qualified local experts. Many leave the local job market to work for international organizations. Through their activities, these organizations create what Mandel calls a "para-state", offering high salaries and interesting working opportunities to pull local experts out of the job market. These actors who lay the foundation for models of *transformation* are thereby unavailable for jobs in state institutions, thus leaving *transformation* to those who do not make it into the more prestigious para-state.

As shown above, an anthropological view on *transformation*, such as that offered by Humphrey or Mandel, succeeds in pointing out the shortcomings of the theories and models of transitologists. Thus, anthropology has much to offer as a discipline; its analytical tools can be used in future discussions as well as in the elaboration of new models and theories argued for by Thomas Carothers and others. Some of its contributions are long-term fieldwork instead of short-term consultation; an actor-centred approach instead of one focusing on institutions; and an understanding of history, not as a legacy,

---

9 See Hann (ed.) 2002; Humphrey 2002; Verdery 1996.
10 Humphrey 2002: 59.
11 Ibid.: 56.

which is dragged along and hinders progress, but as something that is instrumentalized and actively makes use of the opportunity to position oneself in the present. Last but not least, anthropology offers a pluralistic conception of culture in sharp contrast to the often-deterministic use of the term within transitology. In the context of transformation studies, the term culture has come to be used whenever transitologists have had to describe and explain why the behaviour of local actors deviated from their assumptions. The concept of culture has more or less been regarded as a primordial constant, which is not subject to change and hinders *transformation*.[12]

An anthropological perspective, however, can do more than simply deconstruct assumptions made by others. It may also give an alternative point of view on the phenomenon of *transformation* itself. In this article, it is argued that *transformation* is a powerful rhetorical instrument in Kyrgyzstan. Looking at the rhetorical use of the concept rather than regarding it as a real-life phenomenon enables us to illustrate the instrumental character of the term and the manifold ways in which it is utilized in post-socialist Kyrgyzstan. This is not to deny that states like Kyrgyzstan are experiencing serious problems and have been subject to massive political, economic, legal and social changes since their independence. What is being suggested here is that the analysis of the concept of *transformation* needs to be looked at from a different perspective.

Looking at transformation as a rhetorical instrument – an alternative approach

While scientific theories and models of *transformation* are subject to more and more critique from both outside and from within the sub-discipline, the general use of the concept of *transformation* is increasingly being used. In the course of the past 20 years, *transformation* has become one of the most commonly used terms alongside *good governance*, *democratization*, *sustainability* and *development cooperation*. Like these concepts, it has been converted from a purely scholarly term to a slogan, which is frequently used in the rhetoric of politicians, international organizations and the media. How can this development be explained?

Since the mid-90s, the use of the term *transformation* has been of an increasingly self-evident nature, despite the lack of a proper definition and not knowing what exactly is understood by it. A few practical examples shall explain this argument: since 1992 the European Bank for Reconstruction and Development (EBRD) has been publishing a *Law in Transition* report in which the current state of legal affairs in transitional countries is described. The World Bank has been publishing a *Transition Newsletter* in which it informs about its activities in transitional countries. For Central Asia, the US

---

12   See, for example, Brunner 1997: 103 ff.

Agency for International Development (USAID) opened an *Office of Market Transition*, an *Office of Social Transition* and an *Office of Democratic Transition*.[13] International and national conferences have been devoted to the problem of *transformation* throughout the past decade. Recent examples of such preoccupations are *Transitions and Inequality in the 21st Century* (Utah, September 2004); *Economies and Politics in Transitions: Central Asia and Beyond* (Almaty, October 2004); *Dynamics of Transformation in Central Asia* (Rome, November 2004). Moreover, a large number of research institutions have been established recently, or have reoriented their focus towards *transformation*, for example, the *Frankfurt Institute for Transformation Studies* or the *Stockholm Institute of Transition Economics*. Numerous journals and newsletters, such as the Czech online-journal *Transitions online*, or *The Journal of Communist Studies and Transition Politics*, are committed to the topic. The concept of *transformation* can also be found in an innumerable amount of monographs[14] about social change in post-socialist states, as well as in travel literature and even fiction.[15]

The general usage of the term *transformation* did not go unnoticed by anthropologists, such as Chris Hann or Catherine Verdery. While Hann argues for the investigation of how discourses on *transformation* influence social practice,[16] Verdery exposes the ideological meaning behind concepts such as *privatization*, *market*, *rule of law* and *civil society*. She analyses metaphors frequently used in transformation studies, such as *shock therapy* or *big bang* (a synonym for this therapy), and claims that, while the first term envisions Western experts as doctors, the second has turned them into God.[17] Both authors have pointed at the usage of *transformation* as Western rhetoric. The anthropologist Kevin Latham,[18] however, has referred to *transformation* as a rhetorical tool, which has been employed in socialist countries as well. In his research, he emphasizes the use of the term *transformation* in Chinese media discourse and assesses the concept as being highly relevant to the Communist Party. His argument is based on the premise that, through the concept of *transformation*, the party is able to sustain the impression that the country is moving in the right direction. In order to disseminate the rhetoric of *transformation* throughout the country, the party relies on the media. Journalists, however, do not only blindly execute tasks imposed upon them, but also actively shape the concept of *transformation* with their own personal hopes and wishes. While Latham has been one of the first researchers to point out the importance of *transformation* as a local concept in socialist countries, he does not deliver an explanation for the predominance of it.

---

13 Mandel 2002: 412.
14 Cf. Di Palma 1990; Lijphart and Waisman 1996; Linz and Stepan 1996; Pribán, Roberts and Young 2003.
15 A recent publication of well-known Russian writer Victor Pelewin carries the title *The dialectics of the transition period: From nowhither to nowhere* (2004).
16 Hann 1994: 236.
17 Verdery 1996: 205.
18 Latham 2000, 2002.

In this article, it is held that the concept of *transformation* has become such a widespread phenomenon in post-socialist Kyrgyzstan, because the local population was already familiar with its usage in socialist political discourse. The success of the concept of *transformation* in Kyrgyzstan is not only due to the high degree of familiarity of the country with Western theories and models as propagated through international organizations. Significant parallels can also be traced between the perception of overall social change as developed in transitology and the concept of social *transformation* as first verbalized in the theory of Karl Marx,[19] and, as later reinterpreted and amplified, in statements made by the Soviet party secretaries. Therefore, it was not necessary to export the concept to Kyrgyzstan after the country's independence, because a socialist version of it already existed there.

What Akaev and Marx have in common

Karl Marx's view of social change can be subsumed into his model of stages, according to which society has progressed from a primitive society to a slaveholder society, to feudalism and then to capitalism in order to reach the final stage of communism.[20] As in the conception of social change in transformation studies, Marx also viewed social change as a strictly linear development. According to Marx, history unfolds in consecutive or overlapping stages of different levels of production. The achievement of a new stage of social development is envisioned as being always linked with class struggle for access to and the distribution of resources. Inter-class fights lead to the collapse of the old system and to the attainment of a new stage. Only when the final stage of communism has been reached, will all grievances cease.[21]

When the Soviet Union was founded in 1922, the first party secretary, Vladimir Lenin, advanced Marx's teachings, which he declared as "almighty, because they are true",[22] by emphasizing the role of the party as the organ responsible for implementing social progress. According to Lenin, only a firmly organized cadre party would be able to guide the proletariat to its victory. He also modified the model of stages as developed by Marx and added the stage of *stamocap* (state-monopolistic capitalism) as a particular form of capitalism to the model. After Lenin, Joseph Stalin again modified the model of stages by proclaiming that one could not wait for a worldwide revolution to reach the last stage of communism, as Lenin had previously argued. Instead, he opted for an immediate intensification of the class struggle; thereby declaring ethnic cleansings, show trials and the Gulag-system as legitimate means to achieve this end. He viewed social change as inevitable

---

19 See "Die deutsche Ideologie", in: MEW 3: 17 ff.
20 Marx referred to socialism as an economical "transitionary stage" which he ranked between capitalism and communism (see Kritik des Gothaer Programms, in: MEW 19: 28).
21 MEW 19: 21.
22 LW 19: 3.

and predestined and described the forthcoming uprising as the "disentanglement from knots of fate".[23]

Lenin and Stalin had almost unrestrained access to the media and both had for a while occupied the position of chief editor of the daily newspaper *Pravda*. Published articles as well as appeals for protest meetings in *Pravda* levered the policies undertaken by the party secretaries. With the media functioning as an instrument of the Soviet revolution from its very beginning, Lenin and Stalin ensured that their activities and vision of the future of communist society were spread throughout all countries and republics of the Soviet empire. Especially Stalin used the media for propagandistic ends.[24] The local population, therefore, did not have to read Marx in order to become familiar with the concept of social change as evolving in linear stages. It can be assumed that the citizens already knew of the stages through the interpretation provided by the respective Soviet party secretaries.

Even up until shortly before the break-up of the Soviet Union, the preoccupation with the role of social change as evolving in a linear manner proved to be useful in legitimating actions introduced by the head of the party. In 1985, Mikhail Gorbachev took up the position of General Secretary of the Communist Party and started a radical political, economic, legal and social reform, following Western-style models. While he broke with almost 70 years of Soviet tradition, he tried to link his undertaking to the Soviet past to show that reforms were still being carried out in the name of the Soviet people. Speaking on behalf of the party, Gorbachev's protégé, Lukyanov, explained the new approach as follows: "We are constructing a law-based state in a Soviet form, that is, in the form that the people have chosen as a result of the Great October Socialist Revolution".[25] Gorbachev travelled throughout the Soviet Union in order to promote his reforms and his speeches were published in *Pravda*.[26] In his speech of 16 February in 1987 in the Kremlin, he criticized the economic, social and moral decay of the country, a situation that left no option other than to initiate radical reforms and far-reaching democratization (Russ.: *demokratizaciia*) of society. According to Gorbachev, the sole alternative, which remained, was that of a "revolutionary transition".[27] He not only demanded this revolutionary attitude from the deputies of the Kremlin to whom he was giving the speech, but also from the general population. In his speech, the people (Russ.: *narod*) were given the significance Marx had attributed them with: Gorbachov refers to them as "the most important factor of the *perestroika*".[28]

---

23   Stalin 1950 [1905]: 160 ff.
24   See Hollander 1972.
25   Cited after Huskey 1992: 34.
26   It had been common procedure to publish speeches of First Secretaries of the Communist Party since the 1930s.
27   See Gorbachev 1987.
28   Ibid.

As pointed out, the original model of stages as developed by Marx has been changed and instrumentalized by different Soviet party secretaries for their own political ends. Although only a few of Marx's original formulations have made it into the rhetoric of the party heads, a general understanding of social change has taken place in a linear way, and the ability to implement this through revolutionary means prevailed throughout all of the Soviet era. The current rhetoric of *transformation* in the post-socialist state of Kyrgyzstan can therefore be viewed as the continuation of older practices. It is applied in post-socialist contexts because of the relevance it had acquired in the Soviet period. President Askar Akaev, in particular, used the concept of *transformation* as a rhetorical instrument for his own ends. Like the party secretaries before him, he relied on the role of the media as a broker and multiplier of the concept. When instrumentalized in this way, the term *transformation* – as used in the local Kyrgyz context – obtains quite another meaning than the one thought of in the theories and models of transformation studies. Which meaning is involved here will be shown in a case study which was conducted in spring 2003, namely that of the Kyrgyz constitutional reform.

The case of the Kyrgyz constitutional reform

On 2 February 2003, the Kyrgyz citizens were called upon to go to the polls to make two decisions: whether a new version of the Kyrgyz constitution should be adopted, and whether president Askar Akaev should remain in office until the end of his term in October 2005. According to the Kyrgyz Central Election Committee, out of the 86.68 per cent who cast their vote, 76.61 per cent voted in favour of the new constitution, and 78.74 per cent wanted to see Akaev continue his term. The events leading to this referendum are complex and cannot be explained within the limited frame of this article.[29] However, it is important to note that the new version of Kyrgyzstan's constitution did not evolve from serious attempts to reform the state's structure. Rather, the referendum has to be regarded as a clever move by Akaev to calm down the population, as well as the international community, which was alerted to his questionable motives, when, in March 2002, during a demonstration for the release of an oppositionist, five people were shot dead by police and several injured. The incident became known as "The Aksy-event" and was labelled by the opposition and international organizations as a serious breach of human rights. The new version of the Kyrgyz constitution was referred to by Akaev as a "constitution of human rights", and its changed content as a compilation of the opinions of all citizens. The second question posed at the referendum can only be interpreted as a direct move against the opposition, which had united in the course of the above-mentioned events,

---

29 For a detailed account of the constitutional reform, see Kunze 2003; Nelle 2004, and OSCE/ODIHR 2003.

and which began to pose a growing threat to Akaev's integrity, calling for his abdication and general reforms of the state sector. In order to promote the new constitution throughout the country, Akaev made extensive use of the media. In three speeches, held before and after the referendum, as well as through newspapers closely associated with the government, he tried to bias the Kyrgyz population. The concept of *transformation* served him as an important rhetorical instrument. However, the oppositional newspapers also made use of the term.

The concept of transformation in the speeches of Akaev and the Kyrgyz media

The use of the concept of *transformation* in the speeches of the President as well as in Kyrgyz governmental and oppositional newspapers can be illustrated in the case of the constitutional referendum quite clearly. The following analysis shows to what ends the concept of *transformation* has been employed in public discourse. The material analysed consists of speeches held by president Akaev as well as articles from the widely known governmental newspapers *Slovo Kyrgyzstana* and *Vechernii Bishkek* and from the two largest oppositional newspapers *Moia Stolica* and *Res Publica*.[30] Within a time frame of six weeks, starting from 14 January 2003 (with the first speech of President Akaev, in which he makes public the decision to hold a referendum on 2 February) until 21 February (with the reaction of the media after the newly adopted constitution had been signed), a total of 335 published articles were analysed and grouped into the following five different categories: coverage, reader's letters, polemics, interviews with local experts, and pleas from local NGOs, veterans and deputies of the parliament as well as the population and the international community.

During the six weeks analysed, a convergence between the time and the course of the event can be observed: the closer the date of the referendum, the more articles were being published. Attention toward this event was particularly strong in governmental newspapers, reaching a climax shortly before 2 February with almost no other topic being presented in the issues debated. The oppositional newspapers also reported constantly about the upcoming

---

30 *Slovo Kyrgyzstana* is the oldest newspaper in Kyrgzystan; published since 1925, traditionally it acts as an instrument of the government. In it, Akaev's speeches and decrees are printed in their original version and his picture is often placed on the front page. The newspaper is published three times a week with a circulation of 7,000 copies. *Vechernii Bishkek* was founded in 1974 and is the most-read newspaper in Kyrgyzstan with a circulation of 60,000 copies in its weekend edition. This newspaper is also associated with the government: At the time of the constitutional referendum, the son-in-law of Akaev was the editor in chief. The oppositional newspaper *Moia Stolica* was founded in 2001 and is published five times a week with a circulation of 5,000 copies; its weekend edition encompasses 17,000 copies. The newspaper can be described as very critical towards the government, reporting mainly on political topics. *Res Publica* is a weekly oppositional newspaper. Both oppositional newspapers work closely together, since they are often in danger of being closed down because of their critical coverages.

referendum. Regarding the concept of *transformation*, half of the articles in the governmental newspapers and one-third of the oppositional newspaper articles combined the national referendum with the concept of *transformation*. Besides the word *transformation* (Russ.: *transformaciia*), other words were used synonymously in the local context. These were passage (Russ. *perekhod*), period (Russ. *period*), transition period (Russ. *perekhodnii period*), stage (Russ. *etap*), transition stage (Russ. *perechodnii etap*), transit (Russ. *transit*), reconfiguration (Russ. *preobrazovanie*), development (Russ. *razvitie, dvizhenie, vozrozhdenie*), mutation (Russ. *izmenenie, peremena*), step (Russ. *shag*) and way (Russ. *put*).

By grouping the articles into five categories, it became clear that, in the governmental newspapers, the concept of *transformation* was used especially in the categories of readers' letters, polemics and interviews, while the oppositional newspapers made use of it in pleas to the local population before the referendum and in their coverage subsequent to the event. In the following, a qualitative analysis of the three speeches given by the president as well as some of the more striking articles out of the above-mentioned categories show how the concept of *transformation* is used in the local context. As will be shown, it serves two purposes: first, to explain the changes in the new constitution; and second, to refer to changes in Kyrgyz society itself.

The transformation of the constitution

The presentation of changes in the new constitution made by Akaev and the media refers to four new legal provisions. These provisions are human rights, democratization, decentralization and judicial reforms. In Akaev's first speech entitled "The people has deliberated and suggested", the president formulated a new national idea for the year 2003, which is supposed to be reflected in the new constitution: "Kyrgyzstan – Land of Human Rights".[31] According to him, the new constitution not only proclaims to, but also actually puts human rights into common practice. The new provisions were also declared as furthering the processes of democratization and decentralization in the political sector, thus transferring more power to the local regions. He declared that judicial reforms would guarantee the immunity of those judges, who, for a long time, have been subject to critique from within and without the country. In his speech, Akaev also frequently used terms such as *civil society*, *rule of law* and, time and time again, the term *human rights*; he also declared that, should the population accept the new constitution, all these concepts would be realized. When referring to the old version of the constitu-

---

31 It has become almost a tradition for Akaev to formulate a new "national idea" for every year. Interestingly, his ideas are often in stark contrast to social reality. For example, after the inter-ethnic conflict occurring in the Southern part of the country in 1990, he moulded the slogan "Kyrgyzstan – our common house". After the "Aksyi-event" in 2002, his slogan now refers to the supposedly functioning human rights system in the country.

tion, Akaev uses the term "constitution of the transition period" (Russ. *konstituciia perekhodnogo perioda*) and, by comparing Kyrgyzstan's reforms with those of the other Central Asian republics, he has tried to strengthen the impression that the country continues to be the leader in terms of introducing and implementing reforms.

The governmental newspapers *Slovo Kyrgyzstana* and *Vechernii Bishkek* took up Akaev's opinions on the new constitution and duplicated them in all five categories with reader's articles predominantly dealing with the positive *transformation* of the constitution. However, it is doubtful whether these letters actually reflect the opinion of the Kyrgyz population. According to many sources interviewed within the frame of the research presented here, it is likely that these letters were "bought". This habit would also seem compatible with the practice of Akaev, who, shortly before the referendum, had distributed presents, honorary titles and awards as well as raised the salaries of government officials and promised an increase in pensions.[32] On a general note, the governmental newspapers were preoccupied with showing that the new constitution, as well as Akaev's confirmation as president, was the wish of the population. By assigning reader's letters and interviews a prominent position in their issues, the newspapers tried to contrive authenticity. After reading through the letters and analysing the interviews, it becomes obvious that Akaev's statements were never questioned. Also, no other topics or other provisions were ever made the subject of discussions. Thereby, the governmental newspapers tried to show that the Kyrgyz population was united with regard to the referendum – a concept that Akaev had also referred to in his first speech.

However, referring to the new constitution as a *transformation* of the old one was not restricted to the governmental newspapers. In *Moia Stolica* and *Res Publica* as well, the concept of *transformation* was used – although in the opposite way. While the governmental newspapers were eager to show the progress made from the old to the new version, the oppositional newspapers regarded the new version as being more autocratic, as not protecting human rights, as limiting the influence of the population on state politics and as not guaranteeing the independence of the judiciary. In pleas made to the population as well as to the international community, opposition politicians, and NGOs tried to convince the population not to endorse the two questions being posed at the referendum. If adopted, the new constitution would not only have a negative impact on the state sector, but on society as a whole:

"The project for the adoption of a new constitution may cause regressive processes, lead to instability and the continuing polarization of the society as well as hinder the socio-economical transformation of the country".[33] After

---

[32] This piece of information comes from newspaper articles in which Akaev's behaviour was portrayed in a positive way. See for example the article "Present from the President" (*Prezidentskii prezent*), *Vechernii Bishkek*, 21 January 2003.

[33] From "The South and the North raise objection" (*Jug i Sever vyražajut nesoglasie*), 21 January 2003, in *Moia Stolica*.

the referendum, the oppositional newspapers, in their coverage, referred to the newly adopted constitution as a regression (Russ. *otkat*) to undemocratic and authoritarian regimes.

Despite these different assessments made by Akaev and the media, it is striking that concepts such as *civil society*, *democratization* and *rule of law* were not made subject of discussions, but rather taken for granted. For example, what is understood by the term *civil society* was never questioned. The subject of discussions only dealt with whether or not these concepts would be realized in the new version of the constitution. This observation applies to the concept of *transformation* as well. Whereas Akaev and the governmental newspapers regarded the new version as guaranteeing the progressive development of the country, the oppositional newspapers saw in it a guarantee for its continuing decay. All of them, however, had an understanding of the concept of *transformation* as developing in a linear way. The direction in which the country was "transforming" was merely disputed. In the same way, both types of newspapers gave an account of the new constitution as the cornerstone of Kyrgyz history. The point, therefore, is not only that the constitution was transforming, but also that Kyrgyz society itself was viewed as being "in transformation". In Akaev's speeches, as well as in the media discourse, the event of the constitutional referendum was linked to the development of Kyrgyz society.

The transformation of Kyrgyz society

Already in his first speech, Akaev not only referred to the *transformation* of the constitution, but also extrapolated – out of its possible adoption – consequences for the development of Kyrgyz society. According to him, "The new constitution will guide our country further on its ways to democracy, economic affluence, peace and national unity".[34] In the following weeks, these formulations turned up frequently in the governmental newspapers. Especially in the categories of coverage, reader's letters and interviews, the referendum was linked to the above-mentioned concepts. In his second speech entitled "Ahead of us lie high goals and difficult tasks" given on 5 February 2003, shortly after the referendum, Akaev iterated the four positions mentioned earlier (human rights, democratization, decentralization and an independent judiciary) and declared them realized. He again emphasized that this result had only been achieved because of societal consensus. According to him, Kyrgyzstan has entered a new stage, which he calls the "period of stable development" (Russ. *ustoichivoe razvitie*). In retrospect, he regarded the strong position of the president – as it was defined in the old constitution – as justified: "The bygone period was hard [...]. Especially in this period a strong presidential power was needed, being able to protect the country from all

---

34 Extract from Akaev's first speech, 13 January 2003, in: *Slovo Kyrgyzstana*.

possible commotions and warranting a peaceful political and socio-economic transformation of the whole society".[35] In the adoption of the new constitution, he saw a sign indicating that Kyrgyzstan was not deadlocked, but actively working towards its *transformation*. In his speech, he linked the adoption of the constitution with the year 2003 and referred to it as the year of "Kyrgyz statehood", which had been recognized as such by the United Nations. He regarded the history of Kyrgyz society, its thousand years of old tradition and its wisdom as a guarantee for the future of the country. These formulations were taken up by the governmental newspapers as well, and were most explicitly duplicated in a letter by some Kyrgyz citizens, which was addressed to Akaev directly and published in *Slovo Kyrgyzstana*:

> "We, as deputies of the Kyrgyz society, attach in the recognition of the year 2003 as the year of Kyrgyz statehood by the UN a large importance for our young Kyrgyz state. We are striving to erect a democratic society according to your national idea 'Kyrgyzstan – Land of Human Rights'. The legal basis for the further development of our state will be the new constitution, adopted through the referendum this year. It will serve as a symbol for the striving of our people towards stable development (Russ. *ustoichivoe razvitie*) and growth. We need, now more than ever, peace and national unity in our society".[36]

After the ceremony for the signing of the constitution on 18 February, Akaev gave his third speech, "Learning to live according to the new constitution". He called it a "historical" day. According to him, the new constitution had already contributed to a new quality of statehood and facilitated the *transformation* of the republic to a "higher orbit of historical development" (Russ. *na bolee vysokuiu orbitu istoricheskogo razvitiia)*. Having gone through a period of *transformation*, Kyrgyzstan had now arrived at the most effective and dynamic form of government. In the future, the "spirit of political ascent and societal enthusiasm" would need sheltering. In this regard, Akaev again appealed to overall societal consensus.

It is noteworthy that Akaev creatively plays with the concept of *transformation* in his speeches by describing the old constitution as the "constitution of the transition period" and claims that the country has left this period behind and has reached a stage of "stable development". The new constitution is regarded as an instruction on how to live in this new epoch, and Akaev tries to give the impression that the shady past has been left behind. Instead of succumbing to the Westernized forms of *transformation*, he creates a Kyrgyz version of it: neither *shock therapy* nor *transition politics* are used as slogans in his speeches. By developing his own concept, he rather distances himself

---

35 Extract from Akaev's second speech, in: *Slovo Kyrgyzstana* 5 February 2003.
36 Extract from the reader's letter "Time for an over-all societal council" (*Vremia obshchenarodnogo soveta*), in: *Slovo Kyrgyzstana,* 20 February 2003.

from the failed reformative attempts of the international community. In his speeches, the new constitution is referred to as the visible evidence of the successful *transformation* of state and society alike.

In the oppositional newspapers as well, the new constitution was considered more than just a legal document. Opposition NGOs equated the document with the destabilization of the socio-political situation in the country. Many of their pleas made prior to the referendum appealed to the "historical responsibility of the voters for the next generation".[37] In the name of "peace" and "unity", they called for the rejection of the new version. Another congruity between the statements made in governmental newspapers and the oppositional newspapers is the voiced appeal to the "wisdom of the Kyrgyz people". In many articles, the Soviet past was made the subject of discussion. Compared to that period, the situation in current Kyrgyzstan was described as being a lot worse: "The Republic has regressed fifty years. The citizens see no hope for their future. Where are our leaders, where is our independent development (Russ. *nezavisimoe dvizhenie*) that can help us progress?"[38] The Soviet past was instrumentalized in the oppositional newspapers in positive and negative ways: first, by comparing the former welfare state with the current state, as in the example cited above and, second, by describing the new constitution as "pro-Akaev" and comparing it to the "Stalinist constitution" of the past.[39] The oppositional newspapers thereby appealed to the collective consciousness of the older Kyrgyz generation. As done in the governmental newspapers, the oppositional newspapers associated the referendum with the *transformation* of Kyrgyz society. The conception that the development of the society is hindered by the new constitution shows that, also in oppositional newspapers, historical development is viewed in a linear way. In contrast to *Slovo Kyrgyzstana* and *Vechernii Bishkek*, however, the concept of *transformation* ceased to be used immediately after the referendum. The rhetoric of *transformation* in the oppositional newspapers, as having the power to be effective, only aimed at calling attention to the negative changes occurring in the state sector. Although it does not represent a constant feature of reporting, it nevertheless has to be regarded as a tool the government uses. Despite the fact that the oppositional newspapers, including its readers who are critical of Akaev, are familiar with the concept, the governmental newspapers continued to refer to the concept of *transformation* throughout the whole six-week period. As shown, it was Akaev who, most of the time, invented new meanings and made use of them in his speeches. This calls for a more thorough investigation as to how the president personally biased the concept of *transformation*.

---

37 See article "Dear Kyrgyz citizens!" (*Uvazhaemye Kyrgyzstancy!*) in the oppositional newspaper *Moia Stolica*, 17 January 2003.
38 Excerpt from the plea "Akaev has outwitted everybody once again" (*Akaev provel vsekh eshche raz*), in: *Moia Stolica*, 17 January 2003.
39 See for example the article "Notes of an observer ... or propagandistic trick?" (*Zyametki obozrevatelia: ... ili propagandistskij triuk?*), ibid.

Akaev's personal use of the concept of transformation

Akaev's use of the concept of *transformation* in regard to the constitutional referendum shows significant parallels to the way it was used in the Soviet period. His justification that, during recent years, a strong presidency had been necessary resembles statements made by Lenin who argued for a strong "party cadre" in order to convey the revolutionary consciousness to the proletariat. Furthermore, Akaev also sees himself as a visionary and main initiator of reforms.[40] His evolutionary historical model of society described in his speeches and distributed by the media can be compared to the way Stalin viewed social change. Like Stalin, Akaev talked of Soviet society and portrayed the development of Kyrgyz society as historically unavoidable and rooted in fate. In the end, he – like Gorbachev – legitimized his proceedings by referring to Kyrgyz citizens as the actual "reform engine". He declared that the Kyrgyz populace was the catalyst for the new constitution. Like the Soviet party secretaries before him, Akaev has unlimited access to the media. Besides the press, most television channels and radio stations are either directly under the control of the government, or in the hands of his extended family. Oppositional media is constantly struggling with repression and false allegations, leading to defamation lawsuits, bans and prohibitions.

By using the concept of *transformation*, Akaev tied in former historical concepts of linear social development as first verbalized by Marx and later significantly shaped by the Soviet party secretaries for their own political needs. By combining the "transformation of the constitution" with the "transformation of society", Akaev linked his own political ambitions with a socialist, historical model of development, which must be considered as still being prevalent in the consciousness of the Kyrgyz population. As in the past, it is the media that has helped distribute this rhetoric, with journalists at the same time buying in to it and thereby actively shaping it.

As the party secretaries before him, Akaev affixed his own seal on the concept of *transformation*. His formulation of "reaching a higher orbit of historical development" can be regarded as stemming from his scientific background as a physicist: he uses terms inspired by the natural sciences in order to explain his model of *transformation*. Since the beginning of his term in office, he has published extensively on this topic. In his first book entitled "The transition economy in the eyes of a physicist" from 2000, he developed his own mathematical approach on how to end the transition period in Kyrgyzstan. One year later, he published the book "A remarkable decade".[41] In 2002, "A difficult way towards democracy" and "Kyrgyz statehood and the

---

40   During a conference of the Center for Strategic & International Studies in Washington, DC in September 2002 Akaev declared: "In terms of democratization, among the post-Soviet countries, the Kyrgyz Republic – and I put it quite reasonably – is one of the leading countries. And I do not want to minimize my personal role in this process." Cited in: Regine Spector 2004: 3.

41   Akaev 2001.

national epos Manas" were published. Here as well, the *transformation* of Kyrgyz society is prevalent in his arguments prognosticating the future development of the country. Moreover, Akaev has given his model of *transformation* a national touch. In his speeches, he tried to legitimize his actions regarding the new constitution, by linking the political event directly with the Kyrgyz population: he referred to the people as wise (Russ. *mudryi*) and independent (Russ. *nezavisymyi*). Governmental newspaper articles focused especially on the Kyrgyz mountaineers, who, according to legend, symbolize independence and wisdom. By referring to these qualities, Akaev connects aspects of Kyrgyz identity and national consciousness with the upcoming political event. Both Akaev and the governmental newspapers portrayed the day of the referendum as a "historical" event. He also spoke of the "symbolic significance" of the celebration of the 22-century-long history of the Kyrgyz state in 2003 and the fact that the UN had acknowledged the year as such.[42] Akaev also deemed the 125th anniversary in 2003 of the capital Bishkek as symbolic.

Eventually, the day of the national referendum was declared a public holiday. Governmental newspapers published articles on how the national rice dish *plof* had been cooked for the eldest, how sporting events and concerts had been scheduled and how throughout the country people were celebrating. An author of the governmental newspaper *Vechernii Bishkek* suggested that the day of the referendum be elevated to an official holiday: "Patriots of the Fatherland Day".[43] To understand these statements, one has to bear in mind what role elections played during the Soviet period: elections were regarded as the regular confirmation of the Communist Party's existing state of affairs, which had already been decided on; and they legitimized the continuing existence and rule of the Party itself. The reforms as initiated by Gorbachev in the 1990s did not change this custom very much: the existing system was only modified, but not abolished.[44] Concerning Akaev's increasingly authoritarian managerial style, it can be assumed that he, quite willingly, accepted this Soviet tradition of regarding elections as an instrument which is used to acknowledge the status quo. The proclamation of "national unity", which Akaev frequently referred to in his speeches, can also be explained in this context: in Kyrgyzstan, elections continue to be viewed as an occasion to demonstrate the unity of society and the people's support for the president.

---

42 Akaev and the governmental media ignored the fact that, in the resolution of the UN, the allegedly 2200-year old existance of the Kyrgyz state is not mentioned at all.
43 See the article "Hello, patriot!" (*Zdravstvui, patriot!*), in: *Vechernii Bishkek*, 3 February 2003.
44 See Rose 1998: 39 ff.

Conclusion

In this article, it is argued that the concept of *transformation* can be looked at from quite a different perspective than has usually been applied in the branch of "transformation studies". Rather than regarding *transformation* as a real-life phenomenon, which is associated with a "third wave of democracy"[45] occurring in post-socialist countries, in this article the instrumental use of the term, as a rhetorical tool in public discourse, has been explored in the case of the Kyrgyz constitutional referendum. As the result of a qualitative analysis of speeches and newspaper articles on the referendum, one can sum up that the rhetoric on *transformation* constituted a high percentage of the media coverage of the constitutional reform. Following Akaev's lead, governmental newspapers used the term *transformation* as well as other key terms, such as *human rights, civil society, rule of law* and *democratization*, and thereby distributed these concepts to the wider Kyrgyz public. Journalists of the oppositional newspapers also framed their pleas and opinions with the help of the concept of *transformation*. As the anthropologist Kevin Latham has argued in the context of Chinese media discourse, it is the creative use of the concept by journalists themselves rather than the simple carrying-out of commands that ensures the successful distribution of the rhetoric.

Moreover, it is argued in this article that *transformation* is used in such a predominant way in Kyrgyzstan, because a socialist version of the concept already existed many years prior to its independence, thereby constituting a part of the historical legacy of the country. However, this legacy is not being handed down unchanged; it is being employed in new ways according to the will of the ruler.

If one distinguishes between the use of the concept of *transformation* and the meanings attached to it, it becomes evident that the concept itself has never been questioned in Kyrgyz public discourse. Regarding the way it was used in the constitutional referendum, according to linguist Georg Stötzel,[46] one could speak of *transformation* as a *non-controversial* concept. Stötzel maintains that controversial concepts are those linguistic-political conflicts, which are carried out in public, because they carry with them polemic images or certain non-universal ideas.[47] If one transfers Stötzel's concept to the way the concept of *transformation* has been employed in public discourse in Kyrgyzstan, it becomes clear that no such linguistic-political conflicts were present. Rather, the meaning of *transformation* was taken for granted and essentially not questioned at all. What was questioned, however, was the way it is supposed to be carried out and whether the country was progressing or relapsing.

---

45 Huntington 1991.
46 Stötzel 1995.
47 Stötzel, for example, analyses public debates in Germany on the topic of "Gastarbeiter" (foreign workers; literally "guest workers"). Embedded in the term is the assumption that these workers, who came to help rebuild Germany after World War II, at some time have to go home again – as guests usually do.

To sum up, the concept of *transformation* may shape reality, because it is able to legitimize those actions as exemplified in Akaev's political ambitions. As the term has not only been employed by the president, but also in the media, the rhetoric of *transformation* therefore constitutes an important part of public (and also private)[48] discourse about the future political, economic, legal and social development of Kyrgyzstan, thereby influencing the activities of the people as well.[49] However, the concept of *transformation* should not be mistaken for reality itself. Viewing *transformation* as a consciously and unconsciously employed rhetoric has proven to be fruitful in showing the instrumental character of the term and its manifold uses in a post-socialist context. Future research into exploring how social change is experienced in the post-socialist republics in question should take this rhetorical dimension of the concept of *transformation* into account rather than fall victim to it.

Bibliography

Bernhard, Michael. 1996. Civil society after the first transition: Dilemmas of post-communist democratization in Poland and beyond. In: *Communist and Post-Communist Studies*, 29(3), pp. 309-330.

Brunner, Georg. 1997. Rechtskultur in Osteuropa. Das Problem der Kulturgrenzen. In: Brunner, Georg (ed.), *Politische und Ökonomische Transformation in Osteuropa*, 2d. Ed. Berlin: Arno Spitz GmbH, pp. 103-124.

Carothers, Thomas. 2002. The end of the transition paradigm. In: *Journal of Democracy*, 13(1), pp. 5-21, available at: www.journalofdemocracy.org/> (accessed on 3 May 2005).

Di Palma, Giuseppe. 1990. *To craft democracies: An essay on democratic transitions*. Berkeley: University of California Press.

Gorbachov, Michail. 1987. Iz rechi M.S. Gorbacheva na vstreche v Kremle s uchastnikami mezhdunarodnogo foruma "Za beziaadernyi mir, za vyzhivanie chelovechestva". In: *Pravda*, 48, 17 February.

Hann, Christopher. 1994. After Communism: Reflections on East European anthropology and the 'transition'. In: *Social Anthropology*, 2(3), pp. 229-249.

Hann, Christopher. 2002. Abschied vom sozialistischen "Anderen". In: Hann, Christopher (ed.), *Postsozialismus. Transformationsprozesse in Europa und Asien aus ethnologischer Perspektive*. Frankfurt a.M.: Campus, pp. 11-26.

Hollander, Gayle D. 1972. *Soviet political indoctrination: developments in mass media and propaganda since Stalin*. New York: Praeger.

Humphrey, Caroline. 2002. *The unmaking of Soviet life: Everyday economies after Socialism*. Ithaca; London: Cornell University Press.

---

48 Within the frame of the research project described here, interviews with Kyrgyz legal experts such as judges, lawyers and teachers of law were conducted in order to analyse the use of the concept of "transformation" in the local population. Evidently, legal experts frequently used the concept of "transformation" in order to position themselves in a situation they referred to as unstable and unsafe. While the interviewees suspected Kyrgyzstan of becoming an autocracy (with the new constitution being a first step in this direction), their hopes, however, were framed in the rhetoric of "transformation" describing a better future. An important result of these interviews was that, while the respondents viewed their own position in the process of the political "transformation" as insignificant, they did not wait for outside assistance when designing their own personal future.

49 See Wells 1996.

Huntington, Samuel. 1993. *The third wave: Democratization in the late twentieth century.* Norman: University of Oklahoma Press.
Kunze, Thomas. 2003. Die Geschichte einer Verfassung: Machtsicherung für Präsident Akajew oder Stunde Null der Opposition in Kirgistan? In: Konrad Adenauer Stiftung (ed.) *Auslandsinformationen,* 5, pp. 46-57
Latham, Kevin. 2000. Nothing but the truth: media, power and hegemony in south China. In: *China Quarterly,* 163, pp. 633-654.
Latham, Kevin. 2002. Den Konsum überdenken: Soziale Palliative und Rhetorik der Transition im postsozialistischen China. In: Hann, Christopher (ed.) *Postsozialismus. Transformationsprozesse in Europa und Asien aus ethnologischer Perspektive.* Frankfurt a.M.: Campus, pp. 317-344.
Lenin, Vladimir I. 1916. Drei Quellen und drei Bestandteile des Marxismus. In: *Werke,* 19, pp. 3-9, available at: www.marxists.org/deutsch/archiv/lenin/1913/03/quellen.htm (accessed on 3 May 2005).
Lenin, Vladimir I. 1916. Die sozialistische Revolution und das Selbstbestimmungsrecht der Nationen (Thesen). In: *Vorbote,* 2, available at www.mlwerke.de/le/le22/le22_144.htm> (accessed on 3 May 2005).
Lijphart, Arend/ Waisman, Carlos H. (eds.). 1996. *Institutional design in new democracies: Eastern Europe and Latin America.* Boulder/ Oxford: Westview Press.
Linz, Juan J./ Stepan, Alfred. 1996. *Problems of democratic transition and consolidation: Southern Europe, South America, and post-communist Europe.* London, Baltimore: The John Hopkins University Press.
Marx, Karl/ Engels, Friedrich (MEW). 1962. *Werke – Schriften und Artikel,* Vol. 4 and 19. Berlin: Dietz.
Mandel, Ruth. 2002. Das Säen der Zivilgesellschaft in Zentralasien. In: Hann, Christopher (ed.) *Postsozialismus: Transformationsprozesse in Europa und Asien aus ethnologischer Perspektive.* Frankfurt a.M.: Campus, pp. 401-424.
Merkel, Wolfgang (ed.). 1994–2000. *Systemwechsel,* 5 vols. Opladen: Leske & Budrich.
Merkel, Wolfgang. 1999. *Systemtransformation: Eine Einführung in die Theorie und Empirie der Transformationsforschung.* Opladen: Leske + Budrich.
Merkel, Wolfgang/ Puhle, Hans-Jürgen/ Croissant, Aurel (eds.). 2003. *Defekte Demokratien,* Vol. 1: Theorie. Opladen: Leske & Budrich.
Nelle, Dietrich. 2004. Verfassungsreform in Kirgisien. In: *Verfassung und Recht in Übersee,* 37, pp. 133-141.
OSCE/ODIHR. 2003. *Kyrgyz Republic Constitutional Referendum 2 February 2003. Political Assessment Report.* Warsaw, available at: www.osce.org/documents/odihr/2003/03/1381_en.pdf (accessed on 3 May 2005).
Pribán, Jiři/ Roberts, Pauline/ Young, James (eds.). 2003. *Systems of justice in transition: Central European experiences since 1989.* Aldershot: Ashgate Publishing.
Rose, Richard/ Mishler, William/ Haerpfer, Christian. 1998. *Democracy and its alternatives: Understanding post-communist societies.* Oxford: Polity Press.
Sachs, Jeffrey/ Lipton, David. 1990a. *Creating a market economy in Eastern Europe: The case of Poland. Brookings Papers on Economic Activity 1.* Washington D.C.: The Brookings Institution.
Sachs, Jeffrey/Lipton, David. 1990b. *Privatization in Eastern Europe: The case of Poland. Brookings Papers on Economic Activity,* Vol. 2. Washington D.C.: The Brookings Institution.
Spector, Regine A. 2004. *The transformation of Askar Akaev, President of Kyrgyzstan.* University of California, Berkeley, BPS Working Paper Series, available at: http://istsocrates.berkeley.edu/~bsp/publications/ 2004_02-spec.pdf (accessed on 3 May 2005)
Stalin, Josef W. 1950. Bürger! In: *J. W. Stalin Werke,* Vol. 1, Berlin: Dietz Verlag, pp. 160-163.
Verdery, Katherine. 1996. *What was Socialism and what comes next?* Princeton: Princeton University Press.
Wells, Susan. 1996. *Sweet Reason: Rhetoric and the discourses of modernity.* Chicago: University of Chicago Press.

Farkhod Tolipov

Power, Nation-Building, and Legacy – A Comparative Analysis of Central Asian Leadership*

Introduction

The first leaders of the post-Soviet and newly independent Central Asian states are very interesting phenomena in terms of their roles, images, status and personality. Their accession to and retaining of power, their ruling of the respective countries and their soon-to-be ending presidencies play a crucial role in shaping the political systems of these young states, and will leave a deep trace in the overall process of nation and state-building in Central Asia.
Against the background of the very complicated and rapidly changing post-cold war international system and the formation of the so-called *new world order*, the five presidents and their respective states, which at the same time constitute one common region, play an important role in shaping the statehood of their nations. They not only have to conceive and consolidate the sovereignty and cohesiveness of their countries, but must also successfully integrate them into the international community.
The following analysis of the leaders and their respective regimes deals with questions such as: What are the power resources of presidents and their political regimes? What types of leadership exist? Who are those leaders who share a common background that dates back to Soviet period? Do they shape the common future of Central Asia?

Kazakhstan

Power

The Supreme Council of the Kazakh Soviet Socialist Republic appointed Nursultan Nazarbaev, born on 6 July 1940 – former First Secretary of the Communist Party of Kazakhstan – president on 24 April 1990. In the national elections of 1 December 1991, he was elected president. In the referendum of 29 April 1995, his presidential term was extended to the year 2000. However, on 8 October 1998, the parliament of Kazakhstan decided to end his tenure in 1999 and in the next presidential elections, on 10 January 1999, Nazarbaev was, once again, re-elected.

---

* This article was written before the political events in Kyrgyzstan in March 2005 and in Uzbekistan in May 2005 took place. The editors decided to publish it as a document which reflects a certain moment in history. For current developments in Kyrgyzstan and Uzbekistan, see the articles by Berg and Kreikemeyer in Part IV of this volume.

By and large, Nazarbaev has a particular place in the political landscape of the former Soviet sphere. He was very popular with the Soviet people and still plays a particular role in the political processes of the Commonwealth of Independent States (CIS). Thus, in 1994 he introduced the idea of a Eurasian Union at a meeting with the staff and students of the Lomonosov University in Moscow.[1] In 1995, the Eurasian Economic Community (EURASEC) was established as part of the CIS, representing the first step toward the realization of a Eurasian Union. It currently consists of five CIS states: Russia, Belarus, Kazakhstan, Kyrgyzstan and Tajikistan. However, EURASEC is incomplete in the geopolitical, economic and collective security sense.[2] In addition, at the 47th session of the United Nations in 1992, Nazarbaev initiated a Conference on Interaction and Confidence-Building in Asia (CICA) – something similar to the OSCE for Asia.[3] The idea emanated from a very simplistic and straightforward perception of the political, geopolitical and civilizing processes of a vast and fragmented Asian continent. There is some evidence that this project is too ambitious and is thus doomed to be a failure. In February 2003, Kazakhstan and the Ukraine launched a new initiative called the Organization of Regional Integration (ORI) with the participation of Russia, Kazakhstan, the Ukraine and Belarus.[4] As Nazarbaev pointed out, this group covers 90 per cent of the CIS economy and thus has great potential. However, more than two years after the appearance of the new sub-integration institution little is known about its activities and neither analysts nor the mass media pay much attention to it.

Generally speaking, Nazarbaev has proclaimed a so-called multi-vector foreign policy. Stemming from this conception, he tries to balance Kazakhstan's foreign relations with the great powers – primarily the Russian Federation, the People's Republic of China and the United States – as well as with neighbouring countries, primarily Uzbekistan. With respect to domestic policy, Nazarbaev's personal ambitions are reflected in the 1997 adoption of the "Programme Kazakhstan 2030" designed as a strategic development plan for Kazakhstan.[5] It aims to develop the rule of law, market-economy and social self-governance within a 35-year framework. Yet, the development of a constitutional government in particular still seems to be a distant prospect, since Nazarbaev practices an authoritarian style of leadership instead of strengthening political and economic pluralism. Frequent changes in the cabinet of ministers ordered by the president are only one indicator of this situation.[6] Due to the continuing importance of clan relationships shown in the persis-

---

1   See Kukeyeva 2004: 6.
2   For more details see: www.eurasec.org.
3   The CICA was finally established at the Almaty Summit, Kazakhstan, 3-5 June 2002 by signing the Almaty Act. For more details see: www.bits.de/NRANEU/CentralAsia.html.
4   See Center for Non-proliferation Studies, 2003: 4 f.
5   The programme was adopted on 11 October 1997. Nazarbaev's address to the nation is available at: http://www.president.kz.
6   For other examples of presidential power being exceeded in Kazakhstan see Issenova in this volume.

tence of the "*zhuz*" division,[7] the struggle for power is more a matter of rivalry among clans than a democratic competition between opposition political groups.

Political power in Kazakhstan is closely interlinked with the control of economic resources, namely, the production and export of oil. Nazarbaev naturally tries to take advantage of this abundant national resource and, moreover, has admitted to the truth of corruption allegations in relations with foreign oil companies. His abuses of power have caused the investigation process, which is presently ongoing in the US, and, as a result, the freezing of the related Swiss bank account(s). This scandal has become known as "Kazakh gate". It is no coincidence that the term "petrocracy" is used by some Western analysts to portray the interrelations between oil and political power. Wayne Merry notes "these examples of oil-rich but probity-poor states demonstrate that money flow can prolong a 'big man' in power for years, but the regime will ultimately fail due to the corrosion of social peace and the inability of the ruling clique to keep a firm grip on political realities".[8]

Although Nazabaev has already announced his candidacy for the 2006 presidential elections, he is also looking ahead to the time following his presidency. On 27 June 2000, the two houses of Kazakhstan's parliament passed the controversial "Law on the First President of Kazakhstan" in the second and final reading. In accordance with this law, Nazarbaev has been given lifelong immunity from court prosecution. His oldest daughter Dariga – a proprietress of the media empire Khabar and leader of the Asar party[9] – is often mentioned as a potential heiress to the "throne", as is her husband Rakhat Aliev, who was chief of the internal security service and later the head of the OSCE delegation and ambassador of the Republic of Kazakhstan in Vienna.

Nation-building

One important dimension of the overall development of nation and democracy-building in Kazakhstan, as well as in other Central Asian countries, is the existence of sizable diasporas and/or enclaves of nationals from neighbouring states. Kazakhstan is home to more than 120 ethnic groups, among them nearly 30 per cent Russians, nearly four per cent Ukrainians and

---

7   The Kazakhs are divided into three clan groups/hordes called "*zhuz*". The Great Horde (*ulu zhuz*) is dominant in the south of Kazakhstan, the Middle Horde (*orta zhuz*) in the north and east, and the Junior Horde (*kishi zhuz*) in the west. Nazarbaev is said to have roots in the Great Horde. See: Olcott 1997: 29.
8   Merry, 2004: 39.
9   Parliamentary elections were held on 19 September 2004. Three parties and one party block of twelve participating political organizations reached the established minimum requirement of seven per cent of the votes and could nominate their representatives for the seats in parliament. The largest party following the elections is the one of the president, "Otan" (43 per cent); second is that of the president's daughter "Asar" (19.5 per cent). The opposition party "Ak Jol" and opposition block AIST got 16 per cent and eight per cent of the votes, respectively.

two and a half per cent Uzbeks and Tatars each.[10] This makes the question of nationality in Kazakhstan important and sensitive. If one considers that ethnic Kazakhs compose about only half of the country's population, then it becomes obvious that the diaspora factor can carry with it an external/regional dimension.

In his address to the nation on 4 April 2003, Nazarbaev reiterated one central problem: ensuring the present population growth.[11] He emphasized the necessity of implementing a governmental programme focusing on an increase in the birth rate and a decrease in the mortality rate by improving healthcare and by increased immigration – primarily from among ethnic Kazakhs living abroad or the so-called "oralman".[12]

Yet, the nation-building process in Kazakhstan cannot aim solely at revitalizing the Kazakh nation, but must instead create a Kazakhstani[13] nation. Thus, in addition to his efforts to increase the number of ethnic Kazakhs, Nazarbaev pays special attention to the needs of the Russian population and increasingly underscores the importance of close relations between his country and neighbouring Russia.

Legacy

With respect to the future political development of the country, one cannot overlook the dichotomy of Kazakhstan as the nation-state and the Kazakhstan that is part of Central Asia. Although this dichotomy is pertinent to all Central Asian countries, Kazakhstan represents a special case because its exposure to the geopolitical implications of the Soviet dissolution was what propelled the republic into independence in the first place.

The political and social legacies of the current regime will depend on two external factors: one, Russian influence and two, Uzbek influence. It was not by accident that Nazarbaev proclaimed a multi-vector foreign policy. Kazakhstani self-determination as a state and as a nation is and will likely continue to be complicated by a number of factors. Its internal cohesion and the unity of the region are interrelated. Moreover, the current leadership has an historical responsibility to recognize that, together with Uzbekistan – with its higher population and more homogeneous demographics – Kazakhstan may act as a catalyst for more regional integration and bring about democracy and national prosperity in a country that plays an integral part in the fate of the region.

---

10 See http://www.eamedia.org/eamfhome.php.
11 The Russian wording of the original speech is available at www.president.kz.
12 "1991 [...] Kazakhstan initiated a program of 'Kazakhization' to improve the percentage of ethnic Kazakhs and to offset the large-scale emigration of ethnic Russians and Germans. Ethnic Kazakhs were promoted in the government bureaucracy, educated in their language, and invited to return home. They are referred to by the government as oralman." Lynch 2005: 36.
13 The adjective ending –stani in "Kazakhstani" is used to refer to citizens of Kazakhstan regardless of their ethnicity. This also applies to the adjective Uzbek versus Uzbekistani.

Kyrgyzstan

Power

Askar Akaev was born on 10 November 1944 in northern Kyrgyzstan. In 1987, he was elected vice president of the republic's Academy of Sciences and, in 1988, he was elected its president. Following the political crisis in Osh in the autumn of 1990, Akaev was elected president at the session of Kyrgyzstan's Supreme Soviet on 27 October 1990. In the first election after independence in 1991, he was re-elected president. In the next presidential elections, which were set for 24 December 1995, Akaev received 71 per cent of the votes. Despite a constitutional provision limiting the head of state to two terms in office, Akaev ran for president again in 2000 and received 74 per cent of the votes.

At the beginning of the transition process the international community regarded Akaev as one of the most liberal leaders in Central Asia. However, after several years of being in power, Akaev has turned more and more to an authoritarian style of leadership and has continually reduced the power of the parliament. As Merry points out, "Kyrgyzstan's President Akaev is a great disappointment to many in the West who naively saw him as a Jeffersonian democrat in the heart of Asia. Sadly, a better parallel is Zimbabwe's Robert Mugabe, who also won many admirers in his early years before his agenda narrowed to maintaining personal power."[14] Governmental persecutions of political opponents and the re-election of Akaev in October 2000 gave reason for many observers and human rights organizations to express harsh criticism of the president and the policies he had thus far adopted. The sentencing of the former vice-president and opposition leader, Feliks Kulov, before the presidential elections in 2000, undermined Kyrgyzstan's reputation as the only country in Central Asia, which had achieved a certain democratization. Scott Horton, a lawyer in New York and president of the International League for Human Rights, said the following in a New York Times interview: "After studying this case for some nine months, I have come to the conclusion that the prosecution, trial and sentence were all politically manipulated. [...] You could hardly imagine stronger evidence of judicial misconduct."[15]

In the meantime, the president's extended family has accumulated important economic resources. Kathleen Collins alleges that Akaev's clan "controls the national bank and the security forces", while his wife's clan "controls the ministries responsible for gold mining and privatization".[16] But Akaev's wife Mayram is not only involved with economic activities she is also among those mentioned as would-be successors to the presidency. Most likely,

---

14 Merry 2004: 38.
15 Frantz 2001.
16 Collins 2002: 146.

Akaev will be the first among the Central Asian leaders to surrender his office to his successor in the presidential elections in autumn 2005. Both the upcoming parliamentary and presidential elections in Kyrgyzstan in 2005 will cause the political climate of the country to heat up considerably. Debates on future candidates for the office of president of this Central Asian "isle of democracy" in the "sea of autocracies" will become more prominent. Urmat Sovetov, member of the "*Ar-Namys*" party anticipates that, if Akaev once again announces his candidacy for the post, a real revolution rather than a "Rose Revolution", such as the one in Georgia, may take place.[17]

Furthermore, Akaev has (also) prepared himself for the time following his presidency. As early as 2003, he drafted a law on "On Guarantees for the Activity of the President of the Kyrgyz Republic". The law was adopted within an unusually short period of time during the parliamentary session on 26 June 2003. It defines the privileges, immunity and material protection of acting and retired presidents and their families. In addition, it creates a special status for the "First President of the Kyrgyz Republic", i.e. Askar Akaev, and special privileges for him and his family after his retirement. This status includes the right of the retired "First President" to maintain a secretariat and staff, funded by the state budget and defined in size only by himself, as well as the right to continue addressing the people, the parliament and the government "in important cases". Such a situation could create a kind of parallel or shadow presidency after the retirement of Akaev, which he has declared as final after the end of his term in 2005.

Nation-building

Like many newly independent states, Kyrgyzstan's elite, ideologists, and the president himself have been eager to seek out new national symbols for the nation-building process. The cultural restoration of the ancient Manas epos[18] is one of the most important components of national identity. It was not by chance that, from the beginning of independence, Akaev advanced the concept of Kyrgyzstan as "our common home". The country is geographically and ethnically divided to a visible extent. According to data from 1999, the three largest ethnic groups in Uzbekistan are the Kyrgyz (65 per cent), Uzbeks (14 per cent) and the Russians (twelve per cent).[19] Interethnic relationships in the country are of strategic importance. Russian, for example, was given the status of an official state language, and Osh, a city with one-third population of Uzbeks in the south of Kyrgyzstan, was made a "second capital". In addition to ethnic identity, regional identity in combination with belonging to a certain clan plays a very important role in Kyrgyzstan. Three

---

17 See Sovetov 2004.
18 The Manas epos is named after the Kyrgyz hero Batyr-khan Manas who protected Kyrgyzstan against invaders.
19 See http://cia.gov/cia/publications/factbook/geos/kg.html.

groups of clans dominate political and economic life: The *Sol* wing unites seven clans from the north and the west of Kyrgyzstan, including the *Sarybagysh* clan to which the president belongs. The *Ong* wing is a large clan from the south, and the *Ichkilik* wing consists of several smaller clans from the south.[20] Resources are distributed among these three wings, but lie mainly in the hands of northern clans, including the president's clan and his wife's. The shifting of the informal balance of power among the several clans was one of the causes for the unrests in southern Kyrgyzstan in 2002.[21]

Legacy

What legacy will President Akaev and his political regime leave behind? Most likely, Akaev will be the first among the Central Asian leaders to surrender his office to his successor in the upcoming presidential elections. One should take into consideration the dichotomy between the Kyrgyz-Kazakh and the Kyrgyz-Uzbek relations. The gist of the matter is that different kinds of relationships exist between Kyrgyzstan and each of these two neighbouring countries. The Kazakhstani influence may push Kyrgyzstan closer to Russia, whereas the Uzbekistani influence may pull the country in closer toward the Central Asian region itself. It remains to be seen which influence will prove to be greater.

Tajikistan

Power

Emomali Rakhmonov was born 5 October 1952 in the province of Kulob. He graduated from the faculty of economics at the Tajik State University in 1982. Since 1990, Rakhmonov has been a deputy of the Supreme Soviet of Tajikistan and, in 1992, following the resignation of Rakhman Nabiev, he was elected chair. In this manner, he became *de facto* head of state. After the re-establishment of the presidential system, he was elected President of Tajikistan on 6 November 1994 and re-elected in November 1999.
The current state of affairs in Tajikistan can be characterized as authoritarian. Tough rule has seemed to be the clear consequence of civil war, which revealed the existence of divisive and radical elements in Tajikistani society between 1992-1997. The civil war reflected different aspects of power struggles both from within and from outside the country. The demands for the inclusion of both Islamic and secular groups in a government coalition contributed to the outbreak of civil war. Different regional and ideological groups fought for political influence. Domestically speaking, the conflict

---

20 See Olcott 1997: 132 f.
21 For details see: Khamidov 2003.

revolved around a struggle for power between the Leninabad province in the north and the Kulob province in the south. In the period up to 1997, more than 50,000 people lost their lives.

The peace process finally started in 1997 with a peace accord between the government and the United Tajik Opposition (UTO) and with the establishment of a Committee for National Reconciliation (CNR) supported by the international community. The opposition gained a significant number of government posts per quota (30 per cent), and former UTO parties like the Islamic Renaissance Party were legalized.[22] But this solution for balancing diverse political interests seems to be rather fragile. In the very recent past, President Rakhmonov has made several attempts to limit the influence of the Islamic Renaissance Party as well as that of his former allies, and has been quite successful in consolidating his power. He has not expanded his circle with a broader-based government, but rather with people from his home town, Danghara. In doing so, he has hindered the appearance of an alternative leader within the political elite.[23] The absence of public protest after the parliamentary elections in February 2005 is suggestive evidence of Rakhmonov's currently strong position.[24] The next presidential elections are scheduled for 2006.

Nation-building

The reference point for nation-building in Tajikistan is associated with the epoch of the Samanid dynasty (875-999) which is portrayed by the current government as the Tajiks' golden age. On the 8th anniversary of Tajik independence in 1999, two years after the end of the civil war, the so-called National Unity memorial complex was opened in Dushanbe. It includes an 11-meter high statue of Ismail Samanid, the leader of the Samanid empire (892-907).[25] The importance of the Samanid epoch for Tajikistan is based on two elements. First, it was the last time that "the bulk of Iranian lands became the domain of an Iranian ruler".[26] Second, during this period, the region experienced a cultural and economic blossoming.

Yet, the identification with the Samanid Empire also creates problems with neighbouring Uzbekistan. In the Soviet Union, the Tajik Autonomous Soviet Socialist Republic (ASSR) was originally grouped as part of the newly established Uzbek Soviet Socialist Republic (SSR). Later, it was made the Tajik SSR. The region of Leninabad in the Ferghana-Valley, which originally belonged to the Uzbek SSR, was given to the Tajik SSR in 1929 to provide the

---

22 Akiner/Barnes 2001.
23 International Crisis Group 2004.
24 The OSCE stated on 28 February 2005 that "Elections in Tajikistan fail to meet key international standards"; see: www.osce.org/item/8940.html.
25 See Nourzhanov 2001.
26 Ibid.

Tajik economy with an industrial base. Territorial claims over Uzbekistan by nationalists in Tajikistan make waves from time to time.

Anti-Uzbek sentiments do exist among political and intellectual elites, although it seems that such sentiments are more politically than culturally or socially inspired. In June 2000, during his first official visit to Tajikistan, the Uzbek president Islam Karimov gave an emotional speech before the Tajik intelligentsia and advanced the idea that Tajiks and Uzbeks are one people, who speak two different languages. Besides the significant positive effect that this statement had on the public of both countries, it was also seen as a first sign of rapprochement between the two countries.

In addition, one should not forget about the regional fragmentation inside Tajikistan. As mentioned above, the Leninabad region was added to the Tajik SSR later on. Yet, during the Soviet era, Tajikistan was ruled by people from this region. After 1992, the rulers came from southern Tajikistan (Kulob region) and, additionally, after 1997 from Gharm. Currently, people from Sughd have very limited access to political positions. The same holds true for people from the Gorno-Badakhshan Autonomous Region (GBAO). Establishing a Tajik nation, despite huge regional differences and strong regional identities, remains a future challenge for the Rakhmonov regime.

Legacy

Since the break-up of the Soviet Union, of all the Central Asian countries, Tajikistan has suffered the most in every sense: economic decline, civil war, external challenges and geopolitical games. This is why one can expect the most complicated political legacy from the current "transition period".

In any case, Tajikistan's development as a state and as a nation will – to a decisive degree – depend on the leadership's behaviour towards its Central Asian neighbours. Just as its modern nationhood was caused by the division of the region in the early 20th century, its modern statehood is owed to the dissolution of the Soviet Union. Its future survival, identity and prosperity are inexorably tied to the rest of the region.

Turkmenistan

Power

Saparmurad Niyazov was born 19 February 1940 in Ashgabad. In 1985 he was appointed First Secretary of the Communist Party of the Turkmen SSR. He headed the Council of Ministers from 1985 till 1986 and, on 13 January 1990, he became speaker of the Supreme Soviet of Turkmenistan. On 27 October 1990, Niyazov was elected president of Turkmenistan. After the dissolution of the Soviet Union, he was prime minister from 1991 to 1992;

and on 21 June 1992 he was elected president of the now independent Turkmenistan for a five-year term. In 1993, Niyazov proclaimed himself to be "Turkmenbashi", meaning "the Leader of all ethnic Turkmen". His term of office was extended to five years in a national referendum on 15 January 1994. On 28 December 1999, he was proclaimed president for life by the parliament.

Niyazov's regime is perhaps one of the best examples of what Max Weber labelled "sultanistic regimes"[27] and, as such, authoritarian and undemocratic. His cult of personality may be compared to those of Leonid Brezhnev and Joseph Stalin. He commands an extraordinary authority and possesses seemingly unlimited power within his country. Power and national legitimacy are fused in the president's person. To illustrate this, one needs only to recall that Niyazov simultaneously occupies the posts of Chairman of the Cabinet of Ministers, Chairman of the People's Council, Chairman of the Democratic Party of Turkmenistan, Chairman of the Council of Elders, Supreme Commander of the Military Forces, Chairman of the Council of Defence and the National Security Council and President of the Humanitarian Association of all Turkmens in the World.

In Turkmenistan, it is forbidden by law to be in opposition to the president. The two main opposition leaders, Avdi Kuliev and Boris Shihmuradov, have been exiled. As a result, the opposition has been placed in a stranglehold. A number of news reports claim that Shihmuradov was behind the attempted assassination of the president on 25 November 2002, with the help of the Uzbek embassy in Ashgabad. The attempt on the president's life led to the arrest of the opposition's leader.

Nation-building

Turkmenistan has a relatively small population of just under five million. The two major ethnic minorities are Uzbeks, (five per cent) and Russians (four per cent). Most Uzbeks live in the two Turkmen cities of Chardjou and Tashgous, located on the Turkmen-Uzbek border. Inevitably this increases the links between Turkmenistan and Uzbekistan. There has been a sizeable emigration of Russians and Russian speakers due to Niyazov's policies of "Turkmenization" of all spheres of the state and public life, and the adoption of discriminatory laws aimed at that particular group. Turkmen was established as the state language in May 1990 and, in 1993, Niyazov issued a decree on the replacement of the Cyrillic-based alphabet. Later on, several laws and decrees were adopted aiming at eliminating spoken and written Russian in Turkmenistan.

Turkmen are primarily defined by tribal affiliation. The most important tribes are the *Tekke* and the *Yomud*, followed by the *Ersary*, *Salyr*, *Karyk* and the

---

27   See Weber 1978: 231 f.

Choudur. The *Tekke* tribe comes from region of Ashghabat.[28] Although Niyazov as an orphan lacks powerful tribal networks, he is careful about the tribal affiliation of his support base and eager to spread appointments and wealth around.[29] His cult of personality is an attempt at nation-building in a country where tribal differences are significant and complex. It is in this light that we have to see the greatest product of Turkmen ideology, the "Ruhname", (Turkmen for spiritual essay, or holy book) written by Niyazov. In this book, he describes the history of the Turkmen people and prophesises its great and prosperous future, while prescribing how all Turkmens are to lead their lives.

Legacy

The political future of the present Turkmen leader seems to be pointing in two possible directions. First, given his life-time appointment to the presidency and his iron grip on both the country and not least his opponents, it seems that his tenure might easily go beyond those of the other Central Asian leaders. A second and very different outcome is also possible. The very election of new leaders of the other states in the region might prove to be a catalyst for increased and more widespread opposition against Niyazov and could ultimately lead to his resignation.

Uzbekistan

Power

Islam Karimov was born on 30 January 1938 in Samarkand, Uzbekistan. After being raised in an orphanage, he studied engineering and economics in Tashkent. He became involved in politics in 1983 and rapidly climbed the political ladder of the Communist Party. In 1990, he was appointed President of the Uzbek SSR. After declaring Uzbek independence from the Soviet Union, he won the presidential election of 1991 amid protests that the elections were unfair and undemocratic. In a referendum in 1995, his term in office was extended to 2000 and, in the presidential elections of that year, he was re-elected. This took place after a campaign in which the only opposing candidate allowed to run had publicly acknowledged that he supported all of Karimov's policies and that he himself would vote for Karimov. Karimov won 91 per cent of the popular vote.[30]

---

28 See Prazauskas 1998: 54.
29 For more details see Cummings/Ochs 2002: 118 ff.
30 See Eurasianet 2000.

From the outset of independence, Karimov publicly emphasized the symbolism of Central Asian traditions of strong leadership. He devised priorities for both foreign and domestic policy and declared Uzbekistan's "own way of renovation and progress".[31] With respect to Uzbekistan's foreign policy, he settled on six principles: 1) supremacy of national interests, along with due account of mutual interests; 2) equality and mutual benefit, non-interference into internal affairs of other states; 3) openness to co-operation irrespective of ideological outlooks, adherence to universal values, preservation of peace and security; 4) priority of the norms of international law over national ones; 5) development of external ties on the basis of both bilateral and multilateral agreements; 6) non-participation in the politico-military blocks.[32]

Furthermore, Karimov was very eager to establish himself as a regional leader accepting the inheritance of Amir Timur (see below). Karimov's pretension of seizing regional leadership has often resulted in tense relations with Kazakh President Nazarbaev. Sometimes they have tended to obstruct their respective initiatives in regional organizations. In general terms, Uzbekistan's foreign policy orientation seems to be ambivalent. At times, it seems to be rather pro-American and at other times rather supportive of Russian policies.

Karimov has always declared his adherence to democracy proclaiming that sooner or later democratic institutions and a democratic political culture in Uzbek society will take root. Yet, de facto authoritarianism remains strong in Uzbekistan. Although the constitution provides for a presidential system with separation of powers among the executive, legislative and judiciary, the executive branch of power under Karimov's leadership dominates most parts of political and economic life. The existing officially registered parties do not differ from each other with respect to either their programmes or the character of their political activities. They do not display any competition and do not even struggle for power. Their ideological bases are vague; their prestige and influence in the society are invisible. "Real" opposition parties are not registered and continue their activities on an illegal basis. Moreover, they have not so far been able to become a real political force in the country.

Also, in economic terms Karimov intends to create what he calls a state system. His model for building a market economy in Uzbekistan rests on five key principles: the total de-ideologization of the economy, preserving the state's role as the main reformer force in transition, the primacy of law in all aspects of life, sound social policy and an evolutionary manner of transition to a market economy without "revolutionary changes", "shock therapy", or any deterioration in the living standards of the people.[33]

---

31 In 1992, Karimov published a book with this title.
32 The objectives of Uzbekistan's foreign policy course are published at the website of the ministry of foreign affairs: www.mfa.uz.
33 See Karimov, 1993: 37 f.

It is quite evident that Karimov exercises a determining influence on political as well as on economic processes. Yet, contrary to Karimov's rhetoric, Uzbekistan lacks democracy and a market economy as well as a regional leadership role. The concept of the state is very much associated with his person and thus runs the risk of becoming fragile after his displacement. The next presidential elections in Uzbekistan will take place in 2007. Just like his colleagues in neighbouring Kyrgyzstan and Kazakhstan, Karimov is looking toward the end of his term in office. The recently adopted "Law on the Ex-President of the Republic of Uzbekistan" allows him to keep his life-time seat in the senate and to maintain his status as a permanent member of the Supreme Court for as long as he wishes. Yet, the leadership question often causes waves.

Nation-building

As with the other newly independent states in Central Asia, a search for national roots also took place in Uzbekistan. Amir Timur (1336-1405) is considered to have been the first to create a centralized empire on the territory of today's Uzbekistan and is thus the recognized founder of the first Uzbek state.[34] After independence, the statue of Karl Marx in the central square of Tashkent was replaced by that of Timur. Inspired by Timur's achievements, the president declared that Uzbekistan faces a great future and that a regional leadership role awaits the Uzbek nation as the heirs of Timur.[35]

The nation-building process and the creation of a national identity in Uzbekistan are complicated by two factors: First, the importance of regional identity and second, the existence of significant minority groups. Regional and local identity in combination with affiliation to certain influential clans play an important role in gaining loyalty in Uzbekistan. Such a combination often results in an unhealthy struggle for power. The most influential clans come from Tashkent and Samarkand followed by those in the Ferghana-Valley and Bukhara. The far west (Khiva and Karakalpakstan) as well as the far south (Kashkadaryo and Surkhandaryo) are of subordinate importance. The regional groups primarily try to pursue their own group interests at the expense of common, national goals and, to this end, they endeavour to promote the advancement of their members in the state hierarchy. The problem of regionalism and clan relationship is so acute that President Karimov – who himself does not come from a major family – called it a threat to national security. He argued that civil society cannot be strong and well developed if remnants of tribal relationships persist, since it is they who are undermining the unity and

---

34   In 1369, he became Emir of Transoxania and made Samarkand the capital of his empire. Amir Timur is also known as Tamerlane.
35   See Shingleton/McConnell 2001.

cohesiveness of the society.[36] To limit the influence of certain families and clans, Karimov rotates posts frequently.[37]

Uzbekistan contains two important regionally concentrated minorities, the Tajiks and the Karakalpaks. The Autonomous Republic of Karakalpakstan is situated in the west of Uzbekistan. It exists within the structure of the Republic of Uzbekistan and has its own constitution, parliament and president, but the laws of Uzbekistan are superior to those of Karakalpakstan. The Karakalpaks suffer from disastrous environmental problems triggered by the extensive irrigation of the cotton fields, which led to the desertification of the Aral Sea. As already mentioned in the section on Tajikistan in this article, the cities Bukhara and Samarkand are largely inhabited by Tajiks. This fact, in combination with a strong nationalization of politics in Uzbekistan, has led to animosity and suspicion time and time again.

Legacy

Given its strong historical experience in maintaining statehood, and some undeniable social, political, demographic, economic, military and even ideological factors, Uzbekistan seems better prepared not only to complete state-building undertakings but also to secure democratic changes.

Though this may seem a strange and unconvincing idea, Uzbekistan should become a motor for and pillar of democratic change in Central Asia, since it bears special responsibility for the region. Three very important ideas advanced by the president deserve mention from the viewpoint of nation- building: 1) regionalism will lead to globalization; 2) Turkistan is our common home; 3) Uzbeks and Tajiks are one people speaking two languages (mentioned above). The importance of these concepts lies in their inherent regional dimension of national self-determination. So far, these ideas remain unrealised in terms of policy. Perhaps they will be delivered by the next and hopefully more democratic generation of leaders of Uzbekistan.

Conclusion

All five Central Asian leaders are, without doubt, authoritarian rulers of their respective states. The presidential apparatus often plays the role of real, albeit informal, state power, and keeps control as a "coordinator" of legislative and executive power branches. Singular persons always play exceptional and immense roles in authoritarian regimes. In Central Asia, political leaders are affected by Soviet political education and tradition, as well as by Asian psy-

---

36 See Karimov 1997.
37 A recent example – and only one among many – is the replacement of Ismail Jurabekov (Samarkand clan) from the post of the senior deputy premier by Rustam Azimov (Tashkent clan). See Dubnov 2005.

chology and political culture, thus resulting in a complex style of political leadership. Yet, we must be careful about making broad geographical generalizations. The fragmentation of the Central Asian nations into clans and regional and ethnic groupings predetermines, to a great extent, the prevailing mentality of paternalism, a patriarchal political culture and a strong central authority. The latter is believed to have the power and capacity to integrate these clans, tribes and other local groups into one nation, or one state, thus providing a greater degree of security and chance of survival.

All of the five Central Asian presidents have shared the same pattern in their ascent to power. Their nomination was due to Gorbachev's policy of reconstructing the Soviet political system. While their initial power base was the former communist party, they strengthened national identity after their republics gained independence. The five Central Asian states are the only ones in the CIS that have yet to change their political leadership. All of the presidents concerned have been in power for about 15-20 years, as was the Soviet leader Leonid Brezhnev. Yet, none of them seem to seriously care, at least openly, about the merits of a political successor.

Daniel Burghart reminds us of the lesson learned from the past: "The regional leaders must realize that their legacy will be measured by the condition in which they leave their countries, as opposed to their own individual wealth and power. While Tamerlane created a mighty empire, it quickly disintegrated after his death because he failed to establish any viable structure for ensuring its continuation once he was gone."[38] Central Asian leaders should not only consider today's stability, but also political stability after they leave office. It is indeed a moral and political test for them and, at the same time, for the West. The upcoming parliamentary and presidential elections all over Central Asia may prove to be more democratic than the previous ones, and thus could prove to be historical turning points.

Samuel Huntington noted that, after the collapse of communism, the view was reinforced in the West, especially in the United States, that its ideology of democratic liberalism had triumphed globally and was thus universally valid. However, the dominant attitudes toward these Western values in non-Western cultures range from widespread scepticism to intense opposition. "What universalism is to the West is imperialism to the rest."[39] In our case, it is not about inherent incompatibility of Western and Eastern values, but about the unwillingness of certain dominant political forces in Central Asian countries to incorporate democracy which is, by-and-large, not a Western invention. In the very recent past, these countries were socialist Soviet republics. Now, they are all in the process of passing from one politico-economic system to another. What remains obvious, though, is the public confusion about how long the transition period, proclaimed by Central Asian leaders, is going to last. "Nearly a decade ago, the dissolution of the Soviet Union raised

---

38 Burghart 2004: 20.
39 Huntington 1996: 184.

hopes that vast new areas of the globe would come under democratic forms of governance. The five states of former Soviet Central Asia have done the most [...] to dash these hopes."[40]

Central Asian states are undemocratic not because democracy is alien to them; on the contrary, they are not democratic, because they are isolated from each other. Using David Mitrany's contemplation, social activity in the region, in the widest sense of the word, is cut off by state barriers and may, or may not, be combined with similar activities beyond the boundaries with the help of "uncertain and cramping political ligatures".[41] When social activity – which by nature can spread beyond state borders – is cut off at the randomly drawn boundaries dismemberment of national self-identification takes place, and any effort to strengthen national specificity leads nowhere. The irony is that the common threat of terrorism to the countries of the region and common tasks in the struggle against this threat have played what one could call an "angry joke" on the region. Instead of this threat becoming a powerful stimulus for unprecedented regional co-operation, the different countries have begun to use protectionist measures of isolationist character.

Bibliography

Akiner, Shirin/Barnes, Catherine. 2001. The Tajik civil war. Causes and dynamics. In: *Accord: Politics of compromise. The Tajikistan peace process.* (online available at: www.c-r.org/accord).

Babus, Sylvia. 2004. Democracy Building in Central Asia. In: Burghart, Daniel L./Sabonis-Helf, Theresa (eds.). *In the Tracks of Tamerlane. Central Asia's Path to the 21st Century.* Washington: Center for Technology and National Security Policy, pp. 115-138.

Burghart, Daniel L. 2004. In the Tracks of Tamerlane. Central Asia's Path to the 21st Century. In: Burghart, Daniel L./Sabonis-Helf, Theresa (eds.). *In the Tracks of Tamerlane. Central Asia's Path to the 21st Century.* Washington: Center for Technology and National Security Policy, pp. 3-24.

Center for Nonproliferation Studies. 2003. *NIS Export Control Observer*, Monterey, April. (online available at: http://cns.miis.edu/pubs/nisexcon/pdfs/ob_0304e.pdf).

Collins, Kathleen. 2002. Clans, Pacts, and Politics in Central Asia. In: *Journal of Democracy.* 13, 3, July, pp. 137-152.

Cummings, Sally N./Ochs, Michael. 2002. Turkmenistan. Sapamurat Niyazov's Inglorious Isolation. In: Cummings, Sally N. (ed.). *Power and change in Central Asia,* London: Routledge, pp. 115-129.

Dubnov Arkady. 2005. Каримов помиловал своего «серого кардинала». В Узбекистане началась подготовка к смене власти. In: *Vremya Novostei,* 17 February. (online available at: www.vremya.ru/2005/27/5/118619.html).

Eurasianet. 2000. *Turkestan Newsletter,* 13 January. (online available at: www.eurasianet.org/departments/election/uzbekistan/bbu260100.htm).

---

40 Statement by Cassandra Cavanaugh on 12 April 2000 at the joint hearing before the Subcommittee on Asia and the Pacific and the Subcommittee on International Operations and Human Rights of the Committee on International Relations. US House of Representatives. The full text is available online at www.house.gov/international_relations/107/65201.pdf.

41 Mitrany 1975: 118.

Frantz, Douglas. 2001. Fresh dynasties sprout in post-soviet lands as democratic succession withers. In: *The New York Times*, 20 February. (online available at: http://eurasia.org.ru/archive/2001/press_en/02_20_Freshdynasties_eng.htm).

Fomin, Nikolai. 2000. Unhuman "democracy". Following the worse examples president Akayev is likely to face a boomerang effect. In: International Eurasian Institute for Economic and Political Research: *Central Asian Bulletin*, 23 March, (online available at: http://iicas.org/english/publAK_28_03_00.htm).

Huntington, Samuel P. 1996. *The Clash of Civilizations and the Remaking of World Order*. New York: Simon & Schuster.

International Crisis Group. 2004. *Tajikistan's Politics: Confrontation or Consolidation?* Asia Briefing 33, Dushanbe/Brussels. (online available at: www.crisisgroup.org).

Karimov, Islam A. 1997. Uzbekistan on the Threshold of the Twenty-First Century. (online available at: www.uzbekconsul.org/news/Uzbekistan_On_the_Threshold_Of_the_Twenty_First_Century.pdf)

Karimov, Islam A. 1993. *Uzbekistan. Own Model of Transition to Market Relations*. Toshkent.

Khamidov, Alisher. 2003. Kyrgyzstan's unrest linked to clan rivalries. In: *Eurasia Insight*, 6 May. (online available at: www.eurasianet.org/departments/insight/articles/eav060502_pr.shtml).

Kolstø, Pål. 1998. Anticipating Demographic Superiority. Kazakh Thinking on Integration and Nation-Building. In: *Europe-Asia Studies*. 50, 1, January, pp. 51-68. (online available at: http://folk.uio.no/palk/anticipating_demographic.htm).

Kukeyeva, Fatima. 2004. *The Idea of Eurasian Union and Transatlantic Partnership*. Peabody Center for Education Policy. Occasional Paper Series. (online available at: http://peabody.vanderbilt.edu/pcep/papers/kukeyeva.pdf).

Lynch, Maureen. 2005. *Lives on Hold. The Human Cost of Statelessness*. Washington. (online available at www.refugeesinternational.org/files/5051_file_stateless_paper.pdf).

Merry, Wayne E. 2004. The Politics of Central Asia. National in Form, Soviet in Content. In: Burghart, Daniel L./ Sabonis-Helf, Theresa (eds.), *In the Tracks of Tamerlane. Central Asia's Path to the 21st Century*. Washington: Center for Technology and National Security Policy, pp. 25-42.

Mitrany, David. 1975. *The Functional Theory of Politics*. London: Martin Robertson and Company.

Nourzhanov, Kirill. 2001. The Politics of History in Tajikistan. Reinventing the Samanids. In: *Harvard Asia Quarterly*, V, 1, (online available at:
www.fas.harvard.edu/~asiactr/haq/200101/0101a003.htm).

Olcott, Martha Brill. 1997. Kazakstan. In: Glenn E. Curtis (ed.), *Kazakstan, Kyrgyzstan, Tajikistan, Turkmenistan, and Uzbekistan, Country Studies*. Washington: Library of Congress, pp. 1-98.

Olcott, Martha Brill. 1997. Kyrgyzstan. In: Glenn E. Curtis (ed.), *Kazakstan, Kyrgyzstan, Tajikistan, Turkmenistan, and Uzbekistan. Country Studies*. Washington: Library of Congress, pp. 99-194.

Prazauskas, Algis. 1998. Ethnopolitical Issues and the Emergence of Nation-States in Central Asia. In: Zhang, Yongjin/Azizian, Rouben (eds.), *Ethnic Challenges Beyond Borders. Chinese and Russian Perspectives of the Central Asian Conundrum*. Great Britain: Macmillan Press Ltd, pp. 50-69.

Shingleton, William D./McConnell, John. 2001. From Tamerlane to Terrorism: The Shifting Basis of Uzbek Foreign Policy. In: *Harvard Asia Quarterly*, V, 1. (online available at: www.fas.harvard.edu/~asiactr/haq/200101/0101a004.htm).

Sovetov, Urmat. 2004. Революция, но не бархатная. Что ожидает в скором будущем Кыргызстан? In: *Centrasia*. 16 September. (online available at: http://www.centrasia.ru/newsA.php4?st=1095308100).

Weber, Max. 1978. *Economy and Society. An Outline of Interpretative Sociology*. Berkeley: University of California Press.

Atyrkul Alisheva

Kyrgyzstan: The Public and the Authorities*

This article is based on the author's practical experience in a Kyrgyz non-governmental organization. It addresses the role of civil society in the democratic development of the country and analyses its relationship with the authorities – namely that of non-governmental organizations (NGOs), political parties and the local self-government. In addition, based on the example of the OSCE in the Kyrgyz Republic, it touches on topics such as: education for democracy, and the interaction between civil society institutions and international organizations.

Non-Governmental Organizations

Democratization processes that take place worldwide strongly affect post-Soviet countries' political systems and democratic institutions. In Kyrgyzstan, this influence can be observed primarily in the development of civil society. Civil society began to take shape there in the late 1980s, when the first discussion groups were formed. Later, in the early 1990s, such groups were registered as NGOs, while public movements formed into political parties. Among the first politically oriented public movements of the early 1990s was the Democratic Movement of Kyrgyzstan.

At that time, female activists were establishing most NGOs in the Kyrgyz Republic, while men were establishing political parties. During the Soviet period, women, who had only few opportunities to realize their ideas and creative potential, used this opportunity to apply their skills in the non-governmental sector. Currently, NGOs in Kyrgyzstan have found their niche and have successfully resolved many problems of social character. They also make up the most active component of the civil sector and actively deal with social issues that concern the general public, as well as participate in political processes. Leaders of NGOs have gained significant experience through participation in a variety of international conferences and training seminars held both within and outside Kyrgyzstan. Experience shared with NGOs of other countries, support from international organizations and grants provided by Western democracies were among the factors that significantly influenced the development of NGOs in the former Soviet republics. Currently, the active involvement of young people is helping the NGO sector in Kyrgyzstan to grow further.

---

* This article was written before the political events in March 2005. The editors decided to publish it as document reflecting a certain moment in history. For the current developments in Kyrgyzstan, see the article by Berg in this volume.

Political parties

The existing legal environment is quite favourable for establishing public associations and political parties in the country and, as a result, the quantitative growth represented by an increasing number of parties is far ahead of the parties' qualitative development. Early in 2000, as many as 28 political parties were officially registered in Kyrgyzstan, while 2004 saw their number increased to 40.[1] Even though political parties are numerous and well represented in Parliament, it is too early to speak of a sustainable multi-party system in the country. The establishment of a pluralistic party system in Kyrgyzstan is lingering. The numerous political parties in Kyrgyzstan contribute to the country's democratic image favoured by its citizens and the international community, but hardly represent a serious political force. They appear to be a relatively weak component of civil society in Kyrgyzstan.

The social base of a political party can be seen as a key component, and its weakness appears to be the most serious disadvantage of political parties in Kyrgyzstan. As a rule, the leader and the number of members constitute a political party. The experience of some parties has shown that some of members are not necessarily strong supporters of the leader. Therefore, most of the political parties in Kyrgyzstan lack true support.

The results of the 2000 parliamentary elections showed that citizens of the country have no clear position on most of the parties and vote primarily for the leaders they know and have a positive image of. The attitudes toward a political leader are much more important than having information on the party's political programme, social or political strategy. As a result, personification of power has become a distinct feature of political life. This is evidently not enough, however, for a political party to win the elections on either the local or central level. During the past several years, no political party has managed to strengthen its position to the point of becoming a true alternative political force. None of the political parties has a long-term strategy for the development of the country. All political parties lack clear programmes and strategies of political, social and economic development, or at least fail to inform the public about such programmes, as well as involve them in any debate about issues related to the future development of the country.

Although numerous parties are represented in parliament, their impact on political life has been quite insignificant. After the 1995 elections, 12 political parties were represented in the parliament of Kyrgyzstan. In 2000, 14 out of the 28 registered political parties participated in the elections.[2] The Communist Party of Kyrgyzstan, followed by the Democratic Force Union block, were the major winners of the elections. In the course of the elections, it was

---

1   For more information on political parties in Kyrgyzstan see: www.rferl.org/specials/kyrgyzelections/parties.asp (last accessed June 22, 2005).
2   For more details see: ODIHR 2000.

not the political party as such, but more so the elected candidate to the parliament, which played an important role. Therefore, the results of the elections cannot be viewed as an indicator of the attitude of the public toward the political parties involved.

The parties that disagree with the government's policy qualify as the opposition. In many countries, the opposition criticizes the government by offering alternative development strategies and programmes. In Kyrgyzstan, during the last years, none of the opposition parties seriously lobbied for social or political reforms related to developments in the economy, society, or international policy. In fact, none of the political parties has influenced the decision-making on reforms and the political line of the country so far. Thus, the government of Kyrgyzstan has unsuccessfully undertaken a number of country development and poverty alleviation programmes, such as *Araket* (Movement), *Ayalzat* (Women's Initiative) among others within the past ten years. Currently, the government of Kyrgyzstan, with the support of international investors, is implementing the Comprehensive Development Framework 2010.[3] None of the political parties of Kyrgyzstan has offered any amendments or addenda to the programme, and no part of civil society has even attempted to monitor the reforms it foresees.

During the past years, political parties have not offered any significant alternatives to the resolutions of the government. The opposition in Kyrgyzstan is merely oriented against the government and the president. In other words, instead of trying to clearly formulate political interests and priorities, the opposition's politicians express their overall disagreement without offering any alternative solutions. The opposition could markedly increase their impact if they proposed alternative solutions to current problems by presenting their long-term political programmes, while keeping the public informed of their efforts. The immaturity and weakness of some components of society is compensated for by the overwhelming influence of the authorities. Thus, the weakness of the opposition has allowed the executive authorities to gain strength to the point where, instead of further democratization, Kyrgyzstan has been faced with increasingly authoritarian trends.

The international organizations, within the limits of their mandate, should support the elements of civil society, including the opposition forces, which attempt to protect human rights. Yet, expressing their attitude towards the authorities, political parties of Kyrgyzstan appeal solely to international institutions, such as the OSCE Centre in Bishkek, hoping for support from abroad. This manner of appealing to outside forces became quite normal. But, the support of international organizations has to supplement, rather than substitute, internal resources. The key role in transforming the political system belongs in the sphere of civil society itself. As a reaction to this, the OSCE and UN offices in Kyrgyzstan have, within the past several years, been seriously criticized by civil society.

---

3   For more details see: www.cdf.gov.kg.

No one but the citizens themselves can develop political institutions, prevent the government from breaching human rights, and defend democracy. The 2004 regime change in Georgia is an example of an outside force at work. However, it must be noted that outside support in this case was based upon an active civil society, which was prepared for change. In Kyrgyzstan, the most efficient approach to political issues would be to appeal to the public, to the social base of political parties, with the support of the OSCE Centre.[4] This would become a strong impulse for increasing civil society's activities and help develop the potential, activities and political leadership of the individual political parties. It would also act as an impetus to create new leaders within the existing parties. An important aspect of this process would be an improved ability of political parties to accumulate the creative potential of the public.

Parliamentarians that represent political parties virtually never refer to them, so it remains unclear whether such parliamentarians express their own views or those of their party. Thus, upon discussing an important draft Law on the National Language[5] in February 2004, none of the parliamentarians spoke publicly on behalf of their parties. Leaders and followers of parties and NGOs alike belong to the most active group of the population. However, whereas NGOs are aware of the experience and current activities of their counterparts in Western Europe through training seminars, and even receive financial support in the form of grants, Kyrgyzstan's political parties have never been "outside the box" of their own structure and have received no financial support. In addition to the weakness of their social structures, these factors contribute to the overall weakness of political parties.

Parliamentary elections made the leaders of political parties understand that political forces need to be joined and inter-party coalitions established. In September 2003, four political parties disintegrated themselves and decided to establish a joint political party known as *Alga Kyrgyzstan* (Engl.: Forward Kyrgyzstan). Society branded it a "party of the powerful", or "presidential party", since Bermet Akaeva was one of its founders. Formally speaking, the party's membership increased rapidly, because civil servants were forced by local authorities to become members. Since the current majority voting system makes it easier for larger political parties and blocks to win, the party is hoping to outnumber its opponents and thereby win the parliamentary elections. Early in 2004, as many as six opposition parties joined into a single election block called *El Biyligi Uchun* (Engl.: For People Power).[6] The key objective of this block was to overcome the authoritarian style of governance

---

4 This assumption of the author is not in accordance with the OSCE mandate in Kyrgyzstan. See http://www.osce.org/bishkek/mandate/ (remark of the editors).
5 For an overview of the development of the Law on the National Language see http://www.us-english.org/foundation/research/olp/viewResearch.asp?CID=48&TID=1.
6 It consisted of Asaba, Erk, Democratic Movement of Kyrgyzstan, Erkindik, Kairan El and the Republican Party. See: www.rferl.org/specials/kyrgyzelections/parties.asp (last accessed June 22, 2005).

by a peaceful change of regime. However, in between the elections, political parties virtually never engage in any active work with the public. They only become active when elections are approaching. Currently, none of the political parties in Kyrgyzstan can be called a true political force.

Whether the opposition parties will become a political force to be reckoned with, is a moot point. If they join efforts to develop a common platform, they might be able to gain more political importance. However, the party leaders themselves have serious doubts as to the potential success of these efforts.[7] The opposition parties' attempt to join forces has spurred negative reactions from the authorities. On 22 January 2004, the president announced a non-official moratorium on pre-election activities and demanded that all forces concentrate on the resolution of economic issues in the country. Any step made by a politician would be interpreted as a public relations campaign. Despite these attempts, politicians did not stop their activities even for a short while. The moratorium appeared to be one-sided and seemed to hamper the activities of the political opposition. Thus, politicians were concerned whether the moratorium would interfere with their work and lead to the use force against them. Indeed, a moratorium on pre-election activities could well be regarded as an attempt by the authorities to hinder the development of political leaders and political parties, and the participation of the public in policy-making.

The further development of the political system and the strengthening of civil society will not be possible in the absence of a developed party system. Increased civil activities, a stronger opposition and developed political parties could promote democracy and strengthen its rule in Kyrgyzstan. In order to achieve this, political parties need analysts who can realistically assess the advantages and potential of each party and thus develop a framework to strengthen their effectiveness.

Local self-government

Another important step in the political development of Kyrgyzstan is the reform of local self-governance. Self-governance is an important component of civil society and its importance increases under the conditions of democratic development. According to the constitution of the Kyrgyz Republic, local communities shall have governance bodies that are responsible for local issues.[8] The current stage of local self-governance in Kyrgyzstan is characterized by a mixture of complex social, economic and political problems caused

---

7   Jypar Jeksheev, leader of the Democratic Movement of Kyrgyzstan, believes that "In Kyrgyzstan it will never be possible for all opposition parties to join. They still cannot handle their ambitions and can only develop common positions with respect to some issues." Personal interview in March 2004.

8   Constitution of the Kyrgyz Republic, Chapter seven, Article 91. See: www.kyrgyzstan.org/Law/constitution.htm#c5b.

by transition; it reflects the contradictions of the incomplete political development of the country as a whole.

The government programme of de-centralization[9] is aimed at the establishment of local authorities to represent the interests of various social groups and encourage the integration of local communities under the umbrella of their local self-governance bodies. Such integration naturally fosters the development of civil society. In December 2001, the heads of local self-governance bodies were up for election for the first time in Kyrgyzstan. The election took place with the active participation of local communities whose members believed in positive change. However, the elections failed to bring about significant changes in the system of local self-governance. Notwithstanding the conduct of decentralization reforms in Kyrgyzstan, one of the most important obstacles to democratization and public policy development is the high concentration of power within the state's administration.

In developed democracies, local governments are decentralized governance institutions to which the government has delegated some of its powers. The reform of local self-governance institutions is a lengthy process; the first stage of this process in Kyrgyzstan has shown that local self-governance institutions still remain rather an extension of the central power than an independent institution and therefore represent little more than a democratic façade of an authoritarian political system. The reason for this is, first of all, the lack of financial independence, which prevents municipal governments from properly exercising local development policies. Without financial support, local governments cannot successfully carry out decentralization reforms. In addition, the limited range of services, including information services that the local authorities provide, undermines the credibility of and perceived need for local authorities. Furthermore, an authoritarian style of governance is still prevalent in local self-governance bodies. Such authoritarian practices are contradictory to common democratic practice, since they fail to assure transparency and participation of local communities in decision-making. All these factors hinder attempts to achieve the main goal of the reform, namely local development through community mobilization and integration with the help of local self-governance bodies. However, the elections of the local self-governance leaders marked the first step towards democratization in rural Kyrgyzstan and allowed residents of rural areas to gain experience in political processes through participation.

An important problem for further decentralization and democratization is the lacking exchange between various levels of self-governance. At each administrative level, there are bodies of elected representatives – village, district and region *keneshes* (Engl.: council). At the national level, the parliament is referred to as *Jogorku Kenesh*. Each of these bodies is independent from the others. Virtually no vertical relations exist between the members of these elected bodies and they do not co-operate with each other. Meetings are regu-

---

9   For more details see www.cdf.gov.kg.

larly held at the level of local and district bodies. However, no mechanisms exist for vertical relations involving other levels of elected governance bodies. If such vertical links of voluntary co-operation between the local bodies of elected representatives and the supreme legislative authority of the country, *Jogorku Kenesh*, existed, the parliamentary system of Kyrgyzstan would be able to assure greater efficiency in public policy-making.

New public structures aimed at developing and fostering local public policy in the villages of Kyrgyzstan consist of various unions of farmers, which are organized in interest groups. Meetings between these groups and representatives of local self-governance bodies could encourage villagers to actively take part in and effectively influence the process of local decision-making. Democratic reforms and civil participation could be speeded up if district authorities, regional governors and city mayors also played a decisive part in the elections. The direct election of these authorities could contribute to a lesser degree of authoritarian governance practices and corruption, since citizens would be able to express their acceptance or disaffirmation by voting. Thus, the elections of the heads of the district and regional administration could strengthen the legitimacy of these authorities and could encourage the development of political parties and civil society as a whole. The further development of local self-governance structures and civil participation will also depend on the fairness of future elections. Only if fair elections are held, can one expect increased participation of local communities and their desire to join the elected leaders' efforts.

Civil society and the authorities

The attitude of the authorities towards civil society organizations is in fact one of the indicators of domestic policy in a country. Processes and phenomena that occur within governance institutions with respect to opposition political parties and non-governmental organizations mirror the system as a whole. Relations between state authorities and civil society in Central Asian countries appear to be difficult, and Kyrgyzstan is no exception. There is a certain level of mutual distrust between the authorities and civil society. The authorities have difficulties in coming to terms with the fact that their performance and activities have come under scrutiny by the non-governmental sector. As a result, they do not allow civil society organizations to interfere in their work. Unlike the authorities, civil society organizations have long understood that constructive co-operation with government structures will only improve their performance. However, neither political parties nor social groups can truly influence political power in Kyrgyzstan.

When we speak of politics, we distinguish between economic, internal, international, social, education, health care politics, etc. We also apply the term of politics to the processes of election, adoption of laws, meetings and protests. Why is it then that we do not apply the same term to civic activities?

Why is it then that we do not apply the same term to civic activities? Where does the popular phrase "I'm not involved in politics" originate? The answer might be found in our deep-rooted failure to truly understand what politics is about and the tendency to want to distinguish between policy-making and public activities, while in reality the two are indivisible. The attitude of the public toward authorities and the attitude of policy-makers toward the public will only change if the stereotypes inherited from the Soviet past are overcome and a true understanding of politics is gained. Still today, politics is understood as a field reserved solely for politicians and authorities. The failure of political parties to develop their social basis is rooted in this misconception. Such an understanding of policy-making is another reason why the political elite pursues personal, rather than public interests and engages in corrupt practices. For Kyrgyzstan, where the political system has become more authoritarian in the past several years, corruption remains a painful concern of civil society and a threat to democratic institutions. Developing a political culture and boosting policy-makers' abilities to understand that policies are formulated and changed by governments as well as by opposition parties, or other interested actors, could completely overturn existing relations and bring politicians much closer to the public.

As mentioned above, Kyrgyzstan lacks powerful public movements or political parties that could influence government decisions or promote reforms. For this reason, citizens rarely have the chance to participate in decision-making processes and thus feel cheated by the, seemingly, endless chain of mistakes made by the authorities. To some extent, these mistakes can be explained away by the fact that in Kyrgyzstan there has never been such thing as a professional politician. This fact is both a strength and a weakness: On the one hand, if the country is governed solely by "professionals" – law and economics graduates – then public participation will be limited to voting, and citizens' interests will no longer be valued as society's interests. On the other hand, political mistakes have been made due to the absence of government research institutes and independent political survey institutes that could thoroughly analyse the political system of the country and the government's social and political course.

Currently, civil society does not have any influence on economic, social or political reforms in the country. This is mainly because policy-making is almost exclusively reserved for governmental institutions. As a result, government structures turn into a tool with which individuals gain access to material and immaterial benefits, and corruption looms large. For this reason, nothing else can be done for citizens except to keep on looking for individual ways to influence decision-making. During the past several years, a couple of events have shown that protests and rallies have become a common strategy among citizens to express their wants and needs. Civil society organizations consider actions such as meetings and open protests as the most efficient ways to draw attention to the problems occurring in the country.

The increased popularity of these activities can be explained by the fact that citizens not only find it hard to identify their place in policy-making, but also have a hard time making themselves heard. Inaccessible politicians and the absence of effective mechanisms of participation in decision-making are the main reasons why protests remain the public's preferred method. Another serious reason is the lack of credibility in authorities in the eyes of civil society. Finally, the distrust displayed by civil society towards the authorities increases as corruption continues to grow.

It should also be noted that there is no clear division of responsibilities among the authorities. Governance in Tajik is still not rid of the methods inherited from the Soviet period when the Communist Party was in control of all decision-making. An example of such a situation was a demonstration in the south of Kyrgyzstan in March 2002, where police shot down several people.[10] When the conflict was at its peak, civil authorities at all levels (village, district and regional administration), as well as the police, started negotiations with demonstrators. The number of authorities trying to resolve the conflict was so high that later none of them wanted to take any responsibility for the unnecessary deaths of civilians. Any attempt on behalf of civil rights advocates and the population in general to bring the guilty party or parties to justice for the shooting was to no avail. When such a conflict arises, it is the law enforcement agencies, rather than civil authorities, such as administrative bodies, that must act and take full responsibility for their actions. It is impossible to find a guilty party in the absence of a clear division of responsibilities and jurisdiction between authorities. Furthermore, such a division would lead to a better understanding of responsibility for any decision among representatives of the administration and the government.

Criticism of the current authorities comes in waves, and increases when triggered by specific political issues. Political activity can be observed not only in the capital of Kyrgyzstan, but also in rural areas. Occasional civil protests, public demonstrations and rallies can hardly be viewed as local, one-time occasions. Rather, they are the expression of a long-term process of a public becoming more and more active politically whilst searching for ways to participate in the decision-making process.

Another popular way for citizens to call attention to certain issues is by publishing materials in the independent media. However, during the past several years, criticism of government officials by independent journalists has led to court hearings that have resulted in disproportionately high fines and, consequently, has led to the closure of dissenting newspapers. The monopoly of the publishing house *Uchkun* (Engl.: Spark) posed a threat to independent newspapers. Since Freedom House opened its office in Bishkek in 2003, this US-based organization has provided publishing services to the independent media. However, freedom of the press remains a problem which needs to be discussed. Television and radio are the two most efficient channels through

---

10 See Human Rights Watch World Report 2003, http://hrw.org/wr2k3/europe9.html.

which the general public obtains information. First of all, they offer broad coverage and, secondly, many people cannot afford to buy newspapers. Political debates such as those broadcast by the private company "Pyramid" are an efficient way to raise public interest in political life and to influence public opinion. Yet, in 2004 "Pyramid" encountered difficulties corresponding to those of independent newspapers. This led to renewed doubts about whether the independent media is allowed to cover important political events. Thus, up until the parliamentary elections in February 2005, civil society organizations had serious concerns about the authorities trying to isolate the independent mass media from pre-election events.

The need for dialogue between the authorities and society

Non-profit organizations in Kyrgyzstan are represented by a variety of public associations that, to some degree, exert influence on the political processes occurring in the country. When the first NGOs were established, local authorities often felt uneasy about their activities, especially in rural areas. Attempts by local activists to resolve social problems were regarded by government officials as an alternative which posed a threat to their authority and office. Consequently, tensions were released when the government issued an official recommendation to co-operate with the non-governmental sector at all levels. At the level of the government, however, the authorities fostered a rather symbolic co-operation with the public and established pro-governmental NGOs. Such institutions – internationally known as GONGOs (governmentally organized NGOs) – imitate harmonious relations between the authorities and civil society. Such GONGOs appeared for the first time in Kyrgyzstan when international donors offered funding to the government. Unfortunately, they used their funds as a tool to influence the government through civil society.[11] For example, they demanded the signing of an agreement between the government of Kyrgyzstan and NGOs to open an investment project. When the NGOs called for public transparency and monitoring of the project, the authorities hastily established the first Kyrgyz GONGOs to alleviate public pressure and to meet the required conditions. Hence, the government of Kyrgyzstan has at its disposal certain organizations that serve as a camouflage for relations with the international community. The existence of such pro-governmental organizations that agree with everything allows the country to appear democratic to some extent. In other words, the authorities use these

---

11   According to Marina Ottaway, it is not possible to form a political opposition from outside, yet, "if a country receives big foreign aid, the donor states have an economic instrument to demand to hold negotiations on aid through parliament only". Interview of the Washington ProFile agency with Marina Ottaway, Senior Researcher of the Carnegie Endowment for International Peace on 26 March 2004, reprinted in ResPublica, No. 11, 30 March 2004.

institutions as a façade to make them appear as if they held democratic legitimacy.

The interaction between the supreme authorities of the country and the NGOs could have improved their relations, but, unfortunately, the decision-makers at government level in Kyrgyzstan have chosen the path of resistance. It allows them to solve the issue of investments without building proper mechanisms of co-operation with civil society. They use pro-government organizations to report to international investors on their co-operation with the public, when in reality they are not accessible to their civil society. Citizens are reduced to the role of observers who can neither check the authorities nor participate in decision-making on any level.

The influence of the public on political processes largely depends on the level of interaction between politicians and the public. However, the importance of such co-operation is hardly understood by politicians or by the public. Relations between civil society and the government are characterized by insufficient mechanisms for dialogue. If in place, such a dialogue could allow the public not only to inform the officials about their interests and problems, but also to make sure that interests are met and problems resolved. Several attempts of NGOs to establish new relations with government agencies and to involve politicians in their activities have so far not seen much success. To change relations with government agencies, NGOs invite public officials to participate in conferences and round-table discussions. The past several years have shown that changes are beginning to occur in the interaction between civil society and politicians. However, only a few politicians interact with civil society institutions on a continuous basis.

Political interests differ in society. Policy-making, as the mechanism of bringing together the interests of various social groups, can take on different forms. One of them is *meetings* between representatives of public organizations and authorities. Such forums do not aim at the development and adoption of a decision on a specific issue. Rather, they can be viewed as nearly the only opportunity to speak to the supreme authority – the president of the country – and thus to realize the citizens' right to be heard by the supreme authority. A public dialogue with the participation of officials, especially those of the highest level, gives politicians important information on the most significant problems experienced by the population. It also allows citizens to pose questions to politicians or simply be heard. However, such meetings should allow the public not only to speak out, but also to learn about the future plans of the government.

This tradition started in Kyrgyzstan in 2000. The first such forums was initiated by civil society with the active support of the OSCE, and became one way of expressing one's position towards the system of political power.[12] The

---

12   The OSCE Annual Report 2000 states: "Following the visit of the OSCE Secretary General to Bishkek in March 2000, the Government and opposition in general agreed on a national round table. The Centre initiated a series of preparatory sensitization meetings with

authorities began to release tension by holding open, direct discussions with civil society. Such meetings between civil society organizations and the supreme authorities of the country definitely mark a positive step towards the establishment of new forms of interaction between society and the authorities, and may positively influence the process of democratization in Kyrgyzstan. These meetings between politicians and the public show that there is an increasing influence of civil forces on the authorities, and offer an excellent opportunity to attract the attention of government decision-makers to society's most acute problems.

However, only a small part of civil society participates in such forums, while the public in general still feels excluded from political dialogue. As opposition politicians were not included in the first forum, it cannot be called a completely open and honest dialogue between civil society and the authorities. While the first forum came about as a result of public pressure, the government initiated all of the following forums. Thus, this interaction between the authorities and civil society may appear more as a democratic façade.

It is in the interest of various social groups that public forums be held at all levels. By conveying criticism, such forums could significantly contribute to increasing the feeling of accountability among ministries and national committees for the rest of society, as well as to releasing tension and improving the general level of communication between society, the administration and supreme authorities. Without the support of international organizations at the very beginning phase, such forums are hardly possible to set up. With such support, NGOs would be able to initiate the political process. One may then realistically expect that public forums would become an efficient tool of pluralism, which improves the mutual understanding between the authorities and the public.

Despite the first attempts to establish links between civil society and the government, a critical motive for further democratization and change in power mechanisms, as a pluralism of ideas, is still missing in Kyrgyzstan. A variety and pluralism of ideas could be of help in developing the political culture and the party system. Further interaction between the authorities and society should focus on the development of the subjects of the political processes – the unification of people on the basis of common interests. The authorities should support the process by adopting laws to foster the further development of political parties. A functioning party system in Kyrgyzstan will definitely influence decision-making and be able to protect and defend the interests and rights of the social groups they represent.

---

the aim of facilitating the organization of such a round table. Finally, in June, it became obvious that it could not be organized in the original spirit of the OSCE, and the Centre thereafter participated only as an observer in an event organized by the Government". See: OSCE 2000: 62.

Education for democracy

The democratization of both political life and political institutions of any country depends to a large extent on the quality of its educational system. This sector is of paramount importance to the future of any society. Political preferences of the future depend on the current content of education and a society's ability to raise a new generation that shares the same values. In the different post-Soviet countries, different ideals prevail: from Communism and national patriotism to democracy.[13] A gap exists not only between different generations; values of different groupings of young people can vary to quite an extent as well. The review and re-consideration of values in society is reflected primarily by the lifestyle and education of its youth. On the one hand, they are challenged by the realities of the twenty-first century, on the other hand, by their Soviet past. Experiences of the latter can only be addressed and reappraised by disseminating information on democracy. In Central Asia, presently, only the NGOs and international organizations are addressing these challenges. In Kyrgyzstan, it is the OSCE and the NGOs that play an important role in training the public on human rights.

The structure of public education in Kyrgyzstan follows to a large extent the Soviet model: state authorities strictly regulate all education issues. The Ministry of Education supervises all schools and often exerts pressure on them, both in relation to the curriculum and the general environment of the school. Public education institutions remain the most conservative and authoritarian structures of the political system. The Ministry of Education retains its monopoly in the field of general and higher education; it develops policies, decides on the content of education, publishes textbooks, issues licenses, and performs the functions of supervision, monitoring and evaluation. It is necessary to continue democratic reforms in the field of education and, first of all, distinguish between the functions of policy-making and strategy development as well as policy execution.

The government has its own education programme "Cadre of the Twenty-First Century"[14] that allows young people to receive university education abroad. A significant number of students go abroad to study at European and American universities every year. These graduates might bring about changes in the political elite of the country and establish new political relations. Although international organizations and NGOs make an effort to communicate new trends and democratic values to society, significant changes can only be made if the education system as a whole is consistently reformed, both in form and content. In addition to the regular work of the NGOs in the field of civil education, a nation-wide training programme for democracy should be

---

13 "There is a huge gap between generations in Central Asia in their world views, their education and their understanding of political and economic realities." in: International Crisis Group 2003: 6.
14 For more details see: www.gov.kg.

established to strengthen the political culture by making sure the younger generation is given proper information on democracy and their civil rights.

The role of the OSCE

In 1998, the OSCE Centre in Kyrgyzstan was opened. Prior to its opening, OSCE High Commissioner on National Minorities, Max van der Stoel, had actively worked in the country. His activities were closely related to security in the south of the country where issues pertaining to national minorities, particularly the Uzbeks, were addressed. The High Commissioner has visited Kyrgyzstan several times and initiated co-operation with NGOs through the monitoring of inter-ethnic relations in the south. Relations between ethnic Kyrgyz and Uzbeks remained a serious problem in the 1990s as a result of the grave ethnic unrest of 1990. The monitoring revealed the roots of tension. One of them was the inaccessibility of secondary and university education for ethnic Uzbeks. The government of Kyrgyzstan decided to open the Kyrgyz-Uzbek University and a Centre for Textbook Development for Uzbek schools. This decision eased ethnic tensions in the south of the country.
Currently, certain tensions can be observed in the frontier areas of the Ferghana Valley. Numerous problems persist, such as unresolved political issues, restricted freedom of movement across borders, water problems, practices of customs authorities and many others. All these issues have a negative effect on relations between the population of different areas and between different ethnic groups within the same country. These factors pose a threat to the security of the region and to the right to a peaceful life. Many political scientists regard the Ferghana Valley as a Central Asian conflict zone. Thus, activities aimed at improving ethnic relations in the area are particularly important. The co-ordination of the efforts of Central Asian OSCE Centres could be of great help in building and increasing mutual trust among residents of the frontier region. The implementation of joint OSCE programmes in Central Asian states could help NGOs and local authorities co-ordinate their efforts in resolving the cross-border problems and in building "bridges of trust". Joint efforts of the OSCE Centres in the region could include programmes for supporting NGOs and regional Central Asian public forums in the frontier regions. For the authorities of the Central Asian states, such forums could help ease the way towards finding a solution to the transboundary problems, and thus relieve tensions in the region.
In the human dimension, the OSCE mandate does not only include the protection of human rights and security, but also the support of democratic institutions, the development of a vital civil society and the strengthening of the rule of law. The OSCE has been working in these fields from the first days of its existence in Kyrgyzstan. The opening of the OSCE Centre and its active co-operation with civil society, especially at the initial stages of work, in-

creased the capacity of the civil society to interact with state authorities and policy-makers. Thus, one of the priorities of the first Head of the OSCE Centre in Bishkek, Ambassador Jerzy Venclav, was to establish new relations between state authorities and civil society and thus to foster the development of democratic institutions. This initial strategy of the OSCE in Kyrgyzstan was in line with the challenges faced by civil society.

Among the positive factors brought about by the OSCE in the first years of its work in Kyrgyzstan were conferences and round table discussions on various subjects. These discussions and conferences with the participation of public associations, the media, politicians and government officials of various levels, including decision-makers, raised awareness about the importance of political dialogue. Time has shown that the efforts of the OSCE were not futile. A variety of conferences held by the OSCE increased the interest of the public in policy-making and involved more people in political processes. Since the conferences were on specific subjects, representatives of various ministries, state agencies and politicians – otherwise inaccessible to the public – attended them. The platform provided by such conferences allowed civil society leaders to discuss problems and pose questions to high-ranking government officials. This practice of the OSCE showed the importance of such encounters for both civil society and the authorities. The latter were surprised to see the engagement and activities of NGOs and the independent media. Step by step their attitude towards civil society institutions began to change and they acknowledged the existence of a non-governmental sector and civil society as such. This acknowledgement marked the first step towards a transformation of the relations between the authorities and civil society and the government admitted the need to co-operate with NGOs.

The discussions between state officials and the public led to new perceptions on both sides. These were important for the development of pluralism, the adoption of democratic principles of policy-making, and the acknowledgement of civil society by the authorities. In addition, training seminars held by the OSCE Centre for NGOs improved the capacities of civil society. In doing so, the OSCE Centre contributed to the country's development and fostered the trust and respect of NGOs and the independent media in the activities of international organizations.

Later on, however, the OSCE Centre in Bishkek, and especially the second Head of Centre, Ambassador Aydin Idil, changed the strategy and took a more neutral position towards civil society and the government. Not only the OSCE, but also the UN offices in Central Asia changed their focus towards a so-called "policy of balance". Several civil society leaders expressed their disapproval of these changes and started to criticize the OSCE Centre for its activities.[15] While some of them believe that the OSCE works within the limits of its mandate and professionally protects human rights following the

---

15   This estimation was made before the new head of the OSCE Centre, Ambassador Markus Müller, started his work in November 2003.

principles of freedom, prosperity and security, others accuse the Centre of insufficient performance.[16] On 9 July 2003, the leaders of several NGOs even organized a demonstration against an OSCE project aimed at modernizing police forces. They blamed the OSCE for violating its working directives. Even though in most developed countries police forces are well equipped and modernized, the public in Kyrgyzstan viewed this OSCE programme with scepticism, and voiced their opinion against it. The growing distrust of the authorities, their increasingly authoritarian practices and their failure to punish those guilty in Aksy raised public concerns about the security of future meetings.

The stance taken by the public in Kyrgyzstan is understandable. Those engaged in advocating civil rights were convinced that a modernized police would pose a greater danger, especially for the participants of demonstrations prior to important political events. On 27 October 2003, the U.S. Commission for Security and Co-operation in Europe held a hearing on the activities of the OSCE in the field of police reform. Senior Commission advisor Elisabeth Pryor acknowledged the importance of an efficient police force for any society, and the sensitivity of this issue for the countries that are recovering from recent conflicts and experiencing transition to democracy.[17] Indeed, Kyrgyzstan has faced the tragic experience of police beating and the shooting of peaceful demonstrators in the Aksy district in the south of the country. Richard Monk, a senior advisor to the OSCE, who also made a presentation at the above-mentioned hearing, noted that police forces lacked experience and did not know how to act in situations of civil unrest.[18]

It became clear that the negative reaction of civil society to the police projects was, first of all, based on insufficient information provided by the OSCE and the government of Kyrgyzstan who signed a Memorandum of Understanding on the reform of the Ministry of Interior.[19] A public meeting provided in the framework of the OSCE police project, which criticized the technical equipment of the police, showed that the public was well aware of police officers' ignorance of citizen's rights and their lacking conflict management skills.

Important political events, such as the parliamentary and presidential elections, lie close ahead in Kyrgyzstan. At such a time, society expects political changes. Therefore, the OSCE will play an important role in Kyrgyzstan, as it

---

16   Thus, the leader of the "Civil Society Against Corruption" NGO, Tolekan Ismailova, argues that the "role of the OSCE in the region is quite weak, and the OSCE fails to perform its function of human rights protection". Statement at the Forum "Political Parties in the Political System of Kyrgyzstan", organized by the Institute for Regional Studies, 13 April 2004, Bishkek.

17   The verbatim quote of her opening statement: "Having an effective police force is essential to every society, but is a particular challenge to those societies recovering from conflict or undergoing transition to democracy. Some states must attempt both at the same time." US Congressional Briefing on OSCE Police-related Activities, October 27 2003. Transcript available at: http://www.csce.gov/pdf/txt102703breif.pdf: 1.

18   Ibid.: 7.

19   For more details on the police assistance program see: www.osce.org/bishkek/13137.html.

may assure some openness and transparency in the upcoming elections, where people should be able to freely express their will. Equally important is the OSCE's role in ensuring that proper conditions for the participation of interested NGOs in the forthcoming political processes are met, and that open coverage of these processes by the media is guaranteed.

Conclusions

Today, Central Asian countries are in the midst of an economic crisis. As such, they are not only faced with poverty, but also with a threat to their national security. The most serious indicators of such threats in Central Asia today are frequent reshufflings of posts and corruption. The present development of political parties can result in yet another aspect of this threat: ideological monopoly. Thus, the current authorities of Kyrgyzstan have adopted the Democratic Code of Kyrgyzstan[20] as its national ideology. The "recommendations" of the authorities, as to how this document should be studied, are reminiscent of the Soviet methods of introducing documents with an ideological character into school and university curricula.

The openness of a state and its political system depends on the direction of its domestic and foreign policies. Freedom of society can be measured by the pluralism of opinions and ideas and by the people's possibility to express them openly and freely. Any restriction of this freedom, like any other violation of human rights and freedoms, may cause a conflict.

Stability in Central Asia is challenged by factors inherited from the Soviet past, namely by authoritarian governance. However, in the past several years, such challenges related to the values of the Soviet period have become weaker. The political life of society in Kyrgyzstan now consists of a variety of political processes, both organized and spontaneous. Some aspects of society's political life show that people are willing to freely express their position, while the authorities remain reluctant to listen and understand them. The crux of the matter is that people are willing to express their opinions in meetings and at demonstrations, but, when they do so, they risk being shot at by the police. Lack of openness, inaccessibility of authorities to the public, pressure exerted over such important institutions of democracy as the independent media, and other threats posed to democratic values that were adopted by society during the years of independence may give cause to confrontations between political forces and bring about more serious conflicts. Given the state of economic crisis, widespread unemployment and poverty, the transformation of a political conflict into a social one may still prove more of a threat. The most dangerous scenario is ethical unrest in the south of Kyr-

---

20   In 2002, the government developed the so-called Democratic Code of the Kyrgyz Republic and created the Public Council of Democratic Security. See: www.abanet.org/ceeli/countries/kyrgyzstan/oct2002.html.

gyzstan. Violations on part of the authorities in the course of the forthcoming elections of 2005 could become the greatest trigger of instability. It is particularly important to assure that independent media are free to explain the platforms of various political parties and to publish materials that expose corruption. Access to information, especially during the elections, will improve people's abilities to make informed and deliberate decisions.

The strategy aimed at fairness and transparency of elections, freedom of the mass media and judicial bodies from the pressure of state authorities could increase the responsibility of civil society and become an alternative to instability in the country. Only pluralism, democratization of the political system, development of democratic institutions and an improved political culture can assure the security of the country.

Bibliography

Human Rights Watch. 2003. *World Report 2003.* (available at: www.hrw.org/wr2k3/ europe9.html).

International Crisis Group. 2003. *Central Asia: Last Chance for Change?* Osh/Brussels (available at www.crisisweb.org).

ODIHR. 2000. *Final report on the parliamentary elections in Kyrgyzstan, 20 February and 12 March 2000.* Warsaw (available at: www.osce.org/documents/odihr/ 2000/04/1384_en.pdf).

OSCE. 2000. *Annual Report 2000 on OSCE Activities.* Vienna. (available at: www.osce.org/publications/sg/2005/05/14111_280_en.pdf)

ResPublica. No. 11, 30 March 2004.

Part II:
Democratization through External Actors?

Anna Kreikemeyer

Balancing Between Commitments and Co-operation. The OSCE in Central Asia*

The Central Asian states joined the OSCE in 1992. However, it was only at the beginning of 2000 that they advanced to centre stage. At that time, it also became clear that the participating States of that region had growing political and strategic difficulties with the OSCE. A broad disinterest on the side of the mostly authoritarian governments of Central Asia was met with an obvious lack of a concept on the side of the other OSCE participating States. Sometimes there were even rumours of possible withdrawals of single Central Asian participants from the security organization. And from the organisational perspective, since 2005 it has no longer been a sacrilege to think about a possible closure of the OSCE Centre in Tashkent, due to the unco-operative nature of the Karimov regime in the area of human rights.

The main reason for the OSCE's difficult standing in the region was and is its human dimension, one of the cornerstones in the Organization's concept of comprehensive security. At the beginning of the OSCE's engagement in Central Asia the human dimension had indeed been placed, to a large extent, in the foreground. Many of the support projects had been oriented towards keeping OSCE commitments, especially the protection of human rights and respective legislation. On the Central Asian side this sometimes led to the perception of OSCE Centres on the ground as pure human rights organizations. Since the millennium, the OSCE has begun to reverse this misunderstanding step by step and has tried to avoid imbalances between the dimensions by looking for adequate ways of supporting the specific processes of transformation in the region. However, possible indirect effects of OSCE election monitoring on the "coloured revolutions" in Georgia and Ukraine as well as their spill-over to Kyrgyzstan in spring 2005 again highlighted the crucial role of human rights and democratization for the transition of these societies. Thus the attempt of the OSCE since 2000 to reconceptualize and balance its field activities in Central Asia does not mean neglecting the importance of the human dimension. The question arises how the Organization can find its way between commitments and co-operation in its interaction with the regimes in this specific and fragile region of the OSCE area.

The following article, in its first part, recapitulates the development of the relationship between the OSCE and its Central Asian participating States, with special emphasis on the implementation of the concept of comprehensive security. The second part sheds light on specific, political, strategic and instrumental challenges for the OSCE resulting from this concept. Finally,

---

* An earlier version of this article was published in Seidelmann/Giese 2004.

101

recommendations are outlined for a Central Asia regional strategy, which still awaits conceptualization by the OSCE.

Development of OSCE Central Asian relations

The OSCE policy toward the region, roughly sketched, developed in four stages:
1st stage: diversification in the field (1992 – 1999). After the accession of the Central Asian states into the OSCE in 1992, only a small Central Asia Liaison Office, responsible for the whole region, was established in Tashkent (1995). The one exception to this was the OSCE mission in Tajikistan mandated for conflict management (1993). It was only gradually that the OSCE dismissed the idea of treating Central Asia as a region and devoted more attention to the specifics of the single states. On the one hand, the Office for Democratic Institutions and Human Rights (ODIHR) began to negotiate annual memoranda of understanding with single Central Asian governments (Uzbekistan 1997, Kazakhstan and Kyrgyzstan 1998, Tajikistan 1999). On the other hand, from 1999 onward, OSCE Centres were opened in every Central Asian state.[1] At that time, efforts to establish contact and to review the implementation of OSCE commitments with emphasis on activities in the field of the human dimension were dominant. OSCE officers were active in the field of legislation, supported local media institutions or organized round tables with government and opposition members as a political follow up to elections etc.[2] Having worked practically on the ground, the specific transformation conditions in the region quickly became apparent to the OSCE. A report by the then personal representative for Central Asia of the Chairman-in-Office (CiO),Wilhelm Höynck, early on urged a specific and long-term strategy. This prepared the ground for a declaration of intent in the Istanbul Summit Document (1999) to develop a regional strategy for Central Asia.[3]
2nd stage: Shifting to counter-terrorism (2000 - 2002): In this stage, we can observe the first efforts to give the principle of comprehensive security more relevance for Central Asia. According to the understanding of comprehensive security, the emphasis on the human dimension was balanced in a more integrated approach with military-political, economic and environmental activities. The OSCE began to shift its attention towards the security threats in the region and, as a consequence, towards closer co-operation with international financial institutions. In this sense, the Austrian chairmanship organized a

---

1   Cf. Dohrenwendt 1999; Oberschmidt 2001; ODIHR 2001.
2   Cf. footnote 35. For a qualitative overview of OSCE projects in Central Asia cf. Zannier 2003.
3   Cf. Istanbul Document 1999; Höynck 2000.

security related conference in Tashkent on 19-20 October 2000[4] and in response to the armed clashes between Islamist groups and the governments of Uzbekistan and Kyrgyzstan (1999, 2000), the Romanian chairmanship followed with another anti-terrorism conference in Bishkek on 14-15 December 2001.[5]

With the geographic centre of the US War against Terrorism in Afghanistan, Central Asia quickly was placed in the foreground of international security policy.[6] The OSCE immediately reacted to these changes. Especially during the Romanian (2001) and the Portuguese (2002) chairmanships, but also in the subsequent ministerials, terrorism was seen as a collective threat that should be addressed in a comprehensive way. The *Programme of Action* of the Bishkek conference as well as the *Bucharest Plan for Action* of the Bucharest Ministerial (4 December 2001) and the *Charter on Preventing and Combating Terrorism* identify the root causes of terrorist threats as well as strategies and instruments.[7] The OSCE Secretariat tried to strengthen the exchange of information and the co-ordination in a *Roadmap on Preventing Terrorism* (March 2002).[8] Here all OSCE institutions put together projects related to anti-terrorism on the basis of comprehensive security (i.e. projects to foster tolerance and freedom of religion, dialogues between governments and civil societies, legislation monitoring, institution building, training of legal officers etc.). Beyond that, a special representative for the fight against terrorism was named in May 2002, an *Action against Terrorism Unit* (ATU) was established in the OSCE Secretariat and expert meetings as well as workshops were held both by the ATU and the ODIHR.[9]

3rd stage: Criticisms and reorientation (September 2001 – 2004). However, the busy activities in the fight against terrorism could not hide the fact that the regional strategy for Central Asia, envisaged since 1999 was still waiting to be realized. Despite the region's obvious needs, Central Asia got only a tiny portion of OSCE attention. Beyond general structural constraints – a one-year chairmanship, annual mandates for missions in some states and short-term secondments of staff – the OSCE-Centres were usually weak due to the limited number of personnel. Until 2002, the Organization devoted less than five per cent of the total budget to its centres and programmes in the five states and the centres had only about 30 international officers, out of a total OSCE field presence of nearly 3,500.[10] A very critical report of the Interna-

---

4 On the conference "The OSCE and Security Aspects in Central Asia. International Conference on Enhancing Security and Stability in Central Asia: An Integrated Approach to Counter Drugs, Organized Crime and Terrorism" cf. OSCE Austria 2000.
5 "International Conference on Enhancing Security and Stability in Central Asia: Strenghtening Comprehensive Efforts to Counter Terrorism" Cf. Bishkek Conference 2001.
6 Cf. von Gumppenberg 2002.
7 The documents of the ministerials in Bucharest (2001), Porto (2002), Maastricht (2003) and Sofia (2004) are available online at http://www.osce.org/mc/documents.html.
8 Cf. Road Map 2002.
9 Cf. Eggleston 2004.
10 Cf. Nitzsche 2003.

tional Crisis Group and a subsequent hearing with its Director in the Permanent Council strongly recommended that the OSCE decisively determine its course in the region.[11] What was aggravating was that the booming activities of national, international and non-governmental actors in the post-September 11 phase put the question of the specific role of the OSCE even more strongly into the foreground.

While the first decisions that set the course for upgrading the region on the OSCE agenda were already taken in 2002, the Dutch chairmanship (2003) still more decisively than had been the case up to that point, declared Central Asia a focal point of its activities. Since then many high-ranking OSCE politicians and officials have visited the region. The post of a personal envoy for Central Asia of the CiO was filled by the former Finnish president, Marti Ahtisaari, who was especially interested and active in the Ferghana Valley. At the end of 2002, one million Euros from the budget were shifted from the Balkans to Central Asia. What had already been conceptualized in Tashkent in 2000, the strengthening of the first and the second dimensions of comprehensive security, was now being realized with even greater emphasis. The additional money was demonstratively and quickly used for military-political and for economic and ecological projects. However, this should not be seen as a signal of neglect of the human dimension.[12]

Although the attempt of the Central Asian participating States to downplay the importance of the human dimension was widely known, their critique was more subliminal than concrete on a political level. In 2004 this changed. Together with their CIS partners (the Russian Federation, Armenia, Ukraine and Belarus) the Central Asian states issued two statements in Moscow (3 July 2004) and in Astana (15 September 2004), in which they summarized their discontent with the current work of the OSCE.[13] Especially in their *Moscow Statement* they accused the Organization of abandoning the Helsinki principles, primarily the principle of non-interference in internal affairs. In their view the work of the OSCE, especially of the ODIHR was, to a growing extent, characterized by double standards and a selective approach. In the *Astana Appeal* the critique was more focussed on concrete proposals. Among other requests the signatories asked for a still stronger emphasis on anti-terrorism projects, on the adaptation of military-political treaties (CFE, CSBMs) and better balance among the dimensions by more economic-ecological field activities as well as for various changes in the institutional structures of the Organization. In order to exert more pressure to meet the CIS demands the Russian Federation on 13 January 2005 blocked the OSCE budget. The CIS critique was subsequently one of the main reasons for the work of a panel of eminent persons on the reform of the OSCE, in which the

---

11   Cf. ICG 2002.
12   Cf. Nitzsche 2003. The interview of the OSCE Chairman-in-Office with the UN office for humanitarian affairs is available online at http://www.irinnews.org.
13   Cf. Moscow Statement 2004; Astana Appeal 2004.

Kazakh ambassador Kuyanysh Sultanov took part for Central Asia, thus also underlining the Kazakh plea for taking over the OSCE chairmanship in 2009. While the United States put strong emphasis on the importance of the human dimension commitments the Netherlands EU presidency expressed only concern for the CIS critique demonstrating its attachment to the commitments in all three dimensions.[14]

4th stage: Conflict management (since 2005). Since spring 2005 public discontent with the respective leaderships has led to destabilization in two Central Asian countries. In the follow-up of flawed parliamentary elections in Kyrgyzstan, protests in February and March 2005 led to the ouster of former president Askar Akaev on 24 March and the election of Kurmanbek Bakiev as new president on 10 July 2005. On 13 May 2005 the Uzbek government killed several hundred unarmed civilians taking part in a demonstration in the city of Andijan. Depite massive international pressure, President Islam Karimov did not allow the widely demanded international investigation.[15] For the first time since the civil war in Tajikistan the OSCE was again confronted with the tasks of crisis prevention, conflict management and post conflict stabilization in Central Asia. It quickly became clear how much confidence depends upon the respective authorities. While in Kyrgyzstan, dialogue had always been possible, in Uzbekistan the OSCE could hardly cope with the restrictive behaviour of the regime towards international organizations and the OSCE Centre in Tashkent had to balance carefully between OSCE commitments and its fragile stand on the ground. Immediately after the events the ODIHR, for example, published preliminary findings on human rights violations, for which it could collect data only among Uzbek refugees in Kyrgyzstan.[16] It has become clear that the challenge for the OSCE in this final stage consists in finding and keeping political contact with the mostly still authoritarian regimes without giving up its commitments.[17] On 29 July 2005 OSCE Secretary General Marc Perrin de Brichambaut held talks with the Uzbek president and raised again the call for an independent international investigation on the events in Andijan. At the same time he stressed the OSCE's interest in a balanced co-operation and assistance.

Challenges for the OSCE

The following five deliberations are an attempt to cover political and instrumental aspects, which could ease the current search for comprehensive security in Central Asia. It will quickly become clear that some confidence and

---

14 Cf. Bloed 2004; EU declaration 2004; on the OSCE reform see the documents online available at http://www.osce.org/cio/15467.html.
15 Cf. the article of Berg in part IV of this volume.
16 Cf. ODIHR 2005.
17 Cf. the other article of Kreikemeyer in this volume.

courage to take innovative steps as well as commitment from both sides will be needed to find ways for future co-operation and security.

Lack of interest meets lack of strategy

The search for joint solutions through a dialogue in partnership is part of the philosophy of the OSCE. In this respect, the success of the OSCE has been rather limited in the five Central Asian states. Only in those cases where it had been accepted by the governments, was the OSCE really able to make contributions to the reform processes. However, in many cases, it was confronted with a difficult political environment. The potential for tension stems from a wide range of sources, but mainly from authoritarian political institutions and traditional patrimonial culture.[18] Non-democratic governments frequently flout the commitments on which the Organization was built. External actors have not always been welcome in the search for solutions to problems. Host governments have often viewed the OSCE with considerable suspicion. The regional initiatives of the OSCE have not always been welcomed by the Central Asian states; special treatment has not been wanted. In the past, neither the post of a personal representative of the Chairman-in-Office nor an envoy for Central Asia has been regarded as adequate. There has been some resistance on the part of Central Asian hosts; they were reluctant to see more resources committed to monitoring their behaviour in the above mentioned sensitive areas and sometimes there were signals that the OSCE should not take their continued interest for granted.[19] While until summer 2004 it was mostly Turkmenistan that not only criticized the OSCE but also tried to limit its field activities, since the events in Andijan, Uzbekistan too refrains more and more from participating in a dialogue on human rights issues and criticizes this in old Soviet style as an interference in internal affairs.

In many ways, the OSCE, with its unique membership, mandate and field activities, is much better placed than individual states or other international organizations to respond to such difficulties. However, in Central Asia the OSCE has failed to develop a good standing and a long-term strategy. Its low level of activities illustrates the relative lack of interest from the Central Asian participating States described above and the OSCE's institutional limits can be seen as a mirror of this. As the political paths of most of the Central Asian regimes take them further away from the ideals on which the OSCE was founded, the danger for the OSCE is that it could fade into irrelevance. It is against this background that it has to develop a long-term strategic concept

---

18   Cf. the article of Geiss in this volume.
19   "Without a real will by states to embark on a programme of systematic reform, we will be for ever pointing to oases of reform in a desert of repression an authoritaranism." Höynck 2003: 301.

of how it can strengthen its co-operation with the Central Asian governments and help them to fulfill its commitments.

The dilemma between fighting terrorism and protecting human rights

When after the civil war in Tajikistan (1992-1997), violence broke out in armed clashes in Uzbekistan and Kyrgyzstan (1999, 2000) and in bomb attacks in Uzbekistan (1999, 2004) the respective governments quickly complained about the danger of 'Islamist extremism'. Given its security relevance the OSCE had to find answers to this challenge. The Austrian OSCE Chairmanship (2000) clearly condemned the attacks of 1999 and warned of respective security threats. Immediately after September 11, both the Bucharest (2001) and the Porto (2002) ministerial as well as the subsequent ministerials put anti-terrorism high on the agenda: The *Bucharest Plan for Action* especially emphasizes the root causes of terrorism.[20] It soon became clear that from an OSCE point of view anti-terrorist activities needed to take into account their compatibility with human rights. In this respect, the then OSCE Chairman-in-Office, Jaap de Hoop Scheffer, in a seminar of the Netherlands Helsinki Committee on *Human Rights and Terrorism* in The Hague (September 2003), reaffirmed the importance of the human dimension principles.[21] Following that the ODIHR in particular but also the Representative on Freedom of the Media and the President of the OSCE Parliamentary Assembly demanded a more balanced approach to the complicated relationship of human rights protection and anti-terror policy as two different aspects of comprehensive security.[22] Since 2004 the ODIHR has been engaged in developing workshops and projects on the relationship between human rights and 'extremism'/terrorism in the field. The ODIHR also stresses that the unreflected, broad use of the term 'extremism' could lead to a misuse as 'extremism' is not a legal concept and cannot be criminalized. ODIHR experts therefore are active in dialogue projects on newly created anti-extremism legislation with governments of Central Asian states like Kazakhstan. They are also trying to develop preventive field projects, which initiate interreligious dialogues and establish new forms of religious education.[23] In order to avoid 'extremism' being used as a pretext for human rights violations, the ODIHR

---

20 "No circumstance or cause can justify acts or terrorism. At the same time, there are various social, economic, political and other factors, including violent separatism and extremism, which engender conditions in which terrorist organizations are able to recruit and win support." Bucharest Plan for Action 2001.
21 De Hoop Scheffer said that "respect for democracy, human rights and the rule of law were potent weapons in the fight against terrorism and thus ... preconditions for security." The Interview is online available at http://www.ihf-hr.org/booklet/hrt0.php.
22 Cf. Stoudman 2002.
23 Cf. ODIHR 2003. Since 2005 ODIHR in co-operation with the Vienna based ATU has adressed the *Group of Friends of the Chair on Combating Terrorism* and organized a Supplementary Human Dimension Meeting on 'Human rights and the fight agaist terrorism' (July 2005) in Vienna. Cf. online http://www.osce.org/documents/odihr/2005/07/15923_en.pdf.

together with Denmark and Canada organized another workshop on preventing and combating terrorism. Here the organizers pointed out that putting national security issues higher than those of human rights could lead to misuse, human rights violations and conflicts. The neglect of high human rights standards in anti-terror legislation is very problematic.[24]

Balancing the human dimension with the politico-military and the economic and environmental dimension

The OSCE has had to develop a more balanced and co-operative approach toward the Central Asian states. This perception has been formulated in the region since 1999 and has become more and more the common consensus since 2002. The Organization's willingness to understand the specifics of Central Asia has also meant that its general tone has had to be more encouraging instead of instructing. A clear signal was the above-mentioned re-channelling of funds to the centres in the region to support more projects in the politico-military dimension (i.e. security sector reform, border control, organized crime, small weapons, trafficking, drug trade, police education etc.), the economic dimension (e.g. developing small and medium sized enterprises, micro credits, fostering women's participation in business, money laundering) and the environmental dimension (e.g. supporting water management schemes, environmental information on radioactive waste). Since the beginning of 2003 efforts have been made to develop more effective projects and to build up economic development potential. These kinds of cross cutting projects were welcomed in the region and strengthened the understanding of the comprehensive nature of OSCE security co-operation. Also, the personal envoy, Marti Ahtisaari intended to work especially on the inter-relationship between the security dimensions. Particularly since the uprising in 2005 the OSCE Centre in Bishkek has emphasized even more strongly its economic development projects that range from the establishment of an anti-corruption agency to supporting a financial intelligence unit, to small and medium enterprise development, to business training for the socially vulnerable and to developing an investment strategy.[25]

How much contextualization is possible in OSCE human dimension projects?

Despite broad reforms of management and implementation control, the OSCE policy in the human dimension is rooted in the concepts of 1989/1990, which were characterized by far reaching, but mostly illusory expectations of democratization. In the five Central Asian states, the persistence of authoritarian regimes has set barriers to external democratization support. With

---

24 Cf. online at http://www.osce.org/documents/odihr/2004/06/3178_en.pdf.
25 Cf. online at http://www.osce.org/bishkek/14591.html and http://www.osce.org/bishkek/14606.html.

respect to their political systems, we can hardly talk about democratic consolidations: regimes remain in grey zones and seem to stabilize without democratization. Institutional strength is not necessarily linked to democracy; it can also be found in an autocracy. Despite the above-mentioned learning process, the OSCE is not yet fully prepared for dealing effectively with authoritarian regimes, on the one hand, and informal institutions like clan structures, on the other hand. The instrument of election monitoring is certainly of importance in demonstrating how far away the respective governments still are from a real electoral democracy. However, it is of little use in influencing the risky political and social change in bureaucratic and neopatrimonial states.

The question arises where and how the democratization efforts both on the institutional and on the societal level can really be improved. Most OSCE projects are linked to certain prerequisites that hardly prevail in present-day Central Asia. In this respect, better knowledge of informal institutions, typical for the region's institutional landscape and the readiness to constructively integrate this political context without lowering normative standards are preconditions for a political and methodological contextualization of concepts and instruments. While in this respect Ahtisaari stresses the importance of ownership and long time frames for reform, Höynck emphasizes participatory processes on the local level.[26] Based on new qualitative evaluations of the specifics of grey zone regimes the OSCE should also keep in mind one of the results of the single CSCE experts meeting on democratic institutions (Oslo 1991): "It was broadly recognized that democratic government depended on the ability of democratic institutions to function effectively. In order to do so, the structure and authority of institutions needed to be backed by informed and active public support and broadly based acceptance in the society which they serve. A democratic culture was a necessary element for the functioning of all democratic governments, and required permanent encouragement. Where a democratic tradition of long duration has not had the chance to develop, or had been interrupted, it would be necessary to develop a democratic culture, on the local, regional and national level, in order to sustain new democratic institutions. It was noted that the reciprocal relationship between international human rights norms and national practices was important in this regard."[27] With these lessons in mind, a new OSCE experts

---

26 "We have to realise that the reform process is a slow process and accept that. ... we often have a too technical and mechanical approach to development ... change in society requires a change in people's attitudes and values concerning power, work ethics and society as a whole." Ahtisaari 2003, p. 1-2. „The OSCE should be encouraged to place even more weight on participatory processes across the board concerning all OSCE projects, including in particular the efforts related to strengthening local government. A broad spectrum of participatory processes applied at grass-roots' level and based on a 'set of principles and core values' can be of great help in the development of forms and structures of democratic government which are well adjusted to societies in Central Asia." Höynck 2003, p. 306-307.

27 Report to the CSCE Council from the CSCE Seminar of Experts on Democratic Institutions, Oslo, 15 November 1991, in: Bloed 1993, p. 632.

meeting on democratic institution building in Central Asia might be helpful in this respect.

Contextualization does not mean abandoning principles. New efforts to contextualize OSCE instruments can only be undertaken if it is clear that there are distinct barriers with respect to the validity of basic OSCE principles and commitments, especially in the human dimension. The initiation of the *Moscow Mechanism* in the case of Turkmenistan (December 2002) and, at the same time, the continuation of OSCE projects with the Turkmen population, as well as the constant assurance by the Chairman-in-Office that the OSCE is ready to assist Turkmenistan and to build a constructive relationship with that country are demonstrations of comprehensive security in the best CSCE traditional sense.[28] Such clear and careful diplomacy may also be necessary in the case of Uzbekistan.

The OSCE community of values is of universal character, however, it cannot deny its Western origin. Thus, on the normative level, OSCE norms compete with different political and religious orientations. In Central Asia, the OSCE is confronted with, among other things, a specific post-Soviet Muslim population, on the one hand, but also with fundamentalist and radical religions from the outside trying to influence a traditional, patrimonial culture. Here contextualization on behalf of the external actor is necessary. In this respect, the OSCE still lacks a strategy for a systematic dialogue of cultures and should devote more energy to the integration of different norms and principles.[29]

The need for inter- and intra-institutional co-operation

While after September 11, 2001 the political interest in Central Asia grew quickly, this was hardly related to the OSCE. Yet, despite using the OSCE as a platform for security dialogue many states opted to focus on bilateral relations with the Central Asian states. The United States was most active, but also the European Union took on additional foreign policy tasks. Also NATO expanded and adopted more of the soft security issues that were once the OSCE's preserve.[30]

In the Platform for Co-operative Security of the Istanbul Summit (1999), the OSCE strove towards devoting more energy to inner- and inter-institutional co-operation, both on the political strategic level as well as on the project level.[31] Since around 2002 the OSCE in Central Asia seemed best prepared to play the role of a political catalyst given its concept of comprehensive secu-

---

28   Cf. the OSCE rapporteur's report, available online at http://www.osce.org/documents/odihr/ 2003/03/1636_en.pdf.
29   Cf. Seifert 2001; Kreikemeyer/Seifert 2003.
30   Cf. the other article of Kreikemeyer in this volume.
31   Cf. the Platform for Co-operative Security of the Istanbul Summit, online available athttp://www. osce.org/documents/mcs/1999/11/4050_en.pdf.

rity. And at least since then everybody in OSCE circles has stressed the need to co-ordinate and co-operate.[32] However, in practical terms this is sometimes difficult to achieve due to factual constraints or due to de facto inter-institutional competition on the ground. With regard to the inter-institutional level realistically the OSCE has to recognize that it does not have enough financial means of its own and therefore should link its activities to institutions with greater resources. Closer co-ordination with international financial institutions, such as the European Union, the European Bank for Reconstruction and Development, the World Bank and the Asia Development Bank would provide real leverage for the OSCE. Another deficit, closely related to the financial aspect is that the OSCE lacks technical expertise, instruments and respective resources for example in the struggle against drug trafficking, organized crime and terrorism. Here UN institutions like UNDCP are much better equipped and prepared.

As the events in Kyrgyzstan in spring and summer 2005 have shown, the core strength of the OSCE lies in its political capabilities to work both with the authorities and with civil society on the ground and at the same time on the international level for dialogue, conflict prevention and conflict management. The Organization's comparative advantages lie in the comprehensive nature of its security policy. Improvements, however, still have to be made at the intra-institutinal level where OSCE institutions like the ODIHR, the High Commissioner on National Minorities and the Representative on Freedom of the Media could really improve their co-ordination both on the conceptual and on the practical level.

Recommendations for a future OSCE Central Asia policy

As developments since 1992 have shown, comprehensive security with Central Asia in the OSCE cannot be taken for granted. Efforts have to be made on both sides. First of all, every co-operative effort depends on the political will of the sides to co-operate. Understandably, achieving change is a struggle for the OSCE, as it is an organization in which decisions are reached by the consensus of 55 participating States. But if the participating States are serious about the Organization making a difference in Central Asia, political will needs to be created for a significant shift in emphasis. Under the specific conditions of governance in Central Asia, the roles of committed high-ranking personalities in particular should not be underestimated.[33]

---

32 The OSCE Conflict Prevention Centre for example organizes information sharing meetings with international organizations on co-operation in Central Asia. Cf. Zannier 2003.
33 "Will the OSCE be in a position to help the countries concerned, in times of imminent change, to chart a course that uses the opportunities for democracy and avoids the risks of instability? Quiet diplomacy might be the most appropriate tool. To this end a heavyweight personality should be made available, known and trusted in the country concerned and familiar with this country, someone who has the support of the OSCE countries and

Given such political will and decisiveness, a regional strategy towards Central Asia or at least, as Höynck put it, a "road map for OSCE activities in Central Asia"[34] should be based on a complex, long-term and preventive dialogue at various levels. It would, at times, be necessary to integrate contradictory goals. Such a strategy should aim at:

- Strengthening the appreciation of the OSCE by the currently non-democratic leaderships without disregarding OSCE principles;
- Balancing the various dimensions of comprehensive security without loosening the linkages between the dimensions;
- Creating new forms of contact to reach mostly Muslim and patrimonial oriented populations;
- Working out models for an inner and inter-institutional dialogue on the ground without losing sight of the OSCE's profile and principles;
- Fostering co-operation while understanding the current strong emphasis on state and nation-building issues in every Central Asian state.

---

who can also gain widespread support from other international organisations." Höynck 2003, p. 310f.
34   Höynck 2003, p. 311.

Annex: OSCE projects in Central Asia 2002-2005[35]

	Kazakhstan	Kyrgyzstan	Tajikistan	Turkmenistan	Uzbekistan
Human dimension	56	61	59	18	53
Economic and environmental dimension	10	12	7	7	8
Politico-military dimension	2	4	3	3	4
Cross-dimensional	4	5	6	4	4
Total	72	82	75	32	69

country	year	human dimension	economic and environmental dimension	politico-military dimension	cross-dimensional	total
Kazakhstan	2002	7	6	1	1	15
	2003	23	2	1	2	28
	2004	26	2	0	1	29
	2005	0	0	0	0	0
	Total	56	10	2	4	72
Kyrgyzstan	2002	2	3	2	1	8
	2003	27	2	2	2	33
	2004	32	7	0	2	41
	2005	0	0	0	0	0
	Total	61	12	4	5	82
Tajikistan	2002	5	2	1	1	9
	2003	23	3	1	4	31
	2004	30	2	1	1	34
	2005	1	0	0	0	1
	Total	59	7	3	6	75
Turkmenistan	2002	3	4	3	1	11
	2003	1	1	0	2	4
	2004	14	2	0	1	17
	2005	0	0	0	0	0
	Total	18	7	3	4	32
Uzbekistan	2002	2	5	2	1	10
	2003	23	1	1	2	27
	2004	28	2	1	1	32
	2005	0	0	0	0	0
	Total	53	8	4	4	69

---

35   The figures are from a CORE evaluation of 134 OSCE projects in Central Asia from 2000-2005 compiled by John Myraunet. The projects were counted according to the data of http://www.osce.org. The overwhelming number of projects were in the human dimension. Projects that cover the entire OSCE-area are not covered in this list.

Bibliography

Appeal of the CIS Member States to the OSCE Partners, distributed at the request of Armenia, Belarus, Kazakhstan, Krgyzstan, Russian Federation, Tajikistan, Uzbekistan and Ukraine, Astana, 15 September 2004 (quoted as "Astana Appeal 2004"), online available at http://www.belarusembassy.org/news/digests/pr092004.htm.
Ahtisaari, Martti 2003. *Adress at the Permanent Council of the OSCE*. In: PC.DEL/954/03, 5 September.
Balian, Hrair. 2003. *Ten years of international election assistance and observation*, online available at: http://www.osce.org/odihr/documents/speeches_articles/article2_balian.php3.
Berg, Andrea. 2005. *Central Asia quo vadis? Zur fragilen Sicherheitslage in Kirgistan und Usbekistan*. In: Institute for Peace Research and Security Policy at the University of Hamburg/IFSH (ed.): OSCE-Yearbook 2005. Baden Baden (to be published).
Bloed, Arie. 2004. *CIS countries continue to push for a reform of the OSCE*. In: Helsinki-Monitor, No. 4, pp.299-301.
Bloed, Arie (Ed.). 1993. *The Conference on Security and Co-operation in Europe. Analysis and Basic Documents, 1972-1993*. Dordrecht/Boston/London 1993.
Bucharest Plan for Action on Combating Terrorism. 2001. Online available at http://www.osce.org/documents/cio/2001/12/2025_en.pdf. (Quoted as Bucharest Plan for Action 2001)
Delegations of Belarus, Kazakhstan, Kyrgyzstan and Russia. 2003. *On the issue of reform of the OSCE field activities. A food-for-thought-paper*. In: PC.DEL/986/03, 4 September.
Document of the *"International Conference on Enhancing Security and Stability in Central Asia: Strenghtening Comprehensive Efforts to Counter Terrorism"* in Bishkek (14 December 2001). Online available at http://www.osce.org/item/6479.html (Quoted as Bishkek Conference 2001.
Dohrenwendt, Thomas. 1999. *The OSCE Liaison-Office in Central Asia*. In: Institute for Peace Research and Security Policy at the University of Hamburg/IFSH (ed.): OSCE-Yearbook 2005. Baden Baden, pp. 365-374.
Eggleston, Roland. 2004. *OSCE: Meeting in Vienna to review methods for fighting terrorism*. Online available at: http://www.rferl.org/featuresarticlesprint.../9b1e9028-9716-4f8d-98cb-d4fcb3c75ca9.htm.
Eschment, Beate. 2000. Autoritäre Präsidialregime statt Parteidemokratien in Zentralasien [Authoritarian presidential regimes instead of party democracy in Central Asia]. In: *Aus Politik und Zeitgeschichte*, No. B 21. pp. 23-30.
Gumppenberg, Marie-Carin von. 2002. Neue sicherheitspolitische Konstellationen in Zentralasien [New security-politcal constellations in Central Asia]. In: *Österreichische Militärische Zeitschrift*, No. 3. pp. 302-308.
Höynck, Wilhelm. 2003. The OSCE in Central Asia – On the right track. In: *Helsinki-Monitor*. No. 3, pp.300-311.
Höynck, Wilhelm 2000: *Sustainable stabilisation policy in and for Central Asia*. In: Institute for Peace Research and Security Policy at the University of Hamburg/IFSH (ed.): OSCE-Yearbook 2000. Baden-Baden. pp. 215-226.
Hoop Scheffer, Jaap, de. 2003. Interview with the UN office for humanitarian affairs. Online available at http://www.irinnews.org.
International Crisis Group. 2005. *Kyrgyzstan. After the Revolution*. Brussels, 4 May. Online available at http://www.crisisweb.org; (Quoted as ICG 2005a).
International Crisis Group. 2005. *Uzbekistan: The Andijon Uprising*. Asia Briefing 38, 25 May. Online available at http://www.crisisweb.org; (Quoted as ICG 2005a).
International Crisis Group. 2002. *The OSCE in Central Asia. A New Strategy*. Online available at http://www.crisisweb.org; (Quoted as ICG 2002).
Kreikemeyer, Anna, *Präventive Stabilisierung durch säkular-islamische Kompromisse. Dokumente eines islamisch-säkularen Dialogs in Tadschikistan [Preventive stabilization by Islamic-secular compromises. Documents of an Islamic-secular dialogue in Tajikistan]*. In: Anna Kreikemeyer/Arne C. Seifert (ed.). Zur Vereinbarkeit von Islam und Sicherheit im OSZE-Raum [On the compatibilty of Islam and Security in the OSCE area], Baden Baden 2002. pp. 13-30 (together with Arne C. Seifert)

The Netherlands Presidency of the European Union. 2004. *EU Statement in Response to the declaration of member states of the Commonwealth of Independent statse (CIS) with regards to the state of affairs in the OSCE.* In: PC.DEL/633/04 of 8 July 2004 (quoted as EU declaration 2004), online available at http://www.eu2004.nl.

Nitzsche, Alex. 2003. Fresh funding boosts economic-environmental work in Central Asia. In: *OSCE Newsletter*, Vol. 10, No. 3. pp. 7-9.

Oberschmidt, Randolf. 2001. *Zehn Jahre Büro für demokratische Institutionen und Menschenrechte der OSZE – Eine Zwischenbilanz [Ten years of the OSCE Office for Democratic Institutions and Human Rights – an intermediary balance].* In: Institute for Peace Research and Security Policy at the University of Hamburg/IFSH (ed.): OSCE-Yearbook 2001. Baden-Baden, pp. 421-436.

Office for Democratic Institutions and Human Rights (ODIHR). 2005. *Preliminary Findings on the Events in Andijan, Uzbekistan,* Warsaw, 13 May. Online available at: http://www.osce.org.

Office for Democratic Institutions and Human Rights (ODIHR). *Strategy paper.2003. Preventing and combating terrorism. The role of the human dimension,* Warsaw.

Office for Democratic Institutions and Human Rights (ODIHR) 2001. *Central Asia - Inventory of implemented ODIHR projects 1994-2001,* Warsaw .

OSCE Supplementary Human Dimension Meeting *"Human rights and the fight agaist terrorism"* 2005. Vienna online available at http://www.osce.org/documents/odihr/2005/07/15923_en.pdf.

OSCE. The Secretary General. 2002. *OSCE Secretariat's Road Map on Terrorism.* In: SEC.GAL/35/02/Rev.1.

OSCE Austria 2000. *The OSCE and Security Aspects in Central Asia. International Conference on Enhancing Security and Stability in Central Asia: An Integrated Approach to Counter Drugs, Organized Crime and Terrorism, Tashkent, 19-20 October 2000* (unpublished manuscript).

OSCE, Istanbul Document 1999. Online available at http://www.osce.org/about/15853.html.

Sabahi, Farian/ Warner, Daniel. 2004. *The OSCE and the Multiple Challenge of Transition.The Caucasus and Central Asia,* Aldershot.

Seidelmann, Raimund/Giese, Ernst. 2004. Center for International Development and Environmental Research (eds.), *Cooperation and Conflict Management in Central Asia,* Frankfurt.

Seifert, Arne C. 2000. *OSCE and Islam – A Chance for Perfecting.* In: Institute for Peace Research and Security Policy at the University of Hamburg/IFSH (ed.): OSCE-Yearbook 2000. Baden-Baden: pp. 227-238.

Socor, Vladimir. 2005. Moscow Threatens, Slovenian Chair Dithers, Ukraine rallies at OSCE. In: *Eurasia Daily Monitor*, Vol.2. issue 12. Online available at http://www.jamestown.org/.

Statement of Ambassador Alexej N. Borodavkin at the request of the Permanent Mission of the Russian Fedretion to the OSCE, delivered to the 514th Meeting of the Permanent Council on 8 July 2004. In: PC.DEL/630/04 of 8 July 2004 (quoted as Moscow Declaration 2004). Online available at
www.eurasianet.org/resource/azerbaijan/hypermail/200402/subject.shtml - 39k.

Stoudman, Gérard 2002. Finding a balance between ensuring security and protecting human rights in the fight against terrorism. In: *Helsinki-Monitor*, Nr. 2, pp. 281-284.

Zannier, Lamberto. 2003. *The OSCE in Central Asia.* Speech at the OSCE-Information Sharing Meeting with International Organizations and Institutions on Co-operation in Central Asia, 11 June 2003. In: SEC.GAL/107/03 (unpublished manuscript).

Andrea Berg/Anna Kreikemeyer

The ODIHR Human Rights Monitoring and Reporting Training. A Cross National Analysis

Within the framework of the project "Security through democratisation?" which focuses on democratisation policies and their effects in Central Asia, we decided to analyse a concrete activity by external actors and its effects on the target group. The first step was to identify an activity that had taken place in all three of the countries included in the research project. We compared the annual reports of the OSCE Centres in Almaty, Bishkek and Tashkent and finally identified the ODIHR Human Rights Monitoring and Reporting Training – a series of trainings ODIHR conducted between 2000 and 2003 in seven countries of the CIS. After we had developed the questionnaire based on discussions in our working group, Atyrkul Alisheva (Kyrgyzstan), Marina Pikulina (Uzbekistan) and Cyrus Salimi-Asl (with a group of students from the Kazakh-German University in Almaty, Kazakhstan) conducted the interviews during the second quarter of 2004.

Overview of the Human Rights Monitoring and Reporting Training[1]

From 2000 until 2003 the ODIHR NGO Unit implemented its "Human Rights Monitoring and Reporting Training" in close collaboration with the respective OSCE Missions and with the Helsinki Foundation for Human Rights (Warsaw). Starting with Uzbekistan in 2000, the training has gradually been expanded to cover a total of seven countries: Armenia, Azerbaijan and Georgia as well as Kazakhstan, Kyrgyzstan, Tajikistan and Uzbekistan. In each country 20 to 25 participants, including three to four representatives of governmental institutions, were selected to attend the training. In 2002-2003, a total of 150 aspiring and established human rights defenders were trained. The training consisted of three in-country five-day trainings over a period of 14 months and was completed by a mini call for proposals carried out under real competitive conditions. The project proposals submitted by the training participants made up the practical phase of the training. Only the best (ranging from two to four proposals at about 2.000 USD) were funded by ODIHR. The funded proposals were subsequently the object of an expert visit before implementation. Finally, ODIHR, in close co-ordination with the local OSCE Mission, hosted a meeting between the participants after having completed their monitoring reports successfully and the relevant government authorities to present their findings. In a number of instances, these small

---

1   The information in the following section was provided by the ODIHR NGO Unit in 2004.

monitoring projects have actually led to substantial changes and reforms. To highlight these successes and to explain how changes can be achieved with very modest means, the NGO Unit has published a booklet in Russian and English describing these projects.

The series of trainings was concluded in 2003 with two regional conferences, one in Almaty with around 100 Central Asian graduates and the other in Tbilisi, bringing together 67 graduates from the Southern Caucasus region. The idea behind the conferences was not only to assess the effectiveness of the training of the past years and to define future strategies, but also to build a climate of solidarity, confidence and belonging between the many human rights defenders within individual countries and among the neighbouring ones. Indeed, although capacities have expanded over the years, the feeling of "you are not alone" and cohesion among many human rights NGOs are still lacking. These two conferences have proven to be a useful networking exercise, if only by bringing the right people in touch with each other to share similar experiences.

The conclusions of both conferences have pointed clearly towards an urgent need for qualitative follow-up training. Indeed, thanks to its donors, ODIHR has invested three years in building up a solid foundation of human rights defender organisations in the Caucasus and Central Asia. However, more work and training will be needed to enhance the quality and increase the capacity of these organisations to be able to draw up, deliver and advocate for the results of their monitoring reports to international standards in such sensitive fields as human rights education, fair trial and prevention of torture.

The three-pronged collaboration among the ODIHR, the OSCE Missions and the Polish Helsinki Foundation for Human Rights has proven to be a most successful formula in terms of adaptability, greatest impact, cost effectiveness and – not least – visibility.

This project was made possible thanks to generous contributions from the European Commission and the governments of Germany, the USA, Norway, Finland, Italy and Liechtenstein.

Analysis of the questionnaires

A total of 42 participants was interviewed – 14 in each country. Originally 21 participants from Kazakhstan, 21 participants from Kyrgyzstan and 27 participants from Uzbekistan had taken part in the seminar series. However, for a variety of reasons not all of them could be reached for interviews. The questions focused on organisational aspects of the seminar as well as on the content.

Two questions were designed to find out about the link between the participants and the respective OSCE Centres in advance of the seminar. 26 of the participants had already participated in another OSCE seminar while seven were sent by their workplaces. Four participants heard about the seminar by chance and five came in contact with the OSCE Centre by other means. When asked how they got to know of the seminar 27 participants answered that they had learned about the seminar from the respective OSCE Centres. Another eight participants were invited, three got the information from a mailing-list, two from the newspaper, one from a friend and one from another source. It would appear that participation in OSCE seminars leads to further contact with OSCE Centres and to participation in other seminars.

A group of questions focused on the preparation, the structure and the content of the seminar. Half of the participants (50 per cent) got introductory material to prepare for the seminar, nearly one third (29 per cent) did their own preparation and five participants (12 per cent) did not prepare. Four participants (nine per cent) did not answer the question. There was great agreement on the question about the preparation of the trainers. Thirty-five participants were satisfied with the trainers and viewed them as capable and well prepared. Four participants – all of them from Kyrgyzstan – complained that while the trainers were well prepared theoretically, they had little notion of what was going on in the region. One participant from Kazakhstan thought that the trainers were poorly prepared.

Three questions focused on contacts between and the choice of participants. Seminar participants appear to belong to a relatively small group of activists. Prior to the seminar 20 participants knew most of the others and 19 participants knew a few of the others. Only three participants knew none of the others. Consequently, when asked about their contacts after the seminar, only eight participants said they had gained many new and useful contacts while 23 participants had gained a few new contacts. Four participants stated that they had no contact with other participants at all and five participants had contact only with participants from their own country. Two participants did not answer the question.

The selection of participants was predominantly assessed as representative. In general 30 participants shared this view. Yet, while 12 participants from Uzbekistan agreed with this response, only ten participants from Kyrgyzstan and eight participants from Kazakhstan did so. Ten participants said that too few participants from government were invited while nobody was of the opinion that too few participants from NGOs were invited.

The participants seem to be very satisfied with the structure of the seminar. Only one person argued that the seminar took too much time, while 19 were of the opinion that it was beneficial that the seminar had taken place more than once and another 19 thought that all seminars should be split into more parts and follow-up meetings should be arranged. Three participants ticked the answer "other" without more detailed specification.

There was no decisive assessment of the seminars' contents. Twenty-seven participants thought that the seminar dealt with all the important questions in the area of human rights. Ten participants, however, judged that the seminar had a one-sided focus on specific human rights. One participant held the view that in the area of human rights more important questions could have been dealt with. Four participants ticked the answer 'other'. The evaluations of the exchange of experience between trainer and participants differed considerably. In general, approximately one third of the participants were of the opinion, that the seminar was based on the experience of the participants and another third that participants recounted their past experience extensively. Yet, while six participants each from Uzbekistan and Kyrgyzstan chose the first answer and seven participants from Uzbekistan the second, only three participants from Kazakhstan choose answer one or two. Instead, three participants each from Kazakhstan and Kyrgyzstan were of the opinion that participants only recounted their past experience briefly. Only one participant from Uzbekistan agreed with this answer. In addition two participants from Kazakhstan said that experience was shared only during breaks. According to 52 per cent of the participants interviewed, about half of the information provided at the seminar was new to them, while 36 per cent stated that they had hardly learnt anything new. For ten per cent of the participants the information was completely new. One participant did not answer the question.

Several questions were dedicated to the influence of the seminar on the participant's further work. When asked how the seminar had influenced their future work in general, 24 participants said that the seminar had enabled them to develop and implement their own ideas with respect to the monitoring of human rights in their respective countries. Seven participants were of the opinion that the seminar had taught them to conduct monitoring correctly. Four participants from Uzbekistan thought that the seminar had taught them a great deal, but they did not know how to put this knowledge to good use. Six participants marked the answer 'other'. The overwhelming majority of the participants were able to improve their work and knowledge due to the seminar. Sixteen participants said they greatly improved their work and 19 said they improved their work. Two participants gained nothing from the seminar and one participant from Uzbekistan mentioned political obstacles to the improvement of his work. Four participants did not answer the question.

When the participants were asked about the importance of the topic of human rights for their country, all 14 participants from Kazakhstan said that human rights represent a problem in dire need of discussion. Thirteen of the 14 participants from Kyrgyzstan and two participants from Uzbekistan were of the same opinion. Yet, eleven of the 14 participants from Uzbekistan ticked that human rights are already given enough attention. One participant from Kyrgyzstan was of the same opinion. One participant from Uzbekistan said that, the topic of human rights can only be discussed with the OSCE. No participant said that in his/her country there were more important topics than that of human rights.

The participants were quite optimistic about the influence of seminars on the improvements in human rights. Thirty-six of them were of the opinion that seminars lead to dramatic changes and reforms in the area of human rights. Four participants were of the opinion that means other than seminars are needed in order to make changes in their countries. And six participants marked the answer 'other'.

The question of whether the instrument 'monitoring' leads to a better observation of human rights received a very positive echo. Thirty-three participants thought that 'monitoring' was a very good instrument for improving the human rights situation. Five participants argued that 'monitoring' is theoretically a good instrument, but it cannot be applied effectively in their countries. Three of them came from Uzbekistan and one each from Kyrgyzstan and Kazakhstan. Two participants from Kyrgyzstan were of the opinion that instruments other than 'monitoring' are needed and two participants marked the answer 'other'.

According to three quarters of the participants interviewed, the monitoring of human rights leads to greater stability. Yet, five participants thought that the more activity in the area of human rights, the more the situation is destabilized. And three participants were of the opinion that the monitoring of human rights has no impact on the stability.

In general, the competency of the OSCE in human rights issues was judged positively. For 30 participants the OSCE is the most skilled organisation in the area of human rights – twelve participants from Uzbekistan, ten participants from Kazakhstan and eight participants from Kyrgyzstan. Five participants agreed that the OSCE has good experience in the area of human rights. In their view, however, this experience is not applicable in Central Asia. Two participants were of the opinion that other organisations have more experience in the area of human rights, while no one criticised the OSCE for having too little experience with the monitoring of human rights.

At the end of the interview participants were asked to indicate whether they agreed or disagreed with a couple of statements. Here are the results: Twelve participants agreed with the statement that human rights are of interest only to international organisations. Twenty-eight participants disagreed and two did not answer. Interestingly, eleven of the twelve participants who agreed to the statement came from Uzbekistan. Nearly all participants (39) confirmed the statement that in their respective societies human rights are not important. Only one participant rejected this view, while two did not answer.

There was no common opinion on whether human rights are of importance for a particular government. Seven participants from Uzbekistan agreed to the statement that human rights are not important for the government while seven disagreed. Five participants from Kazakhstan agreed, while six disagreed and three did not answer. And four participants from Kyrgyzstan agreed while ten disagreed.

According to 28 participants (seven from Uzbekistan, ten from Kazakhstan and eleven from Kyrgyzstan) freedom of religion is the most important human right. Interestingly, the percentage of participants from Kazakhstan and

Kyrgyzstan who agreed with this statement was higher than that of participants from Uzbekistan. Twelve participants (seven from Uzbekistan, two from Kazakhstan and three from Kyrgyzstan) were not of this opinion. Two participants did not answer.

Thirty-seven participants were in agreement that democracy is an important precondition for stability and security. Three participants from Uzbekistan and one participant from Kyrgyzstan did not agree with this statement. One participant did not answer. Consequently 36 participants rejected the view that the process of democratization has led to greater instability. Again three participants from Uzbekistan and one participant from Kyrgyzstan agreed with this statement. Two participants did not answer.

The majority of participants (37) did not regard democratization as being important only for international organisations. Yet, three participants from Uzbekistan held this view and two participants did not answer.

When confronted with the statement 'Our population is not yet ready for democracy' – a slogan that often can be heard all over Central Asia – 31 participants disagreed and only nine agreed. Two participants did not answer.

Conclusion

In addition to answering the standardized questionnaires all interviewees had the chance to comment on the seminar. Interestingly participants from all three countries underlined the importance of exchanging experience with participants from the other countries. Most of them seem to be interested in more seminars. Additionally, many participants mentioned the wish to include more representatives from local administrations and governmental institutions in such seminars. Especially for Uzbekistan, the dialogue between human rights organisations and the authorities is a process that should be strengthened further, according to the participants interviewed.

With respect to the selection of the participants it would seem, that the same people are invited again and again to seminars and roundtables. Criticized was the fact that several organisations and especially certain governmental institutions were not invited. In the future, more attention should be paid to the selection of participants and to inviting new persons. The author of one of the three country reports wrote: "Among the participants were people who participate in every seminar and are devoted to any subject from ecology to project management."

By and large, the participants seem to be comfortable with the organisation, the structure and the content of the seminar. Strong appreciation was also expressed for the efforts of the OSCE in the area of human rights training courses.

Annex: Questionnaire

1. *How did you get to know of the seminar?*
   a) From the OSCE-Centre.
   b) From the newspaper.
   c) From an emailing-list.
   d) From an invitation.
   e) Via friends.
   f) At another seminar.
   g) Other.....................

2. *How would you evaluate the seminar's preparatory work?*
   a) There was introductory material.
   b) I did my own preparations.
   c) There was no introductory material.
   d) Other.....................

3. *How would you evaluate the exchange of experience between trainer and participants?*
   a) The seminar was based on the experience of the participants.
   b) Participants recounted their past experience extensively.
   c) Participants recounted their past experience briefly.
   d) Experience was shared during breaks.
   e) Other.....................

4. *How would you evaluate the novelty of the information exchanged?*
   a) I have hardly learnt anything new.
   b) About half of the information was new to me.
   c) The information was completely new to me.
   d) Other.....................

5. *How would you evaluate the usefulness of the seminar?*
   a) I was able to greatly improve my knowledge.
   b) I was able to improve my work through the seminar.
   c) Theoretically I would be able to improve my work, but politically this is not possible.
   d) I was not able to gain anything from the seminar.
   e) Other.....................

6. *How would you evaluate your contact to the other seminar participants prior to the seminar?*
   a) I already knew most of the other participants.
   b) I knew a few of the other participants.
   c) I knew none of the other participants.
   d) Other.....................

7. *How would you evaluate your contact to the other seminar participants after the seminar?*
   a) I have gained many new and useful contacts.
   b) I have gained a few new contacts.
   c) I have no contact with the other participants.
   d) I only have contact with participants from my own country.
   e) Other.....................

8. *How did the contact between you and the OSCE-Centre come about?*
   a) I had already participated in another OSCE seminar.

b) I was sent by my workplace.
c) I heard about the seminar and signed up.
d) Other..

9. *How would you evaluate the structure of the seminar?*
   a) It was beneficial that the seminar took place more than once.
   b) All seminars should be split into several parts and follow-up meetings should be arranged.
   c) The seminar took up too much time.
   d) Other.....................

10. *How would you evaluate the importance of the topic of human rights for your country?*
    a) Human rights are already given enough attention.
    b) Human rights represent a problem that is in dire need of discussion.
    c) The topic of human rights can be discussed only with the OSCE.
    d) In my country there are more important topics than that of human rights.
    e) Other.....................

11. *Can seminars lead to improvements in human rights?*
    a) Seminars lead to dramatic changes and reforms in the area of human rights.
    b) Means other than seminars are needed in order to make changes in my country.
    c) Other.....................

12. *How would you evaluate the contents of the seminars?*
    a) The seminar dealt with all the important questions in the area of human rights.
    b) The seminar had a one-sided focus on specific human rights.
    c) In the area of human rights more important questions could have been dealt with.
    d) Other.....................

13. *Can the instrument of 'monitoring' lead to a better observation of human rights?*
    a) 'Monitoring' is a very good instrument to improve the human rights situation.
    b) 'Monitoring' is theoretically a good instrument, but it cannot be applied effectively in my country.
    c) Instruments other than 'monitoring' are needed.
    d) Other.....................

14. *How would you evaluate the preparation of the trainer?*
    a) The trainer was capable and well prepared.
    b) The trainer was well prepared theoretically, but had little notion of what is going on in the region.
    c) The trainer was poorly prepared.
    d) Other.....................

15. *How would you evaluate the composition of the group?*
    a) The participants were representative.
    b) Too few participants from government.
    c) Too few participants from NGOs.
    d) Other.....................

16. *How would you evaluate the correlation between the monitoring of human rights and the stability of a country?*
    a) The monitoring of human rights leads to greater stability.
    b) The more activity in the area of human rights, the more the situation is destabilized.
    c) The monitoring of human rights has no impact on stability.
    d) Other.....................

17. How would you evaluate the influence of the seminar on your future work?
   a) The seminar has taught me to conduct monitoring correctly.
   b) The seminar has enabled me to develop and implement my own ideas with respect to the monitoring of human rights in my country.
   c) The seminar has taught me a great deal, but I do no know how to put this knowledge to good use.
   d) Other......................

18. How would you evaluate the competency of the OSCE when it comes to the area of human rights?
   a) The OSCE is the most skilled organisation in the area of human rights.
   b) The OSCE has good experience in the area of human rights. However, this experience is not applicable in Central Asia.
   c) The OSCE has too little experience with the monitoring of human rights.
   d) Other organisations have more experience in the area of human rights.
   e) Other......................

Indicate whether you agree or not with the following statements:

19. Human rights are of interest to international organisations only.
   a) I agree   b) I do not agree

20. In our society human rights are not important.
   a) I agree   b) I do not agree

21. To our government human rights are of no importance.
   a) I agree   b) I do not agree

22. Freedom of religion is the most important human right.
   a) I agree   b) I do not agree

23. Democracy is an important precondition for stability and security.
   a) I agree   b) I do not agree

24. Democratization is of importance only to international organisations.
   a) I agree   b) I do not agree

25. Our population is not yet ready for democracy.
   a) I agree   b) I do not agree

26. The process of democratization has led to greater instability.
   a) I agree   b) I do not agree

Andrea Berg

Who's Afraid of George Soros? The Conflict Between Authoritarian Rulers and International Actors in Central Asia[*]

If we were to take a close look at the relationship between the governments of the five Central Asian states – Kazakhstan, Kyrgyzstan, Tajikistan, Turkmenistan and Uzbekistan – and various international actors, we would come to the conclusion that the rulers in these countries have been panic-stricken for some time. The cause for this panic can be connected to certain political developments in Georgia, where the so-called "Rose Revolution" in November 2003 led to both the dissolving of the government and new elections, and in the Ukraine, where the so-called "Orange Revolution" one year later swept the opposition candidate Viktor Yushenko to presidency. While in Europe and the United States these events were widely perceived as a victory of democracy, leaders in the post-Soviet region blamed Western-funded organizations for interfering in their internal affairs. In consequence, various factors, hinting at the involvement of international influence,[1] caused the Central Asian presidents to introduce stricter control on international actors as a way of avoiding any risk of such a shift of power.

In this paper, particular focus has been placed on the relationship between the rulers in the Central Asian states and international actors, for example, George Soros' Open Society Institute (OSI) and the Organization for Security and Co-operation in Europe (OSCE). The motivation of this paper is thus less of a theoretical nature; it more so concentrates on identifying a pattern of policies that are employed by the presidents in Central Asia in their relations with international actors in order to retain their power. The main focus is on the developments following the shift of power in Azerbaijan, Georgia and Ukraine and the potential effects this will have on the upcoming presidential

---

[*] An earlier version of this article was published in German in December 2004. See: Berg 2004.

[1] These accusations were aimed particularly at George Soros' Open Society Institute. An article in *The Globe and Mail* on 26 November 2003 was headlined "Georgia revolt carried mark of Soros", cf. MacKinnon 2003. In interviews with the BBC on 15 December 2003 and a Russian TV-station on 1 December 2003, Eduard Shevardnadze even mentioned the name George Soros in connection with the shift of power in Georgia and insistently called on the US influence to be investigated, even though he had at first focused on George Soros. Cf. Antelava, 2003, cf. Pravda 2003. An article by Traynor in Guardian titled "US Campaign behind the turmoil in Kiev" characterized the events in the Ukraine as an "American creation". Cf. Traynor 2004. The Sueddeutsche Zeitung published a portrait of the new First Lady Katerina Yushenko in January 2005, referring to the fact that she has been employed with the US Foreign Ministry, the White House and the US Financial Ministry. Cf. Urban 2005.

elections in Central Asia. The first part introduces the possible scenarios regarding changes in power and of rulers, respectively. Part two focuses on dynastic potentials in Kazakhstan, Kyrgyzstan and Uzbekistan. The relationship between the OSI and the rulers in the Central Asian states is treated in the third part, followed by an analysis of the relationship between the OSCE and the states in question in the fourth part.

Georgia or Azerbaijan as a role model?

In 2004, during personal interviews with representatives of international and local organizations in Central Asia about the future political developments of the Central Asian states, two scenarios were described time and time again, which were founded on either the so-called "Georgian model" or "Azerbaijani model". In the autumn of 2003, parliamentary elections took place in Georgia, and presidential elections in Azerbaijan. Whereas in Azerbaijan the long-planned surrender of power took place relatively free from problems, the president in Georgia resigned only after prolonged protests following elections in which his party had at first been declared the winner. What exactly happened in these two countries?

The Azerbaijani presidential elections on 15 October 2003 were a novelty in a post-Soviet state. For the first time the son of a president succeeded his father. This change of power had been prepared a long time in advance: A constitutional referendum in August 2002 set out new succession procedures, should the president be declared incapacitated. According to the old constitution, the speaker of parliament succeeds the president. Under the new constitution, the prime minister, chosen directly by the president, takes over all duties relating to the presidency. Consequently, the then president Heydar Aliyev pronounced his son, Ilham, prime minister in August 2003. Two months later he would go on to be elected the new president of Azerbaijan.[2] Several newspapers dubbed this development as a "dynastic succession"[3] or "political dynasty".[4] The case of Azerbaijan is not extraordinary, though. In Central Asian states as well, the well-educated and financially successful family members are all preparing to take office.

In Georgia, however, things developed differently. After the results of the 2 November 2003 parliamentary elections were published, opposition members organized demonstrations and called for a repeat of the elections. Two days after the results of the election were made public on 20 November and following weeks of protests, protesters stormed the parliamentary building and forced Eduard Shevardnadze to vacate it. On 23 November, he publicly announced that he was stepping down. The Open Society Institute was accused

---

2   Cf. Lipman 2003.
3   Lipman 2003.
4   Mydans 2003.

of "training" the students and opposition leaders in how to organize demonstrations, support an opposition TV station to help mobilize demonstrators and how to finance the students' movement "Kmara", which led the protests in the streets.[5]

The events in Georgia were widely discussed as a catalyst for political change in the CIS. Thus, in the run-up to the presidential elections in the Ukraine in November 2004, expectations were raised for another regime change. When, on 23 November, the victory of the then Prime Minister Viktor Yanukovich was announced, the supporters of the opposition candidate and former Prime Minister Viktor Yushenko denounced the elections as rigged, and protested until the Supreme Court annulled the elections. In the re-run on 26 December, Yushenko finally won and his campaign became known as the "Orange Revolution".

In the aftermath of this event, discussions turned to the question of where the "Georgian model" would be exercised next. Central Asia, especially Kyrgyzstan, ranked high on the list of possible candidates. A few days after what had become known as the "Rose revolution" or "Velvet revolution" in Georgia, six opposition politicians from Kyrgyzstan sent a letter to the then Georgian acting president, Nino Burjanadze, in which they described Georgia as a role model for Kyrgyz democrats.[6] One year later, after the events in the Ukraine, the Kyrgyz president Akayev argued in an interview that Central Asia had its own unique characteristics and that exporting a "Velvet revolution" there would most likely lead to a civil war.[7] Despite this, opposition politicians in Central Asia were eager to network with, or to copy their "successful" colleagues. "In a symbolic gesture of solidarity", leaders of three different opposition parties from Kazakhstan paid a visit to Kyiv to congratulate Viktor Yushenko on his victory in the Ukrainian presidential elections in December 2004.[8] In January 2005, Andrei Gusak, representative of the Ukrainian civil society organization *Pora*, gave a speech in front of 2,000 people in the centre of the Kazakh capital Almaty;[9] and on 19 January in Bishkek, at a demonstration of 500, the crowd "decked themselves out in yellow to symbolize coming change".[10] Among Central Asian presidents, such acts fuelled their fear of being overthrown and made the threat all the more substantial. Notwithstanding the likelihood of a change in power according to the "Georgian model" in Central Asia, the presidents appear to be taking preventive measures so as to not share the same political fate as their former

---

5   Cf. MacKinnon 2003.
6   Cf. Onica 2003.
7   Cf. Panfilova 2005b.
8   Cf. Yermukanov 2005a.
9   Cf. Karajanov 2005. According to Karajanov "yellow and orange stickers with the slogan 'Go Away' – believed to be a reference to President Nazarbayev – began to appear all over Almaty" in January 2005.
10 Kimmage 2005.

Georgian or Ukrainian colleague. Therefore, they have started to limit, control and vehemently criticize the activities of international organizations.

Dynastic potential

The present-day president of oil-rich Kazakhstan is Nursultan Nazarbayev, the former First Secretary of the Communist Party. His daughter, Dariga Nazarbayeva is head of the *Khabar* media group and her husband, Rachat, was ambassador to Austria. In August 2005, his father-in-law appointed him First Deputy Foreign Minister.[11] In April 2003, Dariga Nazarbayeva founded a political movement called *Asar* (All together), which was transformed into a political party in October 2003; in September 2004, the party took part in the parliamentary elections. Since then, Dariga Nazarbayeva has been a member of the parliament's lower house. So far, she has denied any ambition of ascending to the presidency – at least in terms of the 2006 elections. Time and time again, she has said that her father will remain in office for at least another decade.[12] Yet, since the US courts are pursuing an investigation into the alleged corruption of Nazarbayev in oil dealings between US companies and the Kazakh government – dubbed Kazakh-Gate by the media – the succession question could become urgent earlier than expected.

The daughter of Uzbek president Islam Karimov, Gulnora Karimova, seems to also be harbouring political ambitions. She leads a conglomerate that includes the country's largest mobile telephone provider as well as several nightclubs. Following her divorce from Uzbek-American Maqsudi, she remarried in the summer of 2003. Unconfirmed rumours claim that her new husband is the former foreign minister, Sodyq Safayev. Since 1997, she has worked as a political consultant for the Uzbek Ministry of Foreign Affairs. The year 2003 saw her being named consultant to the embassy in Moscow, arguably to further her political career. Furthermore, there is a warrant out for the arrest of Gulnora Karimova in the US due to her failure to respect a child custody ruling by a US court. In addition, her involvement in trafficking women to the United Arab Emirates was discussed at a 29 October 2003 Hearing in the US House of Representatives.[13] Thus, her candidacy for the Uzbek presidential elections in 2007 does not seem very promising, even though rumours of her father's failing health conditions remain persistent.[14]

---

11 Cf. Yermukanov 2005b.
12 Cf. Kusainov 2003.
13 Hearing before the Subcommittee on the Middle East and Central Asia of the Committee on International Relations House of Representatives, One Hundred Eighth Congress, First Session, 29 October 2003. A protocol of the discussion is online available at: http://wwwc.house.gov/international_relations/108/90361.pdf.
14 Cf. Pannier 2003.

Yet, after the bloody killings in Andijan in May 2005,[15] it is very likely that the succession question in Uzbekistan will be asked very soon.

Prior to the unexpected change of power in March 2005[16] in Kyrgyzstan, the wife of former president Askar Akayev, Mairam Akayeva, clearly displayed political ambitions. She came from an influential clan that oversaw the gold mining area and the privatization of the country, while the former president's clan exerted control over the National Treasury and the security forces.[17] In late May 2003, Mairam Akayeva published a book entitled "Hope has no night. Letters by a president's wife". Local observers noted the start of a campaign to improve her image. In the opinion polls conducted regularly by the research institute Sotsinformbureau on the degree of influence and political prospects of specific persons, Mairam Akayeva, in June 2003, was named third, following her husband and the deputy prime minister, Joomart Otorbayev. Even though she publicly denied all presidential ambitions, she did stress her popularity.[18] In addition, Akayev's son Aydar seemed to have political ambitions to run as candidate for the parliamentary elections in February 2005. Shortly before, he was assigned to head the Kyrgyz National Olympic Committee – a position with many international contacts.[19]

In general, the debate in the Kyrgyz capital of Bishkek in the summer of 2004[20] pointed at two possible developments: One, Akyev would be replaced and a person who acts as a guarantor for democratization and economic progress would take office. Two, he or someone from his family would remain in power, since they have already provided all of their supporters with offices. A new president would put in motion a proper recruiting process, which would only lead to more suffering in the population, qua the building of new networks and favours being distributed.[21]

After reviewing the situations outlined above, it appears that "conducting" elections serves the purpose of maintaining power within the family and thereby follows the "Azerbaijani model". This process of maintaining power is interrupted when international organizations keep adhering to standards for elections, and, prior to elections, hold seminars on elections, election observation and similar topics. Referring to a widely quoted statement by Russian political strategist Gleb Pavlovskii, that the revolution in the Ukraine "did not get punched in the face in time", Daniel Kimmage argues that "Pavlovskii's

---

15 For more details on this event, see the article by Berg in Part IV of this volume.
16 For more details on this event, see the article by Berg in Part IV of this volume.
17 Cf. Collins: 146.
18 Cf. Burke 2003a.
19 Cf. Saidazimova 2005. In Azerbaijan, Heydar Aliyev became President of the National Olympic Committee in 1997.
20 Originally, parliamentary elections were scheduled for February/March 2005 and presidential elections for September 2005. Due to the events of 24 March 2005 and the following change of power, early presidential elections took place on 10 July 2005. For more details, see the article by Berg in Part IV of this volume.
21 Yet, at the moment of re-writing this article it is too early to comment on the activities of Kurmanbek Bakiev, the newly elected president of Kyrgyzstan.

colourful phrase should not be taken too literally; overly aggressive moves could provoke international censure and domestic disgruntlement. Decisions by courts and election commissions to trim opposition prospects in elections, along with efforts to bring to heel Western-funded democracy-promotion organizations and NGOs are more likely to prove the weapon of choice".[22] The following two sections deal with such pre-emptive strategies focusing on arguments and measures by the present rulers against international actors, such as the OSI and the OSCE, who focus on democracy assistance and election monitoring.

The Open Society Institute in Central Asia

Since the early 1990s, the OSI of the George Soros Foundation has been active in the Central Asian states. The Kyrgyz offshoot of the OSI started its work in 1993, the Kazakh in 1995 and the Uzbek in 1996. In Kyrgyzstan, in particular, former president Askar Akayev enjoyed good relations with multibillionaire George Soros, who is one of the main sponsors of the American University of Central Asia in Bishkek. In June 2003, in connection with Soros paying a visit to Bishkek, Akayev stressed that he was a trusted friend of Kyrgyzstan and that his ideas had made their way into Kyrgyz society.[23] This statement seemed to have lost its validity one year later when the state-run media launched a campaign against international organizations, which also included the OSI in Bishkek. On 3 June 2004, the daily newspaper *Slovo Kirgistana* accused international organizations of having an interest in instigating mass popular unrest, in making efforts to weaken the publicly elected and legitimized government, and ultimately in installing a puppet government dependant on foreign powers.[24] A few days later, former president Akayev announced he had no intention of following the footsteps of president Eduard Shevardnadze. He stated that international political practices, which might trigger another "velvet revolution", should give cause to greater concern.[25]

Uzbek president Islam Karimov is a close friend of former Georgian president Eduard Shevardnadze.[26] Just as Shevardnadze, Karimov holds the view that international actors disturb the domestic affairs of his country while claiming to have humanitarian goals. During the spring of 2004, the spokesman of the Uzbek Ministry of Foreign Affairs said: "The reason for not accrediting Soros is that the activities of his foundation are unwelcome in Uzbekistan."[27] This statement marked the preliminary end of a development that had started in early 2004.

---

22   Kimmage 2005.
23   Cf. The Times of Central Asia 2003.
24   Cf. Saralaeva 2004.
25   Ibid.
26   Cf. Herman 2004.
27   Herman 2004.

The news agency *Centrasia* reported on 27 January 2004 that all international organizations and NGOs in Uzbekistan would have to register with the Ministry of Justice before 1 March 2004. Registering with the Ministry of Foreign Affairs would, from then on, only be possible for diplomatic representations and foreign governmental organizations. According to Ilkhom Zakirov, this was done, because, since 1999, the number of international and local NGOs had increased twelve fold.[28] International observers unanimously deemed that the Uzbek government acted this way as a result of the events in Georgia. Even though this affected all international NGOs, the decision was primarily aimed at OSI, the National Democratic Institute, the International Republican Institute and Freedom House, and undermined a 1994 bilateral agreement that would make it easier to register US NGOs in Uzbekistan.[29]

Following a one-month extension to early April 2004 of the deadline for registering, on 14 April 2004 the Ministry of Justice told the OSI in Tashkent that it would no longer be allowed to be registered. The reason for revoking the registration was connected with the OSI's decision to distribute literature to the universities, which in content and meaning distorted the economic, public and political reforms in Uzbekistan as well as discredited government policies.[30] With this decision, Uzbekistan found itself practising the same policies as Belarus, who has also tried to hinder Soros' activities. On 19 April 2004, the OSI put a preliminary stop to their work in Uzbekistan.

The de-facto closure of the OSI in Tashkent is not only an important benchmark for the attitude of the Uzbek government towards NGOs who are critical of it, but it also has significant ramifications for the work conducted by local NGOs. During its tenure in Uzbekistan, the OSI distributed circa USD 22 million to support reforms in the areas of education, culture, health and economic development, which makes it the largest private sponsor in the country.[31] Most of this support was invested into co-operation projects with local NGOs. Therefore, the OSI could be credited for their mere survival. The first signs of the detrimental effects of this on local NGOs were already visible as early as 2004. According to a source within NGO circles, ten NGOs had to discontinue their work in the Ferghana-Valley region alone, due to the loss of OSI funding.[32]

However, international NGOs are not the only ones affected by the actions of the Uzbek government. In early February 2004, the government established a so-called finance committee to control the flow of funds from foreign donors to local NGOs. After a local NGO has received an offer of financial support from an external donor, the finance committee "verifies" together with the government whether the NGO really qualifies for support. According to the testimony of representatives of local or international NGOs, this is to redirect

---

28   Cf. Shekkhar 2004.
29   Cf. Panfilova 2004.
30   Cf. Eurasia Insight 2004.
31   Cf. Open Society Institute 2004.
32   Personal interview in Tashkent, 29 March 2004.

funds to governmental – and quasi-governmental organizations. As a result of a cabinet's decision of 4 February 2004, all local NGOs were encouraged to open an account with either the "National Foreign Economic Bank" of Uzbekistan or the "*Asaka* Bank" and to close all other accounts. The official reasoning behind this decision was that it would create a better overview of money transfers coming into the country and that it would also hinder money-laundering activities.[33] One year later, in an interview with *Nezavisimaya Gazeta*, Karimov stated the following: "We are now researching, which projects get financial means and grants. This is to determine whether a project is humanitarian or its real purpose is to prepare a somehow next 'coloured' revolution."[34]

Another important decision that worsened the relationship between the Uzbek government and international organizations was the revision of Article 157, pertaining to treason, of the Uzbek criminal code of 12 December 2003. The elements of offence for treason now include not only the leaking of state secrets to foreign governments, but also to foreign organizations or their representatives.[35] Representatives of international organizations in Tashkent fear that, with the help of this amendment, pressure can be levied on organizations and individuals who are critical of the government.[36]

The above-mentioned decisions reveal Tashkent's attitude, and thus constitutes a clear warning to all international and local NGOs. Since the spring of 2004, many of these organizations – at least insofar as they have a political agenda – have been able to function only to a limited extent. In the preparations for the 26 December 2004 parliamentary elections, their hands were effectively tied. At first, in Kazakhstan and Kyrgyzstan, the situation seemed to be less tense and was limited to verbal assaults. However, when it comes to securing their grip on power, in these countries as well, the rulers keep a watchful eye on external actors. It had not even been a year since the OSI opened in Uzbekistan, when it was *de-facto* closed on 27 December 2004 and Kazakh authorities launched a criminal case against the Soros Foundation-Kazakhstan.[37] Although Kazakh officials indicated that financial and legal reasons were behind the case, the OSI itself, as well as analysts, believed that political reasons triggered the initiation of the case. According to Yevgeniy Zhovtis, head of Kazakhstan's International Bureau on Human Rights and the Rule of Law, political events in Georgia as well as in the Ukraine have in-

---

33 Cf. Decision No. 56 of the cabinet of ministers, 4 February 2004 "On measures to improve the effectiveness of keeping a record of financial funds for technical assistance, grants, and no-strings aid being received from international and foreign governmental and nongovernmental organizations". (not yet published).
34 Panfilova 2005a. Translation by the author.
35 Cf. Law "On Amendments and Additions to Several Legislative Acts", 13 February 2004. (not yet published).
36 Personal interviews with various international organizations in April 2004 in Tashkent.
37 The case was filed as per Article 222, part 1 of the Criminal Code of the Republic of Kazakhstan "Evasion from tax payments by organisations". See: Press report in Gazeta.kz on 29 December 2004.

creased the Kazakh government's impatience "with what it sees as the [Soros] foundation's interference in the political affairs of post-Soviet countries".[38] At approximately the same time, the Tajik president Rahmonov was cited in the Turkish newspaper *Zaman* as accusing "some international institutions, and especially the Soros Foundation, of acting with the aim to destroy Tajikistan's unity".[39]

While the situation with Soros in both countries has calmed down so far, Kazakhstan – where presidential elections will take place at the end of 2005 or in 2006 – has begun to follow Uzbekistan's footsteps with regard to restricting the activities of international and local non-governmental organizations. On 29 June 2005 – after a year of discussions – the lower house of the parliament in Kazakhstan passed two draft laws: "On the Activities of Branches and Representative Offices of International or Foreign Non-Commercial Organizations" and "On the Introduction of Amendments and Additions into Certain Legislative Acts of the Republic of Kazakhstan on Matters Related to Non-Profit Organizations".[40] Its draft laws veered off in the same direction as Uzbekistan's, i.e. re-registration with the Ministry of Justice of all offices of international and foreign NGOs; financing of foreign or local NGOs only with governmental approval; and requirement to inform the authorities about the amount of financing and its spending.[41] According to representatives of the international community, both laws "do not follow recognized international legal standards and best practices" and "are intended to place unnecessary burdens and restrictions on the activities of foreign and domestic NGOs".[42] Local NGOs argue that the draft laws contradict the constitution and thus urged Nazarbayev to veto them. Because of international and domestic pressure, Nazarbayev submitted both laws for review to Kazakhstan's constitutional council on 13 July.[43] In the meantime, on 20 July, Russian president Putin "spoke out strongly against the foreign funding of Russian NGOs that engage in political activities".[44] The fear of a potential spread of coloured revolutions seems to be growing not only among Central Asian presidents, but also in Russia. And measures are not only being taken to control international and domestic NGOs, but also inter-governmental organizations such as the OSCE.

---

38 Cited in Saidazimova 2004.
39 Cihan 2004.
40 Cf. Flynn 2005.
41 Cf. Pannier 2005.
42 Letter sent to the chairman of Kazakhstan's parliament by several international organizations – Freedom House, International Republican Institute, National Democratic Institute, Internews Network, IFES, International Center for Not-for-Profit Law, American Bar Association, Open Society Institute – on 9 May 2005 (available at www.internews.org).
43 Cf. Flynn 2005.
44 Corwin 2005.

Russian critique of the OSCE is no novelty.[45] The closer the elections in Central Asia are, the louder the voices become that try to limit the influence of international organizations, in particular the OSCE with its focus on observing elections. On 10 June 2004, the then Kyrgyz president, Akayev, surprised the international community with a UNESCO conference in Bishkek by giving a speech that implied a new course in relation to international organizations. A news agency quoted him as saying that "Foreign reactions which have little to do with local realities are often viewed as interfering with internal affairs. But we have to be patient, especially when they [the reactions, eds.] originate from an organisation with the authority of the OSCE."[46]
The height of the Central Asian critique of the OSCE took place on 3 July 2004. On this day, nine CIS members, including four Central Asian countries – Kazakhstan, Kyrgyzstan, Tajikistan and Uzbekistan – signed a statement in which they delivered sharp criticism of the OSCE. The statement was read at the 514th Meeting of the Permanent Council of the OSCE on 8 July 2004 and includes: First, the OSCE is accused of not adjusting to the events of a changing world, and second, of not following the letter of the guidelines as stated in their own documents, especially the principles of not interfering with internal affairs and respecting national sovereignty. Third, the signatories identified an imbalance between the three dimensions of the OSCE. Compared to the military-political and the economic dimensions, the human dimension is given too much emphasis. Fourth, the Organization was accused of having double standards and of employing selective approaches, since it is much more engaged with some of its participating states than with others and, furthermore, does not respect the idiosyncrasies of certain states. In a final point, the field activities, which comprise most of the OSCE spending, were criticized. In the opinion of the signatories, the field activities are ineffective, since they focus solely on the observation of human rights and the state of democratic institutions of any given state, instead of offering help and advice to the respective governments.[47]
Even though many of these arguments had been made by some of the signatory states in various contexts throughout the past year and, as such, do not constitute a novelty,[48] this statement is nevertheless of specific importance. Firstly, the drafting of the document took place in Moscow at an informal meeting of the presidents of Armenia, Belarus, Kazakhstan, Kyrgyzstan, Moldavia, the Russian Federation, Tajikistan, the Ukraine and Uzbekistan.

---

45 In early 2004, Mikhail Margelov, head of the Russian Federation Council Foreign Affairs Committee, wrote an article in which he refers to the OSCE Ministerial Council as being a "meeting place for well-educated alcoholics" and the OSCE itself as a "dump" and "escaped jack-hammer". Margelov 2004. Translation by the author.
46 Saralaeva 2004.
47 Cf. Ministry of Foreign Affairs of the Russian Federation 2004.
48 See also the article by Kreikemeyer in part II of this volume.

Such a meeting is symptomatic for the present-day political development in some states of the former Soviet Union, which, after a decade of rapprochement with the West, now once again primarily turn to Moscow. Secondly, the statement is a sign of the growing self-assertiveness of some CIS states on the international stage – a situation that has been in the making for some years.[49]

Whereas all critical statements toward the OSCE were made by Russia, criticism by a larger grouping of CIS states is indeed a novelty.[50] This seems to indicate the will of the intra-CIS grouping of countries to organize in a more coherent manner. It also illustrates their frustration with the emphasis of the OSCE on the human dimension. Turkmenistan joined the side of the signatories in Vienna, and thus only two CIS states, Azerbaijan and Georgia, did not sign the statement. It is noteworthy that the postulated group identity and collective experience as post-Soviet states ostensibly outweigh the actual discontentment of the Organization's work. According to Radio Free Europe/ Radio Liberty, the spokesperson for the former Kyrgyz president explained that Kyrgyzstan, in principal, had no grievances against the OSCE, but that a certain sense of commitment to its partners within the CIS had made them sign the statement.[51] It seems logical to conclude that, in connection with the upcoming elections in several states, the collective critique of international organizations such as the OSCE will, at least for time coming, balance out the differences between these states; and Moscow's influence over Central Asia will only become stronger.

And if they haven't died (out) they still rule today

The most important goal for Central Asian presidents is to remain in power – at any cost. In order to reach this goal, each president must pay attention to both internal and external factors. Thus, internally they must possess the ability to either fulfil or thwart the expectations of the population, and internationally they must be able to represent the country's national interests.[52] The population expects, following the Soviet pattern, that the ruler provides stability and a passable standard of living. As long as these conditions are provided, the public will not bring to the fore any political demands. Since economic reforms in all three countries have not led to improved standards of living for the majority of the population, but rather to the consolidation of the traditional business elite, the public's discontentment has risen sharply in the

---

49 In this context, it should be noted that Kazakhstan on 18 February 2003 made public that it would work towards getting the 2009 OSCE chairmanship.
50 Admittedly, already 4 September 2003, a paper by Belarus, Kazakhstan, Kyrgyzstan and Russia critical of the OSCE field missions had been published. Cf. Delegations of Belarus, Kazakhstan, Kyrgyzstan and Russia 2003.
51 Cf. Tomiuc 2004.
52 Cf. Hale 1994: 139.

past few years.[53] From the view of the presidents, their goal of maintaining power will be put at risk, because of the work conducted by local organizations in areas such as democratization, the strengthening of civil society, education etc. Due to these activities, it will become more and more difficult to keep the expectations of the public under control. More so, the public will learn how to express their grievances and will pose more and more demands in both the economic and political spheres. Although the fight for democracy seems to be one of the few human rights activities in which the majority of the population takes little or no part, the recent events in Kyrgyzstan very clearly show that the general economic and social dissatisfaction can be easily instrumentalized by certain politicians or other influential persons.[54]

On the international level, the critique raised by international organizations, in areas such as slow-moving reforms, human rights abuses and lack of democratization, affects the esteem of the president and, consequently, weakens his position domestically. Furthermore, this critique can also influence bilateral relations between certain states, as was illustrated by the prompt and demonstrative rapprochement between Uzbekistan and Russia, after the US froze USD 18 million in financial aid for Uzbekistan for the year 2004.[55]

The developments sketched in this paper clearly show that the authorities in Astana, Bishkek and Tashkent – already in the run-up to the presidential elections – are ready to prevent any possible critique with extreme measures. The question remains open as to what extent the populations in question are interested in regime change and whether they will behave under the prevailing circumstances. After a decade of "independence" and after several months of a "new" leadership in Bishkek, it is only obvious that a change in power will by no means necessarily lead to improved conditions for the people.

Bibliography

Antelava, Natalia. 2003. Yesterday's man rues Georgian defeat. In: *BBC News*,15 December.
Berg, Andrea. 2004. Wer hat Angst vor George Soros? Die Auseinandersetzung zwischen autoritären Machthabern und internationalen Organisationen in Zentralasien. In: *Sicherheit und Frieden*, 22 (4), pp. 206-211.
Burke, Justin. 2003. Most Influential Persons in Kyrgyzstan are the President and His Spouse. In: *Eurasianet. Kyrgyzstan Weekly Report*, 30 June.
Cihan. 2004. Tajik Administration Complains about Soros. In: *Zaman Online*, 30 December.

---

53 Whereas the end of the 1990s saw only little criticism of Islam Karimov and, if so, only privately, these days one can hear critical sentiments voiced more or less publicly in the street.
54 Saralaeva titled in a report, focusing on the growing trend towards paying protestors "Rent-a-Mob in Kyrgyzstan". Saralaeva 2005.
55 On July 13 2004, the US State Department made public that Uzbekistan did not fulfil the criteria for receiving aid of up to USD 18 million. The reasons for the decision were lack of progress in the democratization process. International human rights groups assessed this as a step in the right direction. At the same time, though, Washington signalled its continued interest in a narrow/bilateral co-operation with Uzbekistan and confirmed its interest in the region. Cf. US Department of State 2004.

Collins, Kathleen. 2002. Clans, Pacts, and Politics in Central Asia. In: *Journal of Democracy*, 13, 3, July, pp. 137-152.

Corwin, Julie A. 2005. Russia. Will Putin Follow in Nazarbaev's Footsteps? In: *Radio Free Europe/Radio Liberty*, 29 July.

Delegations of Belarus, Kazakhstan, Kyrgyzstan and Russia. 2003. *On the Issue of Reform of the OSCE field activities*, 4 September, non-disclosed document.

Eurasianet. 2004. Uzbek government closes down Open Society Institute Assistance Foundation in Tashkent. In: *Eurasianet. Eurasia Insight*, 18 January.

Flynn, Erica. 2005. Kazakhstan's Constitutional Council due to Rule on NGO-related Legislation. In: *Eurasianet. Eurasia Insight*, 11 August.

Hale, Henry. 1994. Islam, State-building and Uzbekistan foreign policy. In: Banuazizi, Ali/ Weiner, Myron (eds.). *The new geopolitics of Central Asia and its Borderlands*. Bloomington: Indiana University Press, pp. 136-171.

Herman, Burt. 2004. Soros' Foundation Closes in Uzbekistan. In: The Associated Press, 19 April.

Karajanov, , Zamir. 2005. Kazakstan. All Eyes on Kyrgyzstan. Fears of Ukrainian-style "velvet revolution" begin to grow in neighbouring Kazakstan. In: *Institute for War and Peace Reporting. Reporting Central Asia*, 345, 1 February.

Kimmage, Daniel. 2005. Nipping Orange Roses in the Bud. Post-Soviet Elites against Revolution. In: *Radio Free Europe/Radio Liberty. Central Asia Report*, 5 (3), 25 January.

Kusainov, Aldar. 2003. Wheels set in motion for dynastic transition in Kazakhstan. In: *Eurasianet. Eurasia Insight*, 16 September.

Lipman, Masha. 2003. Birth of a Dynasty? In: *Washington Post*, 11 August.

MacKinnon, Mark. 2003. Georgia revolt carried mark of Soros. In: *The Globe and Mail*, 26 November.

Margelov, Mikhail. 2004. Зачем нужна ОБСЕ? Организация, созданная как инструмент улучшения отношений между Западом и Востоком, стала инструментом их ухудшения. In: *Nezavisimaya Gazeta*, 19 January.

Ministry of Foreign Affairs of the Russian Federation. 2004. *Statement by CIS Member Countries on the State of Affairs in the OSCE*, Moscow, 3 July.

Mydans, Seth. 2003. Political Dynasty in Azerbaijan. For the First Time in the Vast Former Soviet Bloc, a Son Will Inherit His Father's Presidency. In: *The New York Times*, 15 October.

Onica, Timur. 2003. Georgia events inspire Kyrgyz opposition, In: *Eurasianet. Georgia Daily Digest*, 25 November.

Open Society Institute. 2004. *Uzbek government forces closure of local Soros Foundation*, 18 April.

Panfilova, Victoria. 2004. Вашингтон обещает лишить Ислама Каримова финансовой помощи. In: *Nezavisimaya Gazeta*, 27 January.

Panfilova, Victoria. 2005a. Ислам Каримов: «При империи нас считали людьми второго сорта». In: *Nezavisimaya Gazeta*, 14 January.

Panfilova, Victoria. 2005b. В преддверии еще одной «бархатной революции». Президент Акаев собирает ресурсы для отражения атак оппозиции. In: *Nezavisimaya Gazeta*, 28 January.

Pannier, Bruce. 2003. Central Asia. Presidents' daughters emerging as unlikely political forces in Kazakhstan, Uzbekistan. In: *Radio Free Europe/Radio Liberty*, 24 September.

Pannier, Bruce. 2005. Kazakhstan. Tough Bill On NGOs Meets with Unexpected Opposition. In: *Radio Free Europe/Radio Liberty*, 28 June.

Pravda. 2003. Shevarnadze accuses Soros of organising a coup d'etat in Georgia, 1 December.

Saidazimova, Gulnoza. 2004. Kazakhstan. Soros Foundation Says Tax Evasion Case is Politically Motivated. In: *Radio Free Europe/Radio Liberty*, 30 December.

Saidazimova, Gulnoza. 2005. For Kyrgyz President, Parliamentary Elections are a Family Affair. In: *Radio Free Europe/Radio Liberty. Central Asia Report*, 5 (3), 25 January.

Saralaeva, Leila. 2004. Kyrgyzstan's Fading Romance With the West. In: *Institute for War and Peace Research. Reporting Central Asia*, 296, 25 June.

Saralaeva, Leila. 2005. Rent-a-Mob in Kyrgyzstan. In: : *Institute for War and Peace Research. Reporting Central Asia*, 391, 28 June.
Shekkhar, Alok. 2004. Минюст Узбекистана проводит перерегистрацию представительств НПО. In: *Centrasia,* 27 January.
The Associated Press. 2004. Uzbeks fear a Georgia-style revolution, 23 January.
The Times of Central Asia. 2003. George Soros' voyage to Central Asia, 5 June.
Tomiuc Eugen. 2004. OSCE. Several CIS States rebuke democracy watchdog. In: *Radio Free Europe/Radio Liberty*, 9 September.
Traynor, Ian. 2004. US Campaign behind the turmoil in Kiev. In: *Guardian*, 26 November.
Urban, Thomas. 2005. Präsidenten-Gattin mit Erfahrung im Weißen Haus. In: *Sueddeutsche Zeitung*, 24 January.
US Department of State. 2004. *Secretary of State decision not to certify Uzbekistan*, 13 July.
Yermukanov, Marat. 2005a. Astana Works To Stave Off Ukraine's Advancing Orange Tide. In *Jamestown Foundation. Eurasia Daily Monitor*, 2 (7), 11 January.
Yermukanov, Marat. 2005b. Nazarbayev Lines Up His Men Ahead of Election Campaign. In *Jamestown Foundation. Eurasia Daily Monitor*, 2 (150), 2 August.

Part III:
Democratization
of the Judicial Sector?

Marina Pikulina

Power Structures and Problems of Law Implementation in Uzbekistan*

Introduction

The Republic of Uzbekistan joined the Conference on Security and Co-operation in Europe (CSCE) on 30 January 1992. At the second meeting of the Ministerial Council in Prague, Uzbekistan declared its willingness to adopt all of its commitments. The President of Uzbekistan, Islam A. Karimov, signed the "Helsinki Final Act" on 26 February 1992 and the "Charter of Paris for a New Europe" on 27 October 1993.[1] The adoption of the CSCE's main documents led to a revision of the constitution in Uzbekistan, since it did not conform with basic international standards, and thus became the subject of criticism by European experts. On 8 December 1992, a new constitution was adopted as well as a plethora of new laws in the following years. In doing so, Uzbekistan theoretically reformed its legal basis. However, I will argue that these reforms took place mainly on paper and that there is a huge gap between existing laws and the level of their implementation. I will further argue that the administrative structure, the lack of separation of powers and the dominance of particular interests hinder the development of the rule of law in Uzbekistan.

The first two parts of the article contain an outline of the existing power structures in Uzbekistan on a horizontal and vertical axis. In the third part, I discuss the issue of drafting and adopting laws, on the one hand, and the implementation of these laws, on the other. The fourth part analyses the effect of legal reforms on economic activities. Part five discusses the role of the OSCE in the reform process.

Horizontal (non)separation of powers

De jure Uzbekistan has a clear separation of powers. The legislature was represented until the end of 2004 by the unicameral parliament (Uzb: *Oliy Majlis*), which was established immediately after gaining national independence in 1991. According to national legislation, the parliament, the cabinet of ministers and the president are entitled to initiate new laws. In practice,

---

* This article was written before the events in Andijan in May 2005. Yet a lot of the problems this article focuses on seem to have a general relevance for the discontentment of the Uzbek population as a whole.
1 See Tiurikov; Shaguliamov 1997: 20.

143

though, only the president and the cabinet of ministers make use of this right, while the parliament remains passive. The parliament thus plays an insignificant role in law-making. Furthermore, the cabinet of ministers often issues decrees that contradict existing legislation. For example, the Constitution of the Republic of Uzbekistan states that only courts have the right to confiscate property or goods.[2] Yet, the cabinet of ministers recently decided that local authorities are authorized to confiscate commodities that have no custom declaration.

The OSCE and other international organizations assist on a regular basis in the democratization of the parliament's activities and the improvement of the professionalism of the parliamentarians. For these purposes, seminars, round tables, discussions and visits of parliamentary delegations to European countries are organized for the members of parliament. Yet, a culture of pluralism and an understanding of democracy in the adoption of laws have not become the norm. The chairman of a committee retains the final say in the decision-making process. In response to the situation, lawyers often criticize the procedure of law adoption that does involve the public. Moreover, remarks and comments of professional law-makers are very often ignored.

The executive in Uzbekistan is represented by the government as well as by the heads of the provincial and the district administration with its subordinated bodies. According to the legislation, the executive works within the framework of the constitution and the existing laws. However, *de facto* the executive authorities also have the right to adopt sub-normative acts that often contradict the constitution and nullify laws approved by parliament. In practice, all basic law violations take place at the level of the executive authorities. Thus, for example, the police do not act according to the legislation, but according to its own internal regulations (Russ: *prikaz*), which are issued by the Ministry of Internal Affairs. Another example is the annual cotton picking campaign. Although the Uzbek legislation prohibits forcing people into cotton picking, local authorities even send children to the fields. The constitutional court rarely intervenes, although it is within its sphere of competence to find and examine such cases.

A special department of human rights has been established in the Ministry of Justice to investigate all cases of law violations and to ensure that all sub-normative acts, issued and adopted by the executive authorities, conform with the existing legislation. This department does not work effectively, however.

According to the constitution, the judiciary is the third branch of government in Uzbekistan and an independent entity. In reality, judges are appointed by the president or by the heads of the provincial and district administration and *de facto* are not independent. The activities of the various courts (criminal courts, civil courts, financial courts, arbitration courts and the constitutional court) are not transparent and corruption is widespread. Under pressure of the

---

2   Chapter XII, para. 53 of the Constitution of the Republic of Uzbekistan.

international community, parliament liberalized the criminal legislation. For example, an article requiring detention for economic and minor crimes was abolished and imprisonment was replaced by fines. A liberalization of the judicial system in general, however, did not take place. This is exemplified by the very limited rights of attorneys.

Vertical (non)separation of powers

In addition to the branches of power mentioned above, there exist three levels of power, the national, provincial and district. The supreme power in both structures is the president with his presidential administration. Although the presidential administration is not foreseen in the constitution and has no legislative responsibility, in practice, it wields unlimited influence on the decision-making processes. Thus, *de facto,* no law can be adopted without the approval of the presidential administration. This is the ultimate authority; and parliament hands over every single law to them for consideration. The administration makes amendments and comments before sending the law to the president. In addition, the presidential administration actively uses the so-called "telephone command".[3]

The internal affairs of the provinces (Uzb: *viloyat*) are the sphere of competence of the respective governor (Uzb: *hokim*), the head of the province's administration. *De jure*, the competencies and responsibilities of a *hokim* are regulated by the current constitution, but *de facto* no one oversees how his decision adds up to the constitution.

Regional, district and local authorities each issue their own sub-normative acts. Practice shows that many laws are ignored and/or adapted to the needs of the local political elite at the provincial level. The provincial *hokim* may issue any decree within the sphere of his competence. Legal authorities in the provinces and districts are sitting on the fence in some respects. On the one hand, they are responsible to the Ministry of Justice and, on the other hand, they fully depend on the goodwill of the province's administration and therefore cannot carry out their functions. The governor is authorized to dismiss any local prosecutor, the head of the police department and the heads of the district administration. In fact, he controls all aspects of the provinces' administration.

According to the constitution, the president is authorized to propose candidates for the post of the *hokim* to the provincial councils, but he in fact appoints and dismisses the *hokims* exclusively. District *hokims* are appointed by the provincial *hokims*. In general, the central government does not interfere with the work of the provincial administration and the provincial *hokim* does not interfere with the work of the district administration.

---

3   The "telephone command" is a verbal order given on the telephone without written submission by a high-ranking official. Often such orders contradict the legislation.

Yet, President Karimov often appoints new *hokims*. In a speech at a session of the cabinet of ministers in Tashkent on 17 February 2003, he blamed provincial governors for acting like "feudal autocrats, thinking they are authorized to force people to work, while paying mere lip service to the law and their obligations."[4] He also held them responsible for the insufficient agricultural output in 2002. Since then, sudden dismissals and rotations have become common; every *hokim* is keen to gain as much personal wealth as possible and to provide his family and friends with posts and access to resources. They rarely pursue specific long-term policies or a political vision. According to an article by Pulat Gadoev, political analysts agree that Karimov "makes sure that no clan can increase its zone of influence" in this manner.[5]

The influence of shadow structures on decision-making and on the implementation of decisions in the provinces impedes the realization of the legislation. The economic elites at the provincial level have close ties with the respective *hokim* and many decisions are taken with consideration toward their interests. Yet, changes in power at the local level often lead to changes in the economic elite circles. Owners of profitable enterprises are essentially robbed by courts, or by the police, and their property is transferred to the hands of the supporters or relatives of the *hokim*.

Reforms are blocked at the provincial level and many laws and human rights are violated. The central government intervenes into the activities of the provincial hokim only when it must protect its own interests. It is not a secret that provincial *hokims* often ask entrepreneurs and enterprises, operating in their province, for money – allegedly for charitable purposes. Needless to say, the government does not control these under-the-table transfers.

Thus, we can summarize power structures in Uzbekistan as follows: at the national level, the president functions as the supreme authority along with his presidential administration. The parliament, the government and the courts answer to him. At the provincial level, the governor (Uzb: *viloyat hokimi*) controls the provincial administration, the provincial council and the provincial courts. The head of a district (Uzb: *tuman hokimi*) controls the district administration, the district council and the district courts. In sum, power structures are very hierarchical and not separated at any level.

Problems of law enforcement in Uzbekistan

There is a certain incongruence between the adoption of laws and their observation in Uzbekistan. International experts agree that the legislation of the Republic of Uzbekistan conforms with international norms and democratic principles. Problems, however, occur because there are insufficient imple-

---

4   RFE/RL 2003.
5   Gadoev 2003.

mentation mechanisms. In the end, citizens cannot assert their democratic rights guaranteed to them by the legislation.

The formation of the current legal system of the Republic of Uzbekistan is based on the constitutional principle of rule of law and on the adaptation of legal doctrines. This process can be characterized as difficult and contradictory. When analysing the reasons for such a situation it is important to determine the weakest sections in the regulation mechanism in order to make improvements.

The legal system can be divided into three sub-systems: legal doctrine, legislative processes and law-enforcing and juridical practice. The formation of a legal doctrine is still in its initial stages in Uzbekistan. After the rejection of the former Soviet legal ideology, there was the need to identify a new legal doctrine based on common international standards, ideas and principles and specific historically developed Uzbek norms and values. Sometimes these components may contradict each other. In addition, an incomplete legal doctrine or legal ideology complicates the interpretation of the law by professional lawyers. It affects both the quality of law-enforcement and law-making activities to a certain degree. The new legal doctrine does not encroach upon legislative acts relevant to the structure of the legislature itself, such as the law "On normative-legal acts of the Republic of Uzbekistan", the law "On preparation of bills", the law "On international agreements" and the law "On the constitutional court of the Republic of Uzbekistan".[6]

As mentioned above, the legislative process in the parliament is under the strict control of the presidential administration. The presidential office monitors all bills being elaborated and discussed in the committees of the Oliy Majlis. The main provisions of the bills are declarative in character, allow a wide range of references and a broad interpretation, and have many gaps. Legal facilities designed to implement these bills do not exist. Any attempt to define more detailed and clear regulations by specialists or representatives of the working groups that are invited to prepare the bills are rejected by the heads of the respective parliamentary committees, or by the representatives of the presidential administration. They are rejected on the grounds that they lack legal tradition or that they do not conform with those regulations of the existing practice. Frequently, bills are adopted even after scientists and other specialists have criticized them. The law "On preparation of bills" does not include regulations on bills that are negatively assessed by experts. In practice, their assessments are ignored.

It is anticipated that implementation procedures will be developed by sub-normative acts issued by the respective department or ministry. Yet, many of these sub normative acts rather reflect singular interests than contribute to the implementation of a certain law. It frequently happens that bills, adopted by the Oliy Majlis and delivered to the president for signing, are "finalized" in

---

6   For more information on the laws of the Republic of Uzbekistan see: http://lawlib.freenet.uz/laws/uzbek/uzlaws.html.

the presidential administration and are published in the press afterwards. In doing so, the parliament is deprived of its possibility to raise any objections.

This means that effectively incomplete and vague laws that cannot regulate public affairs are adopted. Important aspects of regulations are left open to sub-normative acts issued by the executive powers and not by the legislature. These acts reflect the selfish interests of the executive. Furthermore, their period of validity is short (sub-normative acts are changed every year or every six months).

Thus, the public is confronted with the constantly changing "rules of the game". They can never be sure how long a certain rule will be valid. Consequently, the mistrust of power and of the state is omnipresent. While state officials have control over the situation and are able to interpret certain directives according to their own interest, the common people suffer from lack of knowledge, since these directives are not made public. Any request made to state officials, be it tax inspectors, customs officers, policemen or social insurance inspectors, to show their directives and explain the rules under which they are acting, are refused. Often they are unable to explain or give reasonable arguments justifying their actions.

The process of publishing sub-normative acts should also be highlighted. According to the legislation, sub-normative acts must be approved by legal experts and registered with the Ministry of Justice and its provincial and district bodies. In fact, these acts have often come into effect prior to the legal revision and the official registration. Thus, the registration thereof to the Ministry of Justice as well as the legal expertise are reduced to a mere formality and – to put it bluntly – window-dressing.

Several lawyers from the Tashkent Juridical Institute[7] argue that, given the high number of sub-normative acts issued by the customs committee, the state property and tax committee, one can presume a low level of professionalism among the staff of the Ministry of Justice, especially among those who are engaged with the registration and systematization of sub-normative acts. Furthermore, it seems that the Ministry of Justice is not fulfilling its obligations to protect the integrity of the legal system of the Republic of Uzbekistan and to guarantee its non-contradictory character.

All these problems have a direct impact on the implementation of laws. Permanent changes in the legislation and in sub-normative acts have led to disorientation and instability, for example, among the law enforcement agencies. In addition, due to grammar and stylistic mistakes it is difficult to even understand official documents.[8] Up until today, a specific law on state services and its principles does not exist. Low salaries and a wide scope of interpretation of certain laws and sub-normative acts have led to corruption, which has,

---

7   Personal interview with Laviza Kashinskaya, 16 January 2004.
8   State officials and technical staff suffer from the declining education standards as well as the population in general. It is easy to find up to 50 mistakes on one page of a court sentence.

in turn, strengthened the principles of personal support, protectionism and regionalism. In fact, many officials safeguard their own interests rather than state interests.

Another example of weak law enforcement is the work of the police. Police activities have evoked criticism by the international and local human rights organizations. Considering these problems we should take into account that, up to now, the parliament has not adopted any law or provision on police activities. Provisions, regulations and sub-normative acts issued by ministries and departments regulate its activities. These acts and provisions often contradict each other. Thus, the police are often at a loss as to what to do in a certain situation and end up carrying out the commands of the superior officer regardless of the requirements stated by law.

The problems of law implementation do not only hold true with regard to the national legislation, but also with regard to international agreements. The ratification of an agreement by the Republic of Uzbekistan is not always accompanied by its publication, even in the media of the parliament. Sometimes deputies are not familiar with the text of the international agreement they are to ratify. Law application structures (judges, prosecution officers and other officials) responsible for the implementation of international agreements are ignorant of the provisions and therefore are unable to implement them. The diversity of approaches used by the various law structures to implement international agreements makes the situation even more complex.

In addition, it is often unclear whether, after the ratification of international agreements, national laws must be adapted to them, or whether they can be directly implemented and used by the law application structures of the Republic of Uzbekistan. Since this question has not yet been resolved, many international agreements are not being implemented and exist only on paper. In such cases, provisions on how to implement international agreements should be added to the law of the Republic of Uzbekistan. Preferably, the decisions of the plenary sessions of the supreme court and the constitutional court should contain explanations on how the courts are to interpret international agreements.

Legal base of economic reforms

An area of legislation, where the population is extremely affected by the despotism of officials is the economy. More than any other area, it is regulated by permanent changing sub-normative acts and decrees, which often jeopardize citizens' rights.

Five years ago, the government issued three decrees aiming at the improvement of commodity turnover registration and combating non-bank asset turn over.[9] Based on these decrees, commodity producers are bound to cashless wholesale trade with juridical persons and individuals who have certain relevant permits. They are not allowed to sell their goods to buyers without permits even if they offer 100 per cent prepayment. In this way, the freedom of producers is restricted and their work hampered.

If producers do not follow these decrees they are punished with considerable penalties. Any inspecting body is authorized to file a claim against any producer. As a result of this policy, the brain drain from the commodity producing branches increases. It became much more prestigious and profitable to work in institutions, whose main functions are to "seize and divide", for instance, in tax and custom inspections.[10]

Another example of the problems of law implementation in the economic sphere is the registration of enterprises and businesses. Although, according to entrepreneurs, registration is not an insurmountable obstacle any longer, it costs a lot of time and money. The decree "On the improvement of the state registration system of subjects of entrepreneurship", issued by the cabinet of ministers on 22 August 2001,[11] was aimed at simplifying the registration procedure. According to this decree, an entrepreneur has to submit all required documents to the registering organ, which is responsible for coordinating the procedure with tax authorities and other relevant departments. In addition, a timeframe for the registration procedure is arranged. In reality, this timeframe of eight working days for individuals and twelve working days for juridical persons is never adhered to. According to registration bodies, the main reason for the constant delays is the necessity to register entrepreneurs in all relevant bodies. Thus, an applicant has to make a deal with, i.e. bribe, the officials to accelerate the process. Business people know that, for a rapid registration without problems, it is better if the registration body itself prepares their documents. Yet, this strategy is not always successful.

While bribing officials is simply a fact of life for many people, other cases of more serious violations by registering bodies and some officials do occur. It is a matter of common knowledge that entrepreneurs are forced to "donate" money to various state funds focusing on community development and other social needs. Besides the fact that a donation should be a voluntary contribution, many of these entrepreneurs had not even initiated a business at the time of their "donation". According to data from the Ministry of Justice, over 30,000 such violations of the registration procedure were revealed in 2002.[12]

In general, traders and small businesses suffer from day-to-day abuses by the police and the lack of any kind of constitutional state. One instance of this is the 2002 introduction of severe import restrictions, which was meant to force the population to only buy goods originating within the country. In October

---

9   Decrees of the Cabinet of Ministers, 1999, On commodity turnover registration, On combating non-bank asset turnover, On License of export commodity.
10   Laviza Kashinskaya, interview.
11   For the full text of the decree see: http://cr.freenet.uz/legal/20010822.html.
12   See Nazirova 2003.

2003, the government decided that small merchants would only be allowed to continue their sales in registered kiosks and shops, and that they would have to use cash registers.[13] These and other measures have ruined the standard of living of many merchants and their families. The rigorousness with which the police and the tax inspectors are enforcing the regulations and monitoring the sales of confiscated goods has led to more hatred and animosity. Unsurprisingly, this has, time and time again, led to strikes and fights of the merchants and traders.[14]

It should be noted that entrepreneurs and farmers do not always know their rights nor are they familiar with the current legislation. In addition, the representatives of power structures are not aware of the legislation either, and thus act on the basis of sub-normative acts. As a result, we are confronted on both sides with the lack of a legal culture. In consequence, this paves the way for the violation of laws and corruption, and provides many opportunities for contravention of regulations by officials. This tendency is consolidated by a tradition of indisputable obedience of the population to state authorities.

OSCE activities and the representation of interests

In co-operation with other international organizations, the OSCE has paid great attention to the reform of the Uzbek parliament and the training of deputies. As a result, laws adopted in the parliament generally conform with international standards.

In addition, the OSCE launched several initiatives to help reform the judicial and legal system of Uzbekistan. However, the structures of both systems, as well as the way in which laws are implemented, hinder any radical changes. Many of today's attorneys are former investigators and prosecutors, who had to change their occupation for various reasons. However, they are still closely linked to their former colleagues and networks.

Special training programmes are required to foster a political culture among the provincial political elite and state officials. The OSCE and other international organizations do not pay proper attention to the issue of power structure reform. While numerous training programmes are conducted for parliamentarians, representatives of the executive and judiciary branches, as well as local authorities, are not adequately trained. As a result, the activities of the parliament have become more professional, but the adopted laws have not been implemented effectively.

Furthermore, the OSCE has played an important role in forming and strengthening civil society and thus contributed to increasing the participation of a part of the population in the social and political life of its country. What

---

13 See International Crisis Group 2004: 16.
14 For instance, on 1 November 2004, violent mass protests were directed against new market restrictions in Kokand. See Bukharbaeva 2004.

is more, it has increased awareness of their rights. Yet, NGOs still lack experience in co-operating with authorities and with the rural population.[15] A large number of seminars, round tables and workshops have been conducted for representatives of civil society. As a result, civil society has started to demand democratization from authorities. However, the authorities do not understand the finer meanings of the word "democracy". In addition, because many of the NGOs are reliant on grants allocated by international donor organizations, communication with potential local donors is disregarded.[16]

Political parties in Uzbekistan still do not effectively function and play subordinated roles in the decision-making processes. To influence decisions, it is rather useful to address the parliament as such or certain parliamentarians, but not their parties. Financial interest groups, such as business people or farmers have only limited chances to lobby their interests in a civilized manner, i.e. through membership in political parties representing their interest in parliament.[17]

Thus, the significance of informal protests is on the rise. In such cases, NGOs often act as lobbyists and urge parliamentarians to adopt necessary laws protecting the interests of farmers, traders and entrepreneurs, although there are no established mechanisms of lobbyism to fulfil such functions. The same holds true for human rights organizations. In the most unfavourable cases, the protest is expressed through activities of extremist organizations.

International organizations in Uzbekistan, including the OSCE, are very active in the Ferghana Valley. In the three provinces of Namangan, Ferghana and Andijan, they have conducted training events, seminars and round tables. The coordination, however, between all these activities and between local and other international organizations is insufficient. Many programmes are one-time events without sustainability and adequate monitoring. Nevertheless, due to these training events, the absolute and relative numbers of civil activities of the population has increased steadily. However, because the steps undertaken to protest vary, they are not systematic and are not based on a common strategy. People that attended training events and seminars started to protest against various violations of their rights and against social injustices by using various methods starting from signing petitions to blocking roads. By way of their actions, they motivate that specific part of the population that has not participated in the programmes and that does not appreciate the kinds of protests carried out. The same holds true for human rights issues and the involvement of the population in the struggle for their advancement. Many people mix up human rights issues with religious propaganda. Since protests hardly show any effect when conducted in a civilized manner, the struggle for justice turns into more radical forms of protest and even brutal force.

---

15   See also the article by Atyrkul Alisheva in this volume.
16   For more details on this phenomenon see Berg 2003.
17   For more details on lobbyism see the article by Dosym Satpaev in this volume.

Examples of increasing violence are the bomb attacks which took place in late March and early April 2004 in Tashkent and Bukhara. Although Karimov's government was quick to blame Islamic extremists, very different versions circulated among the population.[18] International observers perceived the attacks of Spring 2004 as a relatively clear warning of the hunger for power inherent in the police forces. Other examples that underline the cumulative acceptance of violence by the population are the bombings at the embassies of the United States and Israel in Tashkent in August 2004. According to Igor Rotar, Tashkent residents, who were interviewed about these events, repeatedly said that they could sympathize with the actions, since they simply do not know what else can be done.[19]

Conclusions

For the successful realization of reforms in Uzbekistan, it is necessary that priorities be determined. From our findings, it is evident that there is an urgent need to democratize, first of all, the current power structures and the administration. Without the existence of democratic power structures, there can be no talk of democracy even if a strong civil society and a developed market economy exists.

We should remember that democratization is a long-term process, and that reforms can only be implemented successfully upon consideration of concrete conditions existing in every state and society. One of the conditions preventing the effective implementation of many reforms in Uzbekistan is the low educational background of mid-level officials who participate in the decision-making processes.

The parties represented in the parliament could play a significant role in the reform of the legislation. Therefore, capacity-building for political parties and a clear distinction between the functions of NGOs and parties is of utmost importance. The political parties of farmers and businessmen have been founded only recently in Uzbekistan.[20] However, they do not have their own programme or charter yet, and they are still far from grasping their own roles.

Another disastrous situation in Uzbekistan is the deterioration of the population's living standards. Reforms in the sphere of economy, poverty eradica-

---

18 Ten civilians were killed in the bomb explosion in Bukhara on 28 March 2004. In two further explosions on the same and the following day, three policemen and one child were killed. On the following day, 15-25 people were killed in a shoot-out between police forces and an unknown group. Also, police in a bazaar in Tashkent beat an elderly merchant to death after he refused to give away his goods. See IWPR 2004.
19 See Rotar 2004.
20 In October 2003, The Movement of Entrepreneurs and Businessmen – Liberal Democratic Party was established in Tashkent. Its chairman Qobiljon Tashmatov is a well-known banker and director of the Paxtabank (Cottonbank). The Party of Agrarians and Businessmen of Marat Zahidov and the Free Peasant Party (Ozod Dehkonlar) of Nigora Khidoyatova were denied registration.

tion and reduction of unemployment are those problems requiring rapid resolution.

The former Head of the OSCE Centre Ahmet Erozan[21] determined the main priorities for its activities in Uzbekistan for 2004 as follows: small and medium business development, water recourse management, combating drug trafficking, mine clearing, reformation of the penitentiary system, supporting freedom of the press, assistance to the parliamentary elections and party-building.[22] All these issues are very important for the development of Uzbekistan. Yet, without the reform of the executive branch, without educational programmes focusing on the culture of pluralism and democracy, and without a regional approach in the solution of the outlined problems, the OSCE's activities run the risk of turning ineffective once again.

The prospects of the co-operation between the OSCE and the government of Uzbekistan depend directly on the development perspectives of the Organization itself, particularly on a strategy for its further activities in Central Asia. Many analysts argue that the OSCE has to develop a new approach toward the countries of this region, since the methods currently being applied are not improving the political, economic and cultural conditions in Central Asia.[23] It would be advantageous if the governments of Central Asia took active part in the elaboration of such a strategy in close co-operation with the other participating States of the OSCE.

Bibliography

Berg, Andrea. 2003. Encountering Transition in Contemporary Uzbekistan - A Critical Perspective on Foreign Aid and Non-Governmental Organizations. In: Dreger, Mirka/ Huenninghaus, Anke (eds.): *Social Research on Transformation in Developing Countries - Results of Interdisciplinary PhD-school Participants.* (= IEE Working Paper 171). Bochum, pp. 51-65.
Bukharbaeva, Galima. 2004. Uzbek Authorities Mount Witchhunt after Unrest. In: Institute for War and Peace Reporting: *Reporting Central Asia,* 325, 10 November.
Bulletin of the Oliy Majlis of the Republic of Uzbekistan. 199. 10, Tashkent.
Gadoev, Pulat. 2003. Karimov's Distrust of Feudal Lords Growing. In: Institute for War and Peace Reporting: *Reporting Central Asia,* 182, 13 February.
Institute for War and Peace Reporting. 2004. Uzbekistan. Softly, Softly. In: Institute for War and Peace Reporting: *Reporting Central Asia,* 279, 23 April.
International Crisis Group. 2002. *The OSCE in Central Asia. A new strategy.* Brussels.
International Crisis Group. 2004. *The Failure of Reform in Uzbekistan. Ways Forward for the International Community.* ICG Asia Report, 76, Brussels.
Narodnoye Slovo [eng. Word of the People], 20 October 2000.
Nazirova, Renata. 2003. Государственная регистрация хозяйствующих субъектов: процедуры, проблемы, пути совершенствования (State registration of economic subjects: procedures, problems, ways of integration) In: *Экономическое Обозрение (Economic*

---

21 On 1 February 2005, Ambassador Miroslav Jenca of the Slovak Republic was appointed Head of the OSCE Centre in Tashkent.
22 See OSCE Centre in Tashkent Newsletter, Autumn/Winter 2004.
23 See: International Crisis Group 2002 and the article by Anna Kreikemeyer on the OSCE in Central Asia in this volume.

survey), 6, (available at: http://www.review.uz/archive/article.asp?y=2003&m =59&id= 148).
Organization for Security and Co-operation in Europe. 1996. *Newsletter*, 3, 4, April.
Radio Free Europe/Radio Liberty. 2003. *Central Asia Report*, 3, 8, 21 February.
Rotar, Igor. 2004. Popular Frustration with Karimov fuels Terrorist Attacks in Uzbekistan. In: The Jamestown Foundation: *Eurasia Daily Monitor*, 1, 64, 2 August.
Tiurikov V.; Shaguliamov R. 1997. *Independent Republic of Uzbekistan. Memorable events and dates (1991-1996)*. Tashkent.
United Nations Office for Drug Control and Crime Prevention. 2000. *Summary report of the international conference on enhancing security and stability in Central Asia. An integrated approach to counter drugs, organised crime and terrorism.* (available at: www.unodc.org/pdf/uzbekistan/tashkent_conference.pdf).
United States Mission to the OSCE. 2001. *Statement on Uzbekistan*. 22 February. (available at www.usosce.rpo.at/archive/2001/02/22uzbek.htm).

Sofiya Issenova

Reform of the Judicial System in Kazakhstan: Review of the Effectiveness of OSCE Efforts

The Republic of Kazakhstan has been an OSCE participating State since January 1992. The decision to join the Organization was a result of Kazakhstan's wish to take active part in pan-European processes, which would enable the elaboration and practical application of the principles laid down in the 1975 Helsinki Final Act and in the documents of other international organizations. In January 1999, an OSCE Centre was established in Almaty and has, since then, made major contributions to the reform of the Kazakh judicial system. Literally speaking, the judiciary has significantly influenced the country's political and legal systems, and its level of democracy in general. Securing the independence of the judiciary as a branch of power helps to ensure the effectiveness of a system of checks and balances, and the exercise and defence of fundamental human rights.

Based on its wider concept of comprehensive security, the OSCE has not only been dealing with issues of military security (disarmament, border monitoring etc), but also with human rights. The OSCE's dictum is that security means more than simply the absence of war. For the first time, the Helsinki Final Act included human rights as a salient component of regional security on the same level as armed conflict and political and economic issues. The principles have not been sorted into any hierarchical order, thus preventing any government from asserting that political or economic security comes first and human rights and democracy follow second.[1] Therefore, the general concept of the OSCE supports the assumption that a proper functioning judiciary, which meets fundamental legal democratic principles, is an indication of domestic stability and security.

For some years, judicial reform was the main priority of Kazakh legal policy. Its main objectives became securing the independence of the judiciary, mainly from executive power,[2] improving the court's performance and reworking the judiciary's image. Institutional, structural and organizational changes, which judicial institutions had undergone, received high appraisal from international organizations and legal experts. At the same time, judicial reforms underway still raised administrative and political questions. This article attempts to analyse the challenges and problems encountered in connection with the above-mentioned reforms.

---

1 See OSCE Human Dimension Commitments 2001. p. XIV.
2 The ministry of justice used to be charged with court administration. The Justice Qualification Board was part of the ministry.

When analysing Kazakh judicial reforms, all of the following should be taken into account: their prolonged period of drafting, the comprehensive inter-branch and interdisciplinary nature, and the plurality of actors, stakeholders, people and organizations involved in its implementation.

Based on the above-mentioned aspects, the following article features an analysis of major achievements and challenges related to the implementation of the reform's milestones as well as relevant OSCE efforts. It also provides a review of specific events organized by the Supreme Court and the OSCE Centre in Almaty within the framework of methodological and consulting assistance as well as judicial reform. The concluding part contains recommendations on certain aspects of further judicial reform, prospective sectors of OSCE assistance and general issues of co-operation with the OSCE in terms of judicial reform.

Review of the judicial reform in Kazakhstan

On 20 September 2002, a presidential decree approved the Concept of the Legal Policy of the Republic of Kazakhstan.[3] According to the document, the major successful result of the legal reform in Kazakhstan has been the establishment of the standardized judiciary and a system of measures ensuring the independence of judges. The Concept underlines the following important components:

- the re-organization of courts and a system of law enforcement bodies aiming to increase their remedial performance;
- the introduction of life-long appointment of judges involving all levels of the judiciary community and the staffing of the judiciary;
- the implementation of measures aimed at raising judges' status and level of welfare.

The most noticeable organizational aspect has been the establishment of special institutions to ensure the effective implementation of justice and judicature, i.e.:

- the foundation of the Legal Statistics and Information Centre under the Office of General Prosecutors of the Republic of Kazakhstan which has been tasked with criminal legal statistics functions previously performed by the internal affairs department;
- the Centre for Forensic Medicine of the ministry of justice, which was established on the basis of the Kazakh Research Institute and was transferred from the Committee of National Security, ministry of defence, in-

---

3   Concept of the Legal Policy of the Republic of Kazakhstan 2002.

ternal affairs authorities and customs bodies of appropriate expert departments;
- the institutes of the Committee for Court Administration, the Commission for Judicial Ethics (see appendix I) and the new educational institution, the Judiciary Training Institute (JTI), (see appendix II), which have a special place in the organizational structure of the judiciary.

The concept also stresses the general trend of humanization and refusal of the priority of state interests in relations between the state and private owners. To ensure judicial independence, a series of legislative measures has been adopted, as expressed in the constitutional law "On Judicature and Status of Judges in the Republic of Kazakhstan" of 25 December 2000.[4]

Challenges of the judicial reform

The judicial and legal reform underway in the country has resulted not only in positive developments, but also in a number of challenges and problems, which require a thorough legal, social and economic analysis. It should be noted that the state of the judiciary still causes concern for the Kazakh legal community and for international experts. A few issues are treated briefly in this section.

Regarding the independence of judges, some doubt prevails: the problem emanates from a proper understanding of the concept of independence of the judiciary. The proclamation of any public authority as independent should carry with it the notions of responsibility, accountability, strict order and delineated terms of disciplinary punishment in case of transgressions. In order to effectively check judges who act in an unethical or illegal manner, a procedure of appellation needs to be installed, as well as other mechanisms to maintain the general system of checks and balances among the three branches of power.

Regrettably, today there is an alarming trend, which consists in that judges see, in their independence, their effective freedom to act as they wish without the risk of being held accountable for their actions, often leading to judicial self-will.

The independence of judges in Kazakhstan finds its expression in different forms. Positive independence means a judge is not suppressed, acts by virtue of personal qualities within the limits of the law and enables proper behaviour of other trial participators. Negative aspects of independence can emerge in cases where there is lack of control over the operations of judges. Consequently, this can lead to various forms of abuse. What is lacking in this area are the adequate mechanisms of public control and an accountability infra-

---

4 A brief review of innovations in the fundamental normative legal act is available in appendix V.

structure, which is the basis of independence for any public authority, as well as a proper ethical mindset of the judges.

The status of a judge must be strengthened not only by protection from unreasonable dismissal, external influence on administration of justice or discrimination in terms of being overlooked for promotion, but also by clear, unanimous, well-considered and transparent procedures of filing complaints to a judge, consideration of disciplinary offences and a subsequent dismissal of the judge in question.

The price for misperceiving independence is the result of illegal exposure or unethical acts in relation to corporate ability, both of which are hard to prove from a legal standpoint. Self-regulation and professional solidarity are sometimes connected to negative systems, which are bound in frankpledge. Often judges work in pairs. During the trial they contact the prosecutor on the outcome of a case or prosecutors protect judges. The "telephone command" still rules.[5] The independence of judges cannot be said to be absolute in positive terms. Some judges admit that they are strongly dependant on the executive authorities in certain areas, primarily in the material sense, for example, in the allocation of housing. Also, judges are sometimes appointed to a position by criteria other than residence area. Thus, it becomes difficult for judges to obtain lodging in a new town, thereby deepening their dependence on local authorities. Even though the new constitutional law "On the Judiciary and the Status of Judges"[6] has significantly improved the status of judges, they remain obviously dependant in terms of:

- *Appointment*: the constitution of the Republic of Kazakhstan guarantees that judges of regional and lower courts are appointed by the president upon recommendation of the Supreme Judicial Council, which the president has formed and holds accountable (cf. system of judge appointment in appendix III). It is likely that the court personnel are dependent on high-ranking executive officers. Moreover, they are also dependent on the Justice Qualification Board (JQB), which is considered by some judges as a de facto "division of the public legal departments of the president's administration". Principally, the specifics of the existing political system in Kazakhstan, its centralization and concentration on the president's personality do not leave any doubt as to the dependence of judges on political entities.
- *Logistics provision*: the main focus is on the courts as budgetary institutions funded by national and local budgets, which until recently were distributed by the government and local *akims* (Kazakh: governors). The

---

5 The "telephone command" is a verbal order given on the telephone without written submission by a high-ranking official. Often such orders contradict the legislation.
6 Constitutional law of the Republic of Kazakhstan "On the Judiciary and the Status of Judges of the Republic of Kazakhstan" 2000.

issue of proper housing for judges rests upon the will of local authorities.
- *Internal subordination dependence*: in the existing system, it is likely that chairmen of higher courts will impose their authority upon the judges of the lower courts. For the most part, dependence emerges when judges assign cases for consideration or give references to other judges for further career advances, benefits, vacations, etc. At the same time, there are instances where chairmen of lower or higher courts put pressure on a judge to force a certain ruling in a specific case.

The views mentioned above have entailed general conclusions as regards the extent of the judicial independence in the Republic of Kazakhstan:

- Courts and judges may depend heavily on executive authorities in terms of appointment, in organizational, legal, material and technical matters. Sometimes such dependence may affect procedural matters, where executive authorities may try to suppress court rulings by judges on certain cases to meet the interests of authorities on the outcome of such cases.
- This is an obvious issue of possible direct political influence on judges, given the existing political system, which is based on super-strong presidential powers and a system in which judges are appointed and dismissed by the president.
- As regards the proceeding, judges suffer from having to subordinate themselves to higher judges and rarely to prosecution authorities.
- True independence of the judiciary must rest upon an effective infrastructure of accountability and clear behavioural ethics; equality of executive and judicial power and the availability of certain checks and balances in their relations; similar relations between courts and the office of the public prosecutor; maximization of the extent of dependence between judges of various instances in the proceeding and its minimization in the office administration; material/technical and personal matters; financial and economic self-sufficiency of courts and a high level of education, professionalism and morality among judges.

Unfortunately, trials are usually conducted at a low professional level, which is set by the prosecutors and lawyers who represent the interests of prosecution and defence, respectively. Often, situations arise in which judges investigate matters of a case in order to comply with the adversarial principle, which is mandatory by law. Judges fulfil duties of the parties and expose themselves to unfavourable comments by prosecutors and defence lawyers alike. Reports are often made about the abuse of power by judges, i.e., about judges who have ignored the arguments presented by a party. During trials, decisions are taken in view of interests of relevant public authorities connected to the cases, primarily the executive branch. The distressing conclusion is that the adversarial nature of trials in the practice of justice administration in Kazakhstan is not applied in full. For it to be applied in court cases depends on the attitude of the judge and how he chooses to act as an intermediary between the various parties.

Appointment of judges:[7] Pursuant to the law "On Courts and Status of Judges", the president appoints the judges (see appendix III). Chairmen of courts and boards are appointed for terms of five years. The public legal department of the presidential administration performs the appointment procedure as follows. A judge sends an application to the JQB and sits an exam of 100 questions. If passed (a minimum of 60 correct answers plus a few questions from the JQB), a candidate may wait years for his appointment. Many judges have illustrated that, regardless of multiple vacancies in courts (nearly two to three vacancies on average), the appointment procedure's efficiency has been undermined, as it has not been duly monitored, and, as a result, the workload of judges is increasing.

The problem also lies in the fact that, with the transfer of judge appointment functions to another department, an apparent procedure has not been established to clearly define the criteria of appointment to the post of a judge. In addition, the table showed that all subjects of the judiciary, including the structures which produce appointment recommendations and representations to the president, are directly or indirectly linked to the president, thus corroborating a certain degree of dependence on it and its administrative section, which deals with judiciary staffing. The broad authorities of the staff of the executive power – without being counterbalanced by the legislative power – will always be a source of abuse and pressure. The presidential administration exercises its influence both in terms of appointments and dismissals. Pursuant to Article 4 of the constitutional law "On Judiciary and Status of Judges", the decision on dismissal is formed in a presidential decree prepared by an appropriate division of the administration, while the chairman of the Supreme Court is charged with less significant procedures having to do with the suspension of judicial authorities.

Common challenges of the judicial reform

For a number of years, the state has been trying to implement a series of measures in the context of legal and judicial reform. However, some problems, including the above-mentioned, have demonstrated that matters of principle also require an appropriate analysis and consequent solution.

First, as already noted, researchers and laymen alike have become aware of the political influence of the court. Primarily, this relates to trials against

---

7   "We shall attain transparency in the most delicate issue. Judges will not be appointed by a request or by will of a person; they will pass a test." Mami 2001.

political opponents of the people in power, as well as political influence wielded through the trying of economic cases before the court, where one party is a powerful financial group or an authoritative national or local political figure. Still, the issue of equal protection of the law and court arises when investigating common criminal or civil cases, where a party is a person vested with ponderable political or financial power. As a rule, a judge shall not be exposed to any kind of direct influence; however, knowledge about "who is involved" is enough to make a judge biased. The political dependence of courts, particularly on the president's administration, for the most part, does not cast any doubt. At the seminar "Prevention of Corruption in Courts is a Security (Factor) of People's Trust in the Judiciary", Igor Rogov, deputy head of the presidential administration and head of its public legal department, admitted that the administration itself receives, *inter alia*, civil complaints on gross violations of legality and norms of the code of ethics by judges.[8]

It is obvious that, in many instances, the judicial reform as such has failed to enable true independence of judges from political influence. Although the reform is mostly focused on administrative and structural changes, its importance should not be underestimated. Therefore, ensuring the true independence of judges should become the central goal of the reform of the judiciary, its principles and indeed the entire system of public authority. The improvement and consideration of this issue unambiguously require political will and a systematic approach toward the streamlining of international institutions.

Second, the judicial reform must be seen in the context of a comprehensive strategy both vertically and horizontally. Horizontal comprehensiveness includes, in this instance, the need for adequate reforms of adjacent branches such as law enforcement, executive proceedings, advocacy etc. Otherwise, it is likely that the so-called "funnel effect" will emerge, in which the effectiveness and quality of a reform in a certain field are absorbed, discredited and reduced to zero by sub-standard maintenance and obsolete regulatory mechanisms in other adjacent branches.[9]

Third, the judicial reform is a comprehensive and long-term one. Thus, its impact has been slow to show immediate results. Moreover, the judicial reform requires a long-term strategy in combination with the components of deep monitoring, and an adequate and well-considered methodology of risk and efficiency assessment, as well as the involvement of other actors, stake-

---

8   See Nurseitova 2003.
9   From this point of view, the experience of reform of the Georgian judicial system is a most illustrative example. The government made the decision to organize open exams for judges to ensure more transparency. The Georgian mass media addressed the examination very closely. The impact of this action received high appraisal from both governmental and international experts. Also, the level of access to the Georgian courts became higher and more effective. The trust in judges elected through an open and transparent procedure improved. Unfortunately, the positive effects of the temporary and local measures started to decrease as soon as enforcement agencies, prosecutors and other adjoining institutes remained closed, obscure, inefficient and corrupt.

holders and institutions. An important feature of the strategy should be the clear determination of final goals and priorities. In order to be implemented, the strategy should be based on an assessment of the judicial and legal system, the preparation of a detailed plan, the identification of priorities with assessment of available capacities through coordination with other active donors and a dialogue with other participants at all stages of the process.

Fourth, court independence directly relates to the theory of neutrality of the law. The judicial reform must be seen, inter alia, in the context of the country's economic development, and the reform will no doubt have lasting effects on the investment climate. It is reasonable to exploit the potential for protest of the most financially strong groups of the population, for example that of businessmen, whilst reforming the judicial and legal system. As a rule, their experience in appealing to corrupted courts gives rise to and/or activates alternative forms of justice: arbitration courts. Still, this option will not eliminate the problems experienced by the normal citizen.

Fifth, the issue of accountability of judges is the most problematic and widely debated. Independence of the judiciary, which obstructs the implementation of the accountability principle, remains the main argument of judges. Judges believe that accountability damages the quintessence of independence. International standards and foreign experience support their opinion. In particular, experts note that the accountability issue may be seen in analogy to the status of central banks of countries that are also independent bodies, and still accountable.

Contributions of the OSCE to the judicial reform in Kazakhstan

In the judicial reform the following major actors are relevant:

- state actors (Supreme Court, committee for court administration, judicial ethics commission, judicial academy and others);
- local non-governmental organizations (NGOs), including the Union of Judges;
- foreign embassies, international governmental and non-governmental organizations (World Bank, OSCE, USAID, Soros Kazakhstan, GTZ and others).

Although the OSCE did not play a central role in the process, the analysis of the activities carried out by the OSCE Centre in Almaty[10] illustrates that there

---

10 In 2004, the OSCE Centre in Almaty consisted of 18 persons, including seven technical employees. A relatively small staff of five people worked in the departments on political and legal issues. According to the employees, nearly 80 per cent of the activities of the OSCE Centre in Almaty during these days were dedicated to economic and environmental issues, and the rest to political and legal matters. Interview with OSCE Centre officers 2004.

is an awareness of topical issues and needs at the current implementation stage of the judicial reform. In this instance, the OSCE Centre contributed in terms of consultancy, methodological assistance and organization of training, seminars, conferences and round tables. The focus of the activities has also met some of the major and current needs of the judicial reform (see appendix IV). Meanwhile, some experts have criticized the OSCE Centre for its lack of a systematic approach, not only in the legal field, but in other areas as well. In turn, opposition politicians complain about the lack of a clear position on a wide range of issues of domestic and external policy, overly diplomacy and cautious statements and comments.

In interviews, officers of the OSCE Centre in Almaty and of the Office for Democratic Institutions and Human Rights (ODIHR) presented their counter-arguments.

> "When people speak of an OSCE strategy, they should know and understand some basic principles of the organization. Otherwise, this gives ground to observers talking about a lack of strategy. The strategy should primarily be considered as a process based on principles adopted by the participating States. There is also an ambiguous understanding of the OSCE's role and mission. All over you find different views of the organization and its perceived role, be it as a human rights organization, a global policeman or simply a discussion club."[11]

> "Despite the lack of an outspoken strategy in view of outside observers, the OSCE Centre in Almaty attempts to make OSCE goals and tasks known to the wider public, and clarifies certain issues, such as the interrelation of a wide context of security and democratization processes (female participation in social life, fair elections, independent courts etc.). Another aspect is the fact that these efforts are not always systematic. We should bear in mind that the OSCE is not a project implementation organization, but an organization which is dedicated to a process. Nevertheless, the project work as a complementary and supplementary component can be carried out within the frameworks of technical assistance, which is first of all a political issue. In this context, such projects will focus on a certain issue and raise awareness of state authorities and all stakeholders on that issue."[12]

In response to the question on the prevalence of technical assistance in the structure of OSCE activities as opposed to the lack of focus on political issues, an OSCE officer said that

---

11   Ibid.
12   Ibid.

"the construction of a system where democratic institutions will function, the strategy of the judicial reform should be determined by the state. The OSCE finds it unproductive to follow the way of changing the system. The organization's philosophy adds up to the fact that the change of certain elements of reform of a certain field, judiciary in this instance, may sometimes lead to some positive systemic changes and induce such. At the same time, principal changes should be initiated by the state itself."[13]

In an attempt to analyse the OSCE's role in the reform of democratic institutions and in the search for advantages and disadvantages of the Organization's involvement, the following aspects should be highlighted:

- A unique situation exists which does not allow an objective evaluation of OSCE activities in this analysis. In a way, results depend on the authorities of the participating States and rigid standards exist for them. However, the extent and the pace of approximation of standards also depend on the heads of state.
- Disadvantages may also be seen as advantages: there is a relatively high frequency of replacements of heads of OSCE Centres. In this instance, the activity of certain centres may to a great extent depend on the personality of its leader.[14] Since the OSCE may be considered an institution, there is no clear or obvious strategy of actions. This factor may have both positive and negative implications. The positive side lies in the potential for flexibility and a quick response to the challenges stemming from a real political situation.
- It should be noted that the OSCE has a complex structure with inherent advantages and disadvantages. In the past decade, the OSCE Centres and the ODIHR have evolved. The continued process of re-thinking and the re-distribution of functions entail changes in structure, but not in political priorities. Today, the OSCE must find its niche and stand out against the backdrop of other European institutions.

Summary

It must be admitted that Kazakhstan has made significant institutional, legislative, technical and educational efforts to reform the judiciary. In the same respect, the OSCE efforts undertaken to that end should not be underestimated. The issues of corruption prevention in courts, an increase in quality of court performance and a strengthening of interrelations with the mass media

---

13   Ibid.
14   "It is a guarantee of success, when a person has due understanding and is in the right place, but it would be a catastrophe if a person is no success." Ibid.

continue to be discussed and solved. Permanent institutional changes related to the introduction of the jury, the functioning of arbitration courts and the strengthening of courts' specializations are underway. At the same time, the OSCE Centre in Almaty, in relation to the legal reform, continues to discuss other issues which are relevant to the judiciary such as the abolishment of capital punishment, directorate of public prosecutions, forensic enquiry etc.

Meanwhile, the judicial status quo analysis has demonstrated a general trend of reform and democratization of state power in Kazakhstan. At some level, institutional reforms may be carried out with a focus on administrative, structural or technical matters. However, equally important issues remain in the political field, and a solution of most of these issues is related to the need for overall changes in the political system and constitutional framework. The political will to resolve these issues may be de facto that of the president's only. This trend is also seen in the strategy of the majority of international and donor organizations in Kazakhstan, whose activity has been focused on administrative changes in the context of the existing political system and the super-strong presidential power.

Until recently, the OSCE was the only organization in Kazakhstan to set rigid requirements on political matters of principle. The latest attempt was a series of round tables to discuss the election law. The OSCE attempted to serve as a mediator between opposition and authorities and secure a consensus on political matters of principle. Regrettably, the attempt was not successful and failed to produce meaningful results. Moreover, experts say the results of the event were satisfactory to neither the authorities, nor to the opposition, thus affecting the OSCE's reputation in Kazakhstan negatively.

There are reasons to believe that the OSCE Centre in Almaty reached an inner decision "to change tactics" after having realized that it is not productive to directly change the political system, since "changing certain elements [...] can entail the change of the whole system".[15] It should also be noted that the authorities have criticized the OSCE in public recommendations: "The OSCE activities in Kazakhstan should be more objective."[16] While Kazakhstan declared its intention to chair the organization in 2009, the authorities were not always supportive of the OSCE's political initiatives in the region. This was evinced by their highly sensitive reaction, making it clear that such initiatives were perceived as meddling with domestic policy issues. From this viewpoint, it is obvious that the OSCE focuses on compromises and the administrative component of reforms.

As regards the so-called political issues in the judicial reform, two major aspects have surfaced: first, accountability and, second, the political independence of judges. These issues are indicative of the status quo in which judges are not seen as a strong and independent branch of state power, nor as a counterbalance to the executive. The fact that the president can be sum-

---

15   Ibid.
16   Ibid.

moned to give testimony, as for instance in the US, can be considered utopian for Kazakhstan. Regarding the notorious trials of high-ranking officials, 90 per cent of the population perceive this as politically motivated and see the courts as tools for political reprisals.[17] In this sense, we can understand the statement made by Bryant G. Garth, the Director of the American Bar Foundation: "Some labelled a 'judge' in another country may be a very different kind of person. The label is not enough to separate those called judges from local politics, families, political feuds, or clientelism. Indeed, if we consider the local context carefully, it is clear that we cannot expect the legislative and executive branches of the government to grant complete autonomy to the courts just because it is a good idea to have an independent judiciary."[18]

Concerning future events within judicial reforms, it is recommended that the OSCE strengthen the following components:

- research and diagnostics;
- focus on both administrative and political aspects of the judicial reform;
- activities aimed at a reform of adjacent branches: prosecution, advocacy, investigation, enforcement, etc.;
- use of adequate mechanisms for the monitoring of the judicial reform on the whole and of its own efforts as well as feedback mechanisms;
- co-ordination with all stakeholders, public institutions and international organizations working in the field; OSCE working toward strengthening co-ordination with governmental and public bodies;
- experience in judicial reforms of other Central Asian states.

In the context of the chosen strategy, the following aspects of the reform of the judiciary are worthy of attention:

- training activities for judges in order to teach and introduce anti-corruption measures and mechanisms to the judiciary;
- activities aimed to ensure a more transparent system of appointing judges. This process must be controlled fully by the public and not be the result of a single decision, even after a bureaucratic procedure of representation, review, exams etc.;
- activities aimed at simple access to judicature;
- assistance in training of court personnel in judicature and case management, methods of modernization of court equipment (preservation of archives, judges' registration for case consideration) to avert overload and various abuses;

---

17 Ibid.
18 Garth 2000, p. 23. See also the conclusion of the lawyers committee for human rights: "Judicial independence is the most important measure of commitment – the willingness of the government to take concrete steps to reduce political influence in judicial appointments and court operations....". Van Puymbroeck 2000.

- measures to ensure the transparency of a trial, including the on-line posting of a court judgment;
- exchange of lessons learnt and experience in organizing new institutions such as the jury.

It is important to stress that the OSCE is primarily a political organization.[19] This enables the widespread employment of its political potential in the region to solve a number of issues and also inspire independence of the judiciary from the political arena in Kazakhstan.

---

19 "Unlike many other human rights documents, OSCE human dimension commitments are politically rather than legally binding. [...] They have been adopted by consensus and thus are politically binding on all OSCE particpating states." OSCE human dimension commitments. 2001, p. XV.

Appendix I: The Commission for Judicial Ethics[20]

As a public institution, the Commission for Judicial Ethics has now been operating for over two years under the Union of Judges. The decrees issued by the Commission on reviewed complaints are to be entered into the courts records by the chairman of the city court, an action which might strengthen control measures over the work of judges. Even though the Commission has operated for only a short period of time, officers, citizens and judges have highlighted a number of issues within the institution itself.

- Commission personnel finds it expedient to charge the institution with more effective functions, let alone the right to submit a request to appropriate authorities to discharge a judge for repetitive infractions of judicial ethics.
- The investigation of each complaint takes up considerable resources and efforts. Lists of complaints and applications submitted for consideration of the Commission need to be categorized in order to enable the institution to return uncategorized applications, which were not considered.
- The complaint review procedure must be amended so that a complaint can only be considered once the ruling on a case has taken place. This would ensure that the hearing of the case by the same judge does not produce a biased ruling after the Commission's consideration of a case.
- A norm must be introduced to give judges the right to appeal to the Central Council of the Union of Judges on the rulings of the Commission which recognized infractions of the Code of Judicial Ethics by a judge.
- Commission personnel have made a proposal to include in the Commission both practicing and retired judges, since life and professional experience of the latter may significantly help to standardize tasks.

Appendix II: The Judiciary Training Institute

The Judiciary Training Institute (JTI) was founded on 4 December 2001 by the Supreme Court following a governmental decree of the Republic of Kazakhstan. The curriculum is based on typical errors in the rulings of lower court judges, which the Supreme Court summarized in its relevant conclusions. A standard course at the institute lasts three weeks. In the period of over one year, 452 people, working in the judiciary, have completed the course. Most graduates are judges and chairmen of courts of the first instance. In February 2003, the executive director of the institute of the Central European and Central Asian Legal Initiative in Prague, Joel C. Martin, came to Almaty to review the work of Kazakhstan's JTI. Upon his return, he reported on his work to the Supreme Court, to the Committee of Judicature and to the institute itself and highlighted the following the institute's activities as its strong elements:

- support of the state.
- co-operation with international organizations including OSCE. In November 2001, OSCE/ODIHR invited the new JTI rector, the chairman of the Committee for Judicature, and two judges of the Supreme Court to visit the Bulgarian Judicial Training Centre to conduct observations and gather experience.[21]
- co-operation with NGOs. In November 2002, the OSCE and the American Bar Association/Central and European and Eurasian Law Initiative (ABA/CEELI) carried out a three-day seminar for 24 teachers of JTI on the application of adult training methodology.
- the academic standard of study. The observer noted a relatively high level of teaching.

---

20 See Oleynikova 2003.
21 See ODIHR 2003, pp. 16-19.

The observer found that the following aspects could be improved:

- the material basis is inadequate in terms of equipment and facilities;
- learning materials: JTI should consider the option of gathering, editing and publishing materials elaborated for the institute's courses;
- composition of the curriculum: JTI should train judges in how to avoid typical errors in applying Supreme Court rulings. Also, judges need constant training in the judicature, case management, public relations, judicial ethics and anti-corruption issues.

Appendix III: Appointment of Judges in Kazakhstan

According to Art. 31 of the Constitutional Law "On Judiciary and Status of Judges," judges are vested with authorities in the following manner:

	Election	Appointment	Introduction	Reference
Supreme Court	by senate		by president	by supreme judiciary council
Regional Court		by president		by supreme judiciary council
District Court		by president	by minister of justice	by Justice Qualification Board (JQB)

According to Arts. 31 and 36 the Constitutional Law "On Judiciary and Status of Judges" provides details on the procedure of vesting chairmen of the judicial system subjects with authorities:

Chair	Election	Appointment/ Dismissal	Introduction	Reference
Supreme Court	by senate		by president	by supreme judiciary council
Regional Court		by president	by Supreme Court Chief Justice (chairman)	In view of conclusion of plenary session of the court
District Court		by president	by minister of justice	JQB on Supreme Court representation in view of conclusion of plenary session of the court
Supreme Judicial Council		by president		
Justice Qualification Board (JQB)		by president		

Appendix IV: Review of some innovations in the constitutional law of the Republic of Kazakhstan "On Judiciary and Status of Judges", 25 December 2000

1. Art. 1 of the constitutional law provides the appartenance of Kazakhstan's judiciary to courts, represented by regular judges and a jury trying a criminal case as provided by the law. The term jury, with appartenance to the judiciary, is new to the law
2. The chairman of the Supreme Court assumes wider authorities with the adoption of the new constitutional law. According to the new constitutional law, the chairman of the Supreme Court makes proposals in terms of legislative development to the president of the Republic of Kazakhstan.
3. According to Arts. 30 and 36, the status and the authorities of the JQB have changed. The JQB used to operate under the ministry of justice, which influenced its independence as an autonomous structure. Following the reform, the JQB operates under the presidential administration with the JQB chairman appointed by the president. The president has also charged the JQB with the right to decision-making when selecting a candidate for a vacancy position of district judge.
4. The need for an independent public institution charged with court personnel, financial, material and technical matters with a view to ensure independent court activity was put up for discussion already in the second phase of the state legal reform programme. The establishment of such a public authority aimed to put an end to the practice of charging executive authorities as well as the ministry of justice and its local departments with implementation of court activities, and to align the situation with the constitutional principle of separation of powers and international norms on judicial independence. From this viewpoint, the establishment of the committee for court administration under the Supreme Court of the Republic of Kazakhstan, charged with rights and duties on the implementation of court activities, which were once performed by the ministry of justice, has become a fundamental choice and an important element in ensuring the independence of judges.
5. Art. 28 "Requirements to a Judge" legitimized the compliance of judges with the judicial ethics requirements; the relevant code was adopted on 19 December 1996 at the first session of the parliament of the Republic of Kazakhstan. Failure to comply with judicial ethics requirements may cause the disciplinary and qualification board to consider the possible discharge of a judge. One of the most important innovations in the law has been the establishment of disciplinary and qualification boards charged with the right to review, at their discretion and independently from other public authorities, issues dealing with the encouragement of and responsibility for infractions of legal requirements. The chairman of the Supreme Court now enjoys independence and is entitled to open a disciplinary trial against any judge of the country for reasons provided in the new law.

Appendix V. Events related to Kazakhstan's judicial reform with participation of OSCE Centre in Almaty (2003-2001)

Date	Scale and name of event	OSCE status	Brief description	Participants
17-18 February 2003	International conference: "Problems of Strengthening the Rights of Criminal Trial Participants"	organizer	Discussion of: - accretion of the adversarial principle in the criminal trial in light of implementation of the Concept of Legal Policy; - international standards and foreign experience in criminal trial; - guarantees on rights of suspects and defendants; application of procedural restraints on investigative actions. Defence of childrens rights in the criminal adversarial trial; - issues of the exercising of rights of victims in a criminal trial; - rehabilitation, compensation for harm caused by illegal actions of authorities processing a criminal trial.	Personnel of presidential administration, Supreme Court, office of general prosecutor, constitutional council, ministry of justice, ministry of internal affairs, members of the parliament, ombudsman, heads of institutes of education
25-29 March 2003	Training seminar for judges of specialized inter-district economic courts: "Special Economic Courts in Kazakhstan: Establishment, Court Practice, Development Prospects."	co-organizer: OSCE Centre, Almaty	Discussion of issues of the material and procedural law: tax law, currency regulation issues, customs law, administrative law, and bankruptcy issues.	Personnel of economic courts, staff of the Supreme Court, of the committee for judicature under the Supreme Court, of the academy of the financial police as well as representatives of other departments concerned and academics
26 May 2003	Seminar: "Prevention of Corruption in Courts is a Guarantee of People's Trust in the Judicature."	support, participation	Discussion of mechanisms, forms and methods of preventing corruption in the judicature and issues of ensuring justice transparency, presentation of a programme of automatic case assignment in courts, which later was launched as a pilot project in the Auezov district court in Almaty city with the goal of being implemented in all the courts of the country.	Personnel of public authorities and organizations, international organizations, heads of working groups on legislative matters of the council of foreign investors, chairmen of commissions on judicial ethics, chief of chancelleries and experts of district and specialized economic courts

173

Date	Event	Role	Description	Participants
23-24 June 2003	International conference: "Life Imprisonment: International Standards and Practice."	organizer	Discussion of various aspects of imposition of life imprisonment: requisite changes to the laws in question, individual approach to life-term and long-term prisoners, international standards and practices of treatment of life-term prisoners as well as safety of personnel and convicts in institutions where life-term prisoners will be contained and psychosocial correction.	Personnel of the presidential administration, government, parliament, constitutional council, Supreme Court, office of the general prosecutor, ministry of justice, ministry of internal affairs, ombudsman, representatives from NGOs, international experts, officers of penitentiary services of Russia, Ukraine, Tajikistan, and representatives of diplomatic missions.
19-20 August 2003	Seminar: "Strengthening of Principles of Publicity and Legality Through Strengthening Partnership and Mutual Responsibility of Judiciary and Mass Media".	observer	The seminar produced an analysis of inappropriate behaviour of journalists, judges' bans on audio recording, attitude of trial participants to TV cameras, request for prior agreement of journalist presence at a trial. Discussion of trial media coverage and avoidance of external influence on court rulings, legal responsibility of journalists and mass media for legislative infractions, legal investigation into cases of defamation and insult, protection of honour and dignity, compensation for moral harm, business reputation involving a journalist as civil defendant or accuser. Judges wished journalists would be more active in covering court activity with the purpose of forming a positive perception of the judicature and justice system as a whole in the minds of citizens.	Personnel of the Supreme Court and oblast courts, Adil Soz Fund, Union of Judges, heads of newspapers and broadcasting companies, staff of scientific research institutes under the office of general prosecutor of the Russian Federation, press secretaries of courts, representatives of the European Initiative for Democracy and Human Rights (EIDHR), OSCE observers
11 September 2003	Official meeting	organizer	Discussion of further cooperation and projects	Supreme Court Chief Justice Kairat A. Mami, Head of OSCE Centre in Almaty Amb. Anton Rupnik
10–11 November 2003	Regional conference: "Dispute Settlement as a	organizer – OSCE Centre in Bishkek.		Deputy chairman of the committee for judicature under the Supreme Court of the

Date	Event	Role	Description	Participants
	mechanism of Assistance to small and Medium Businesses in the Commercial Field."			Republic of Kazakhstan, T.T. Kireyeva.
25-26 November 2003	Conference: "Issues and Ways of Establishing a Jury Trial."	organizer - ODIHR and OSCE Centre in Almaty.	Discussion of the introduction of the jury in Kazakhstan along with various models of jury trials in countries worldwide.	Personnel of public authorities, deputies of the parliament, judges, scholars and foreign experts, representatives NGOs
5-6 December 2003	International conference: "Procedural Control in Criminal Procedure of the Republic of Kazakhstan: Current Problems and Development Prospects."	support of ODIHR and OSCE Centre in Almaty	Discussion of conceptual approaches to the reform of the institute of procedural control; role of office of general prosecutors and courts in ensuring the procedural control over criminal procedure; pre-trial procedural control; procedural control over criminal procedures at appeal and supervision proceedings; responsibility of public authorities for violation of rights of citizens during criminal trials.	Personnel of the presidential administration, prime minister, chancellery, ministry of internal affairs, agency of financial police, national security council, ministry of justice, Supreme Court, office of general prosecutor, constitutional council, parliament, ombudsman, research institutes, NGOs, foreign embassies, international organizations
23 December 2003	Official meeting	organizer	Discussion of proposals for joint projects in 2004.	Supreme Court Chief Justice Kairat A. Mami, chairman of the committee of judicature under Supreme Court, V.M. Borissov, Head of the OSCE Centre in Almaty, Amb. Anton Rupnik.
25 September 2001	Official meeting	organizer	Discussion of the stages of reformation of the judicial system.	Supreme Court Chief Justice Kairat A. Mami, Human Dimension Officer of the OSCE Centre in Almaty, Bjorn Halvarsson.
29-30 October 2001	Conference: "Enforcement of Court Decisions in the Republic of Kazakhstan."	assistance	Discussion of problems which have arisen during the enforcement of orders, of new ways of improving the state of enforcement and of ways of learning from foreign experience in the field. Three main reports:	experts on issues of enforcement of court decisions, members of parliament, representatives of central executive bodies, representatives and administrators of local courts,

				(1) issues and ways of improving the enforcement of orders, (2) alternative ways of enforcing writs and other enforceable documents and (3) topical issues of execution proceedings. Based on the results of the conference, a seminar was held on the second day.	senior cour officers, judges from Almaty and Astana courts.

Appendix VI. Activities of the Supreme Court of the Republic of Kazakhstan in the context of the legal reform

1. Supreme Court activities on the introduction of jury trials

The Supreme Court held a series of seminars on the introduction of jury trials and an international scientific and practical conference, whose findings and conclusions form the basis of the concept of jury trial in the Republic of Kazakhstan as elaborated by the Supreme Court.

The concept of the jury is as follows.[22] Every citizen at the age of 25 with no prior convictions is eligible for jury duty. He or she may not be a law-enforcement officer, power department officer or deputy. Jury members are to be paid for their services. Whenever an employed person performs jury duty, a proportion of the average monthly pay shall be paid for the days spent on the jury. If any member of the jury is unemployed he or she is entitled to a minimum pay equivalent to that of a public employee. The list of jury members will be approved in each territorial unit by the akim. Members of the jury will be selected by random. According to Supreme Court Chief Justice Kairat Mami, candidates must be representative of labour groups, public organizations and parties alike.

2. Requisite activities for the introduction of jury trials in the Republic of Kazakhstan

It is suggested that the jury will be introduced in three stages in the Republic of Kazakhstan.

The first stage (2003-2004) consists of normative and legal provisions of court activity with the jury by adopting new as well as improving effective normative legal acts on regulating the status of the jury, safeguard of independence and measures of security of the jury, procedure of formation and criteria for selection of persons subject to inscription in the list of prospective candidates for the jury, procedures of selection and demurrer of the jury, the work quota for juries, jurisdiction of cases to be tried by the jury, list of provisions given which a person will be discharged from office, role of a professional judge etc. Some other issues must be resolved as well: sufficiency of a unanimous verdict by a jury to impose the death penalty, appeal of unenforced verdict passed by the court together with the jury, rights of prosecutors to appeal against acquittal passed by a jury, requisite amendments to the appellate procedure on similar cases and other issues.

The second stage (2004-2005) sees organizational issues solved and the creation of material and technical bases able to maintain a due level of jury activities and the introduction of the jury for consideration of cases on crimes, for which the punishment is the death penalty or lifelong imprisonment.

The third stage (once experience with the jury has been gained, not earlier than 2010) suggests resolving the matter of disposal of all criminal cases on grave crimes to jurisdiction of juries.

3. Activities on improving the transparency of courts

The Supreme Court considered the issue of further development of a single database of court rulings, implementation of an automatic case assignment programme, and receipt of petitions. At

---

22 See Mami 2003, pp. 10-11.

the end of 1999, the council of foreign investors under the president recommended creating an electronic database of court rulings accessible to judges and the general public. The Supreme Court implemented the idea within the frameworks of the project of legal reform supported by the European Bank for Reconstruction and Development (EBRD). From early 2001, to the present, all Supreme Court rulings of practical value have been included in the database available on the official website of the Supreme Court (www.supcourt.kz).

4. Interaction between mass media and courts

Interaction between courts and mass media is a stirring issue. Over the past three years, the Supreme Court, with the support of international institutes and organizations, has held a series of meetings with journalists and judges on such topical issues as their internal relationships and the solutions to their problems. Today, press services are being established in oblast courts.

5. Prevention of corruption in courts

One of the elements in the fight against corruption in the judiciary is a recently developed automatic case assignment programme. The programme was elaborated by the Supreme Court and the committee for court administration in co-operation with experts of the JurInfo company. For a period of half a year, the programme underwent pilot and test procedures in the Auezov court of Almaty city. With regard to corruption, Kairat Mami stressed that there are some misfits amongst the judges.[23] Official statistics show that in 2003 criminal cases were opened against nine judges; 24 judges were discharged for inaptitude. An amount of 2,727 complaints were filed against judges, including 1,044 to Supreme Court with every seventh complaint corroborated. Nearly half of the complaints were filed against the actions of judges of the Karaganda oblast and Almaty city (720 and 565 complaints, respectively). In the majority of the cases, complaints were filed on infraction of legality on administration of justice, red-tape, negligence in case consideration, and failure to comply with work ethic. An applicant may file an appeal against infraction of ethics to oblast commissions for judicial ethics, who carry out office examinations on applications of concerned parties and respond quickly to misdemeanours by judges. Phone numbers of the commission for judicial ethics are available on the information boards of every court and on the Supreme Court official site.

Bibliography

Concept of the Legal Policy of the Republic of Kazakhstan, approved by the presidential decree
    of the Republic of Kazakhstan on September 20, 2002. *Collection of the legal acts of the President and the Government of the Republic of Kazakhstan.* No. 31, p. 336.
Constitutional law of the Republic of Kazakhstan "On the Judiciary and the Status of Judges of the Republic of Kazakhstan", *Kazakhstanskaya pravda*, December 25, 2000.
Garth, Bryan, G. 2000. *Presentation.* World Bank's Global Conference on Comprehensive Legal and Judicial Development. in: The World Bank (ed.). Comprehensive Legal and Judicial Development. Toward an Agenda for Just and Equitable Society in the 21st Century, Washington, DC.
Interviews with officers of the OSCE Centre in Almaty, January, 2004.
Juridicheskaya Gazeta. [Judicial Newspaper], January 10, 2001.
Kazakhstanskaya pravda. [Kazakhstans Truth], October 3, 2002.
Mami, Kairat. 2001. On themis balance. *Caravan weekly*, No 20.
Milestones of the judicial system reformation performed, interview with Chief Justice of the Supreme Court Kairat A. Mami, *Jurist,* No. 6, pp. 10-11.
Nurseitova, Torgyn. 2003. Themis to assume more responsibility, *Juridicheskaya Gazeta.* No. 24.

---

23   See ibid. p. 8.

ODIHR. 2001. (ed.). *OSCE Human Dimension Commitments. A reference guide.* Warsaw. Online available at http://www.osce.org/documents/odihr/2001/01/1764_en.pdf.
ODIHR 2003. (ed.) Experts proposals for the Advanced Judicial Training Institute. *Jurist*, No. 6. pp. 16-19.
Oleynikova, Olga. Does a professional need emotions? *Juridicheskaya Gazeta*, December 24, 2003.
Puymbroeck, Rudolf V. van. 2000. (ed.). Rethinking the Process and Criteria for Success. Lawyer's Committee for Human Rights, 2000.
The World Bank (ed.). *Comprehensive Legal and Judicial Development. Toward an Agenda for Just and Equitable Society in the 21st Century*, Washington, DC.

Dosym Satpayev

Creating Mechanisms for Social Lobbying in Kazakhstan

As practice shows, in most democratic political systems, precisely lobbyism is the most prevailing and optimal form of interaction between various social groups and structures of state authority concerned with solving social problems. In contrast to political parties, pressure groups are the most practical mechanism for the presentation and assertion of the local interests of narrow social groups. One can completely agree with Gilbert Almond who is of the opinion that pressure groups in Kazakhstan played a significant role in the process of articulation of social interests and in the establishment of important communicative links between the political system and civil society. According to David Easton, pressure groups, as well as other institutional organizations, articulated social interests and played the role of mediator in transforming requirements into political demands. These groups generally work in areas that deal with civil society, from which spontaneous impulses often come, and in the political system, which controls the decision-making processes.

At the same time, the different types of groups have their own ways of articulating their interests. This is done either by means of official or more informal channels. The choice of one over the other depends on the level of openness of the political system, the quantity of the actual points of access and the de-facto opportunities for using them. As many political scientists consider, favourable conditions for lobbyism depend on just how plentiful the opportunities are to affect state authorities, as well as on the quantity and quality of these access points – in other words, it depends on the structure and type of political system.

The following article describes the current state of lobbyism in the Republic of Kazakhstan by distinguishing between two models of lobbying the corporative and pluralist way of lobbyism, and by analysing current legal efforts as well as preconditions both in the political system and in society. Finally, it shows possibilities for external actors like the Organization for Security and Co-operation in Europe (OSCE) to support the creation of a new system of lobbyism in Kazakhstan.

Corporative and pluralist ways of lobbyism

In democratic political systems with true separation of powers, points of access are adequate enough to define the activity of interest groups. As for the majority of post-Soviet political systems, including Kazakhstan, lobbyism is not the preferred channel of communication between the authorities and civil society, since the legal framework for it is absent. The determining characteristic of the post-Soviet sphere is that, in major cases, social interest groups are not able to act as pressure groups and exert influence on the decision-making process, whereas those pressure groups that are actually influential do not express the social interests in question. To better understand the current difference between democratic and post-Soviet systems, it is helpful to differentiate between a corporative and a pluralist variant of lobbyism.

Corporative variant

Corporative interest intermediation can be described as an exchange or deal between influential lobby groups and political power structures. This implies that the authorities are in collusion with one or some of the biggest pressure groups, who, generally speaking, have been advancing the interests of oligarchic capital in an informal way. In other words, these groups agreed upon who will get the definite benefits, privileges and protection in exchange for its political loyalty to the state power structures. This kind of corporatism is an integral part of a closed political system. Its members are unable to apprehend the majority of external impulses from the surrounding social environment. In a corporatist political system, the absence of inter-institutional communication ties, combined with the neutralization of the "feedback loop" in closed political systems, presents favourable conditions for institutional groups with particular interests in gaining momentum and influence. Within such a framework, structural lobbyism is preserved in oligarchic corporative behaviour and, as such, it does not play a positive role in the democratization processes of the country. This way of conserving patron-client relations is only viable with the absence of reliable channels of communication between society and the state power. It takes place at the expense of the active involvement of the institutions of civil society in lobbyist activities, as well as that of social pressure groups and political parties.

At present, the activities of the institutional pressure groups in Kazakhstan are directly connected with the active pressure to convert political power into property as well as with the redistribution of already divided spheres of influence. Nevertheless, one should not regard the corporative form of government with mere reproach and rigid criticism. Notwithstanding the negative aspects, such as the danger of setbacks in the democratic development, corporatism may – if combined with pluralistic interests – have some positive sides to it as well. First, the state only takes into account the opinions and interests of certain groups, namely those who have the access and resources that are important to large social groups. This de facto monopoly on access to state structures can lead to a more fluent and effective decision-making process. Second, corporatist lobby groups are interested in bringing in the support of oligarchic capital, for example, to regions where the oligarchs are the main employers. The very struggle between corporatist interest groups is of use to the regime, which is based on the plurality of influence groups, none of which can monopolize any power. It would be far worse if all interest groups joined forces, since they would pose a threat to the weak political institutions. The struggle thus compensates for the lack of publicity and control of public power.

Pluralist variant

A second way of representing group interests is the classical form of pressure groups from a great number of lobbying actors, who have turned lobbyism into a competitive activity. However, what is important in this respect is not the number of interest groups, but the quantity and quality of access points to the power structures, which are used as main channels of pressure. An increase in such points means growth in the decentralization of power. Hereby, the necessary background for electoral forms of support for institutions could be created and this would in turn lead to increased legitimacy and a further increase in the level of political participation by certain social groupings. A rise in the number of competitive lobbying groups, who use different methods of influence on public-power institutions, the openness of the political system and the strengthening of social control could make the mechanism of lobbyism adequately transparent. Moreover, it is likely that public elections and respective electoral campaigns will create conditions that are conducive for large financial-industrial groups to actively lobby their interests in such a way that they become significant political sponsors. This would constitute one of the classical impacts on power in connection with liberalizing political relations.

Lobbyism in post-Soviet Kazakhstan

The Kazakh political system developed along the lines of transformation, from post-totalitarian bureaucratic corporativism (a group form of lobbyism that arose during the deconstruction period, when the old stable systems were destroyed) to anarchical or 'wild lobbyism' in the post-Soviet period at the end of the 1990s. Studying the main features of lobbyism in Kazakhstan includes paying attention to the informational function of pressure groups, their place in the Kazakh political system and their role in the political decision-making cycle. In this respect, it is helpful to turn our attention to a scheme of political communication developed by Karl Deutsch, who distinguishes between

- effectors: performers of decisions, bureaucracy;
- receptors: receiving blocks, coding, selection of information and data processing;
- and memory and values: political experience and traditions.

In Kazakhstan, the right to the circulation of political information has been violated. All levels of selection and filtration of incoming information are characterized as having a positive effect. Quite often, external information simply does not reach the centre of decision-making. As a consequence, the centre often uses inaccurate or wrong data about external facts, which lead to inappropriate reactions to requirements put forward by external agents. This creates a time lag and hampers the forestalling of complicated situations.

When faced with a scarcity of fresh information, the political system in Kazakhstan relies on its memory and values, in which the post-totalitarian political traditions of interaction between the authorities and society are conserved. In Western political systems, the system of decision-making is based on various sources of information from different pressure groups. In Kazakhstan, the communicative channels between the centres of decision-making and the surrounding environment are not as numerous. Communication networks and the main sources of information are inside its political system. In order to be effective, the major Kazakh pressure groups should be linked to this sphere.

At present, two main forms of political communication in the framework of lobbyist activity can be regarded as typical for Kazakhstan: First, communication is made possible by means of using informal contacts, which is also known as straight or external lobbyism. In this communication type, the mediator is the person who controls the "know how" and the "know who". This kind of communication has been actively used by institutional pressure groups working inside the political system; however, this way is barred for major social groups, who are not part of the political system. Second, contact is made through the mass media (indirect lobbyism). Trying to influence public opinion in favour of the question in case creates the needed pressure on institutions of political power. This form of communication is used in part by NGOs, but the problem is that, in many cases, the mass media are either under state control, or are being used as a weapon in the fight between different financial and industrial lobby groups, on the one hand, and political elite lobby groups, on the other.

In connection with this, the author's Assessment Risks Group (ARG) held an experts poll in December 2002 among representatives of NGOs, deputies of both chambers of the parliament, of the administration of the president and of the constitutional council. The respondents participated in a two-day seminar on "How to lobby social interests in the state power bodies". The overwhelming majority (85.7 per cent) of the experts questioned answered that lobbyism is part of the political system in Kazakhstan. The governmental lobby, pressure groups representing the interests of foreign companies and the tribal lobby were named the three most influential pressure groups in Kazakhstan. The largest group of respondents among the experts (36 per cent) considered the role of pressure groups in Kazakhstan to be a negative factor due to the belief that their influence proliferates corruption. In this view, the most popular method of lobbyist activity is using informal channels, that is, channels based around family and personal ties. The second-most prevalent opinion was that pressure groups act on the prejudice of state interests.

Analysing these results, we can observe that, in Kazakhstan, public awareness, in the majority of cases, is still at the level of stereotypes: the procedure of lobbying itself is perceived to be a constituent part of the development of corruption procedures. However, after studying the problem more in depth, we can say that this kind of lobbyism also has a communicative role in social interactions. In the opinion of American political scientists, lobbyism has long since shifted from corruption into information in the democratic political systems. This is also true for Kazakhstan, where social pressure groups are important channels of communication and information exchange between society and the various branches of power.

The results of an ARG study on the role played by pressure groups in Kazakhstan in June 2003 clearly illustrates their influence.[1] Based on the analysis of the results (see annex I), the most substantial factors of risk are the issue of authority succession, an excessive bureaucracy and corruption, an uneven distribution of income, a decrease of the legitimacy of the state authority, a destabilization of activities of influential pressure groups and a high level of and the lack of transparency in the political decision-making process. These results do not allow any room for optimism among those who already consider NGO activities to be influential, simply because NGOs are prominent in numbers. The quantity of NGOs has not yet been transformed into quality. In many cases in Kazakhstan, as in many other post-Soviet republics, the third sector presents itself as simply separated NGOs who prefer to do their own business. This has happened against the backdrop of maintaining the leading role of the state, whose interaction with NGOs has not been based on trust and mutual understanding for a long period of time.

The main problem of NGOs is that, with having passed the first stage of organizational legalization and having found their own social niche, they have no experience to help them make public their participation in the political decision-making process. We can not talk about the existence of a third sector, as it is still impossible to try to uncover and express social interests without having mechanisms for their defence against the authority. Raising the issue of a dialogue between the third sector and the authority, we have to talk about concrete mechanisms and a tool kit for such an interaction, i.e. a

---

[1] Among the participants were representatives of foreign investment companies, Kazakh political scientists and foreign experts studying the political and financial processes in Central Asia in general and Kazakhstan in particular.

legal and legitimate framework for "social lobbying". By "social lobbying" we understand the process of purposively influencing institutions of political power from the side of NGOs and those social organizations that express social or other public interests.

Example of the law "On lobbying of legislative acts"

The draft law "On lobbying of legislative acts" was developed by the representatives of Kazakhstan's third sector and has passed the following stages: elaboration of variants, processing proposals from the representatives of NGOs, discussions with various groups of interests, lawyers and scientists, participation of those interested in the draft advancement and forming a favourable public opinion on the concept of lobbying and draft advancement at all government levels.
In spite of the fact that the draft law had actually passed all the legislative stages, it had not been approved by the Kazakh parliament. The reason it was not passed is that it had been delayed for a long time during the consultation procedure with representatives of the authorities: ministry of justice, members of the government and of the presidential administration. Taking into account the presence of high-ranking opponents within the authorities, there was a lack of control on the side of the initiators, who should have recognized the possibility of counter-attacks on their initiative beforehand.
Given this new initiative, in the view of legal experts, possibilities for lobbying already exist in Kazakhstan. According to the juridical scholar, G. Sapargaliyev, from a legal point of view, there is a definite legal basis for social lobbying in Kazakhstan. Article 33 of the constitution says that the citizens of Kazakhstan have the rights to participate in the management of state affairs via its representatives and to address them personally as well as send an individual or collective announcement to the state. The legal foundation of lobbying is constituted by normative legal acts, which define the status of all state bodies. According to the constitution, citizens have the right to address the president not only in issues of personal importance, but also in issues of public significance, in particular, questions of legislative improvement. Within the framework of the laws "On the parliament of the Republic of Kazakhstan and the status of its deputies", "On the regulation of the parliament", "On the regulations of the upper and lower chambers of the parliament" and of the law "On legislative acts", NGOs can participate in the decision-making-process. Furthermore, NGOs can take part in the elaboration of and discussion of drafts as well as exert influence on the legislative establishment.
According to presidential representative, Zh. N. Baishev, there are many opportunities for social lobbying in the bicameral legislative system of Kazakhstan. This situation creates additional points of contact for lobbyists. There is a large number of committees in the *mazhilis* (Kazakh: lower house of par-

liament) and in the Senate, where a smaller number of deputies is involved, whose opinions may be influenced effectively. The role of the parliament's speakers should not be underestimated, as they are not only responsible for holding the sessions, but also for deciding when it is suitable to vote. Lobbying during parliamentary hearings can be successful, since it takes the shape of different types of seminars and scientific-practical conferences on the issues of concrete draft laws under discussion in which respective deputies are participating. Lobbying can also be effective via deputy groups and unions as well as via informal groups of deputies.

Despite these views the draft law should be further improved. In order to successfully promote it, serious study should be devoted to the following: studying the laws, which are directly and indirectly related to the subject of interest as well as the corresponding literature; talking to scientists and specialists, who are engaged in solving these problems; mastering the nuances of the legislative process by attentively analysing the activities of the state bodies as well as parliamentary deputies and the draft work of the government; arranging contacts with those deputies of the *mazhilis*, who are able to help, both with their own support, as well as with brokering the support of their colleagues; and last but not least making the public aware of the issues.

Details of the draft law should be given a closer look. Many instances require a more detailed elaboration; in particular, the articles devoted to the legal status of the lobbyist or the lobbyist organization. The text of the draft law has to be more precise as regards the requirements of registration and the indication of responsibilities of the lobbying side. One of its very weak points is that the scope of activity of the draft applies only to the legislative branch, despite the fact that most lobbying groups act in the vertical structures of the executive branch. Here an additional negative factor might be the frequent cadre rearrangements within the government.

The law should not be considered as more than just an instrument whose effectiveness is proportional with the openness of the political system. In any case, a legal control of lobbying activities would serve a declarative purpose and signal that, within this framework, corruption will not be tolerated. Even though this draft law has plenty of weak points, its mere existence illustrates that the problem has matured, as well as the way it has been handled. Adopting it will have the following effects: first, it will acknowledge the presence of lobbyism as a constituent part of political life in Kazakhstan; second, it will allow for the introduction of lobbyism into the legal frameworks; and third, it will provide stimulus for the creation of a mode of transfer of opinions and ideas from the side of civil initiatives to that of the state. A significant proportion of the experts interviewed said that adopting the bill will create favourable conditions for the lobbyist activities of the different social groups. The law on lobbyist activity control will establish the rules of registration for all pressure groups that are active within state structures.

For this reason, the third sector has to overcome some weak points as well. Despite the theoretical opportunities for the NGOs to constitute an active presence in the lobbying process, the political realities are far from conducive to this end. Firstly, the majority of NGOs have only vague notions of the decision-making procedure as well as the finer points of the legal sphere. Secondly, unlike other former Soviet republics, perhaps with the exception of Russia, the character of the political system in Kazakhstan is far from that of Western states. This is illustrated by the fact that Kazakhstan's lobbying groups generally do not work in the corridors of parliament, but rather those of the executive. However, activities within the sphere of party politics and the rise of a new political parliament creates additional favourable conditions for the development of social lobbying. This concerns, in particular, the parties *Ak Zhol* (Kazakh: wise path) and *Asar* (Kazakh: all together), both of which have already made attempts at utilizing the parliament as a venue for the lobbying of their initiatives. Therefore, the passing of this law would play an important role in increasing the status of the third sector in the process of political decision-making. The acknowledgement by the authorities and NGOs of the legal and justified status of lobbying as an important mechanism and channel of communication will create a basis for dialogue. Both parties, authorities and third sector forces should be interested in such a development.

Fostering social lobbying – the possible role of the OSCE

ARG's scientific research on the issue of lobbyism in Kazakhstan was conducted with the support of the Soros Foundation Kazakhstan and the Eurasia Foundation. As the resulting analyses only constitute the initial stage, more laborious work still remains in the area of the practical realization of those proposals and recommendations made during the spadework. Naturally, many factors depend on the third sector itself and on a favourable political situation in Kazakhstan. However, this work can only be realized in collaboration with a strong political partner and a stable financial basis. One of the main partners among Kazakhstan's NGOs in the creation of an effective mechanism of social lobbying may be the OSCE. The following factors could be favourable in advancing an optimal mechanism of social lobbying through the support of the OSCE:

- Forming a mechanism of social lobbying is a constituent part of the democratization process in Kazakhstan. Here, the OSCE has an important role to play, especially in the initial stages. Certainly, in this respect, it is important to keep in mind the framework of OSCE possibilities in order to really contribute to an acceleration of this process. The range of external actors is limited here.

- Another factor would be OSCE support in the evolution of a republican political system towards openness of dialogue with the civil society. Concrete steps in this direction have already been taken with the first Civil Forum in the history of Kazakhstan, which was an indicator of the fact that the political elite cannot but admit the existence of the third sector, which not only provides work for Kazakhstan, but is able to stand as a viable alternative channel for spreading single-purpose information and work on numerous local-level problems, which state authorities cannot or do not have the time to deal with.
- The OSCE has the ability to act as a productive bridge between state powers and NGOs. Given the peculiarities of Kazakhstan in the third sector, less politicization and a considerable potential for co-operation with the state power could ease the mediating role of the OSCE. Thus, it could become a more concrete bridge between the NGOs and the authorities, which are ready to accept initiatives from below.[2]
- Another important factor is the international experience of the OSCE in supporting different civic initiatives with the purpose of expanding and strengthening democratization. Here, Kazakh NGOs can profit from a considerably large data base on the OSCE's work on different levels of political and socio-economic development as well as on the specific practical methodologies.
- The last but no less important factor, which expresses the OSCE's participation in shaping social lobbying mechanisms, is the financial opportunity of the organization. This factor is extremely important in the realization of long-term projects, which cannot rely on one-time grants only, but require long-term support.

In the following, an outline of two models of social lobbying will be sketched. The models show lobbying at the local and national level in the development of which the OSCE could support the Kazakh third sector.

Social lobbying at the local level

Before working on a mechanism of social lobbying, the local authorities' absence of responsibility with regard to the following has to be taken into account: the population, the strong dependence on *maslikhats* (Kazakh: local councils) and on *akims* (Kazakh: governor), the absence of mechanisms of interaction between authorities and NGOs, and the absence of NGO coordination for addressing the authorities. In order to develop problem-solving alternatives, local self-government systems, which are based on the election

---

2   In this respect it is very important to take into consideration a previous unsuccessful experience of the OSCE in Kazakhstan. The issue in question is the failed attempt of the OSCE to mediate between Kazakhstan's opposition and the state power in 1999-2000. The reason is that the OSCE had not been precise enough in determining its ability and that of the other party to carry on a dialogue.

of representatives and executive bodies, would have to be created. Furthermore, the population should have the opportunity to recall officials; the activities of the authorities should become more transparent; the activity of the civilian population should increase; the electoral system should be reformed; electoral commissions should be removed from the jurisdiction of the executive authorities; the power of the representatives' bodies should be strengthened in order to better control the activities of the executive bodies; and hearings should be opened in *maslikhats* with the participation of civil society. On the side of the third sector, an NGO coalition should aim at combining their efforts to solve current local problems. NGOs should also publish their own printed material and draw attention to their activities via the mass media. Thus, they should create socially important joint projects together with state bodies.

In order to work out a real mechanism for social lobbying, civil self-consciousness has to be awakened by the introduction of a local self-government system. Furthermore, the law on local self-government has to be improved, and the draft law "On lobbying of legislative acts" has to be adopted. Public relations activities have to be started in order to engage civil society in broad discussions on the problems of democratic participation. In addition, better working conditions for NGOs have to be created. And finally, in order to strengthen the interaction between the bodies of local self-government, NGOs and the population, the results of these steps should be monitored and assessed.

Social lobbying at the national level

Before working out a mechanism for social lobbying on the national level, communicative ties between state bodies and NGOs should be improved. In order to achieve a better structure for these relations, some legal barriers should be removed first. The structures of political decision-making should become more open and the public control of them should increase. In order to work out a real mechanism, the notion of "lobbyism" and the role and competencies of lobbyists should be defined for Kazakhstan. The lobbying procedure as well as the exact sphere of lobbying should be determined. "Influential" people could be of organizational help in the realization of lobbying due to their authority. This is especially the case with meetings and negotiations between representatives of social interest groups and members of the state authorities. On the local level, a public relations campaign in the mass media would also be useful. Again, the results of these activities should be monitored, analysed and assessed.

The OSCE could contribute to both local and national efforts to establish mechanisms for social lobbying by organizing respective training activities for representatives of NGOs and for state employees, and by discussing the respective local and national models with them. The main aim of such trainings would be to get rid of stereotypes and find common points of contact. To achieve the latter, it is necessary that work with NGOs and state structures be carried out parallel to each other.

Besides this, the OSCE should engage in informational work with the mass media. The mass media, in turn, should possess clear notions and perceptions of the respective problems and the ways in which they may be solved. This might be carried out in part, again, by arranging specialized seminars for journalists and by writing publications on the theme at hand. The regional director of the Public Humanitarian Fund for Sociological and Political Research and Head of "Central Asia Consultants", L.V. Balatskaya, presented a valid argument when she stated that interest movements constitute the main part of a multi-faceted process of democratization. This process does not begin at the parliamentary level, though.

Finally, the prospects for social lobbying in Kazakhstan will depend on which of the two main types of interest advancement (corporative or pluralistic) prevail. At best, it will come to additional points of access for lobbying actors in the political system – meaning a favourable environment for the development of social lobbying will be created. At worst, these processes will be artificially hampered or will succumb to banal formalism. The OSCE, however, can play a positive role in deciding which route the development of social lobbyism should take. In order for this to happen, it is necessary that the OSCE take an active position and support NGOs in trying to become partners of power in the area of problem solving, both at the local and national level. If this does not happen, Kazakhstan will turn to the corporative variant of development, a case in which the trends of social lobbying are very doubtful.

Annex I: *Level of political risks in Kazakhstan*
(January – June 2003)

Risk factors	Quantitative index	Total points
threat of political regime stability	(1) no threat (10) extremely high	6
stability of government	(1) without changes (10) under the threat of change	8
legitimacy of state power	(1) high (10) extremely low	6
legitimacy of the pressure group	(1) constructive (10) destructive	8
opposition testimonial	(1) constructive (10) destructive	5
threat of state stability from outside (intergovernmental conflicts)	(1) no threat (10) extremely high	3
social stability of state	(1) stability (10) extremely tension	5
estimation of total revenue distribution	(1) uniform (10) abrupt stratification of society	7
political succession	(1) in existence (10) completely absent	8
nationalism	(1) completely absent (10) supported by the state	4
bureaucracy	(1) insignificant (10) extremely high	8
contradictions between centre and regions	(1) no threat (10) uncompromising	6
influence from outside by the other states	(1) insignificant (10) substantial	6
illegal enterprise of nongovernmental structures: threat of extremism and terrorism	(1) no threat (10) extremely high	5
organized crime	(1) no threat (10) extremely high	5

Sofiya Issenova

Quasi-Judicial Institutions.
The Ombudsman in Kazakhstan

> "Those, who are appointed to supervise liberties in the state, do not have more socially beneficial and necessary credentials, than the authority to accuse in front of the people or court those citizens who committed criminal acts against the state's liberty."
> (Niccolo Machiavelli)

The ombudsman is one of the most important remedial institutions in the history of well-developed democracies. For new independent states, the establishment of an ombudsman and its effective functioning constitutes a considerable potential for democracy and can thus become an effective tool, lever and catalyst of democratization. Maximum utilization of such a potential should, however, not only contribute to the formation of a remedial infrastructure, but also facilitate the processes related to the reform of the public service, enhance and complete the realization of the citizens' constitutional rights, and should additionally play an important role in the prevention of administrative and political corruption, which can be regarded as a grave human rights violation. In transition economies,[1] the institution of an ombudsman has to become an important tool for the formation of a new political system, and also of the public governance system based on implicit observance of human and civil liberties that are of utmost value for a state.
However, the experience of the ombudsman institution recently established in Kazakhstan demonstrates a different scenario: the ombudsman is quite smoothly adapting itself to the public management system and becoming a specific part thereof, without making any claims for a system-forming body in the sphere of human rights protection. The Kazakh ombudsman does not insist on autonomy from the executive authorities,[2] nor on assuming empow-

---

1   During several recent years, the political, legal and economic systems of the countries that are traditionally referred to as transition economies, have undergone crucial transformations. Due to this, such generic terms as transition economies, post-soviet countries, new independent states, etc. are becoming very conditional and unable to reflect the specific reality of a particular state. The term "Central Asian countries" is also quite conditional and reflects purely a geographical notion.
2   In this case, we mean dependency on the president who, formally and legally, is the highest state official and "stays above" the three branches of the state power. However, actually the political figure of the president is perceived, primarily, as the head of executive power.

erments in investigation procedures. A peculiar process is taking place: the new democratic institution is assimilating to the out-dated political system and its sluggish reform of the public governance system and public service that have, consequently, come close to stagnation.

In this article, we will try to analyse the efficiency of new democratic institutions in the political systems of the new independent states based on the example of the ombudsman in Kazakhstan. Comparable institutions such as Kyrgyzstan and Uzbekistan will be dealt with in order to comprehensively assess the prerequisites for the establishment of the ombudsman institution and its legislative status.

The institution of an ombudsman. Basic status

The ombudsman is an independent national institute created especially to implement remedial functions and promote the ideas of human rights observance. It originated in Sweden in 1809. After World War II, in 1946, the United Nations Organization contributed to the determination of key functions of the national human rights institution of the ombudsman. In the early 1990s, the institution of the ombudsman, as a national human rights institution, spread not only in European countries, but also on the African continent and in the Asia-Pacific region. The ombudsman position was also established in the post-Soviet countries.[3]

Experts relate the wide-spread occurrence of this institution in European countries to the crisis of traditional liberalism in the 19th century, when society required a more accountable participation in public life, expecting provisions of such vital social services as health care, public safety, education, etc. Meanwhile, dependence on the state led to an unavoidable crisis in the sphere of human rights observance by state bureaucratic institutions. Moreover, to resolve the crisis in this state-society relationship, a new public institution was required. It had to be based on the high morale of a particular individual and include a simplified procedure for filing complaints as well as a review, which is free of bureaucratism. It had to be a person that would be an effective mediator in settling disputes between state bodies and citizens.

The ombudsman's work in terms of history and experience in the Scandinavian countries is considerable; the definition of its legal and public status

---

3   In Africa the ombudsman was installed in Cameroon (1991), Chad (1994), Ghana (1993), Nigeria (1996), Senegal (1997), SAR (1995), Uganda (1996) and Zambia (1997). Cf. Report of Dr. Solomon Nfor Gway, chairman of the coordinating board of African national institutes for Human Rights, 3 July 1998. In Asia the Ombudsman exists in India (1993), Indonesia (1994) and Sri-Lanka (1997). In Eastern Europe we have an ombudsman in Bosnia and Herzegovina (1997), Croatia (1990), Hungary (1996), Macedonia (1991), Poland (1997), Romania (1991) and Slovenia (1991). In the CIS the institution exists in Georgia (1996), Latvia (1996); Lithuania (1992), Moldova (1997), Kazakhstan (2002), Kyrgyzstan (2002), the Russian Federation (1993), Ukraine (1996) and Uzbekistan (1997).

refers to the latest period. In world practice, there are no rigid standards with which the ombudsman must comply. It was only in 1993, under the UN aegis, the so-called Paris Principles, where it was formulated that the ombudsman forms the basis for the activities of national human rights institutions.[4] These principles formulate a general standard for human rights institutions, which is to comply with the following provisions: a wide range of powers, considerable attention to the integration of international standards on human rights into national legislation, an institutional status on legislative level, independence from the state in decision-making, strict adherence to the principles of pluralism and incorporation of various civil society groups, and the right to receive and review citizens' claims.

Currently, various countries have various ombudsman functions and models. We can distinguish them

- according to the completeness of credentials: i.e. having a wide range of credentials and paying significant attention to the introduction of international standards into national human rights legislation or having a truncated range of credentials.
- according to the level of legal enactment that establishes the status: i.e. a status defined by law, or by a president or executive body's decree.
- according to the entity for reporting and appointment:[5] the entity is the legislative ombudsman, whose legitimacy is based upon parliamentary decisions and who is responsible to parliament or the executive ombudsman, who, in turn, is a commissioner appointed by the government or the head of government.[6]
- according to the priority of functions to be carried out: the "court-like model",[7] where citizen's complaints are treated; the "procurator-disciplinary model" where the primary task is to exercise legal supervision of government authorities (including courts) and their officials. The ombudsmen are also entitled to initiate legal proceedings against the public on account of criminal offences committed in the exercise of official duties. The "mediation model" where the ombudsman performs the intermediary function in the dispute between natural persons (or private companies) and state bodies. In this case, the ombudsman performs the function not of an arbitrator, but of an intermediary, and can recommend to the state body that it rectify administration errors. The "hy-

---

4   Cf. Paris Principles 1993.
5   Cf. Vedel Kessing 2000.
6   It is required to differentiate between the ombudsman institution and various committees acting as consultancy and deliberative bodies under the head of the state or executive bodies.
7   Citizens complaints about bad governance and maladministration, imperfection of regulatory procedures, exceeding authorities by some officials, lack of access to information. In Europe an ombudsman has the right to handle judicial complaints, including those against the European Court for Human Rights (with exception of its direct judicial functions).

brid ombudsman" combines in various proportions the above-mentioned and other functions.
- according to specialization: the general jurisdiction ombudsman or the specialized ombudsman (for example: on children's rights).

Among the tasks of an ombudsman are the following main functions: to provide simple methods for an unprejudiced and independent investigation of complaints against administrative bodies; to train representatives of administrative authorities in the code of conduct and official standards; and to increase awareness of citizens with respect to rights thereof for effective and fair services from the State. A former governor-general of Australia, Sir Ninyan Stivens, described the main task of an ombudsman as: "You are indeed guarantors of the fact that rights and legitimate interests of citizens are observed properly. And while realizing this you not only assert the rights, but also instruct administrative bodies in such a way that strict observance thereof becomes a second nature of them. Such training mission in my opinion is perhaps the highest aim an ombudsman has to strive for."[8]

The human rights commission in Kazakhstan

In 1994, in the Republic of Kazakhstan, the human rights commission under the president was founded. Since 2003 it works in accordance with the presidential decree of March 19, 2003 "About the Commission on Human Rights under the President of the Republic of Kazakhstan".[9] As a new advisory body, the commission's main objectives were to assist the president in the realization of his status as guarantor of rights and liberties of persons and citizens. Thus, it aims at the improvement of citizens' rights and liberties.
The commission cannot be regarded as an independent national institution because of its legal status as an advisory body under the president. It was created by a personal decree of the head of state. Its operational body –the secretariat – is a sector within the structure of the social and political department of the president's administration. A state secretary coordinates the commission's activities. Besides the constitution and laws, the commission is guided by the secretary's instructions. Based on proposals by the state secretary, the commission's members are approved by the president. At present, the commission's secretariat consists of three persons: the secretary, his/her deputy and a lawyer. Members of this body have basic jobs at companies and participate in the commission's activities on a voluntary basis. The commission does not include representatives of the mass media, NGOs, independent lawyers nor human rights activists. NGO representatives are involved in the framework of an expert's council; however, the sessions are conducted on an

---

8   Source with the author.
9   Cf. Kazakhstanskaya pravda, March 21, 2003.

irregular basis without fixed procedures. The vague status of the commission also predetermines the closed bureaucratic way in which members are appointed and dismissed. Following the requests from the administration, the secretary has to perform duties that are not always related to the duties of a secretary in a commission. Sessions with the required quorum are held occasionally; there are, however, no clear regulations for carrying out these activities.

Obviously, the human rights commission being an advisory body under president is essentially restricted by decree in its powers related to citizens complaints and does not have sufficient authorities to directly protect their rights. Comprised of two or three permanent members, the commission cannot carry out any efficient activities on consideration and resolution of the citizens' complaints. Therefore, it is frequently forced to re-address the complaints of relevant state bodies, whose actions are, at the same time, the subjects of those complaints. In order to resolve the incumbent tasks, the commission has the right to request and receive from relevant authorities and officials the required data, documents and materials, and the right to listen to its sessions and gather information from relevant officials. However, the commission members do not use this right to a sufficient degree. The commission is not empowered to institute investigations on particular complaints. The commission's resolutions are purely of recommendation character, while the sole subject of these recommendations is the president. The procedure for the implementation of these recommendations is not specified by the decree. It is difficult to say for sure whether the president's acts are based on the recommendations given by the human rights commission, as there are no tools to monitor the activity thereof. Furthermore, as an advisory body under the president, there are no procedures to monitor the implementation of the recommendations issued. However, researchers have noted that certain state institutions are becoming more attentive to the commission's recommendations, which is related not only to the prestige of the president's administration, but also to the increase in the general level of legal consciousness and awareness of the importance of human rights and liberties. On the whole, this body's activity is not public, and consequently, citizens are simply unaware of its existence and powers.

The commission's competence covers the compilation of annual reports and special papers on the observation of human rights and liberties, and putting forward proposals in the form of recommendations on streamlining tools to ensure human rights protection. These are then brought to the president's attention. The commission's annual report is not published and is a document for administrative use. The commission's report can be circulated to the ministry of internal affairs and to international organizations (UN, OSCE). According to OSCE employees, though the commission is unable to monitor the human rights situation using its own facilities – with the exception of the information obtained from complaints – the report reflects quite acute impartial facts on human rights violations by state authorities. Perhaps, this aspect predetermines the non-disclosure of the reports. At the end of 1998, a republican newspaper published an abridged version of the report on the observance of human rights and liberties for 1997.[10] Extracts from this report were primarily concerned with the status of social and economic rights and liberties in Kazakhstan.

Besides annual reports, the commission compiles special papers on the observance of the requirements specified by international legal documents ratified by the Republic of Kazakhstan. In 1998, Kazakhstan ratified the Convention against Torture and Inhuman or Degrading Treatment or Punishment. The human rights commission, jointly with law-enforcement bodies, prepared an official report on the effects of this convention in Kazakhstan, which was delivered to the UN in April 2001 along with an alternative report by Kazakh NGOs.[11]

The establishment of an ombudsman in Kazakhstan

The limitations of the human rights commission's functions and its inadequate response to the actual needs of society has led to the establishment of an ombudsman institute. During the period of 1998-2000 in Kazakhstan, a large-scale UNDP and OSCE project on the development of national human rights institutions was implemented. This project constituted a framework for the draft law "On the National Ombudsman in the Republic of Kazakhstan"[12] – a result of the joint efforts of international institutions and national state bodies. According to both parties, the draft law should meet two contradictory requirements: on one hand, the new institution should comply with the constitution and should not require amendments thereto; on the other hand, it should comply with the Paris principles' requirements (1993) and the international standards of the UN and the OSCE.

The following concepts for an ombudsman are laid down in the draft law:

- defender of citizens' liberties against abuse of power by public officers;
- provider of strengthened accountability of executive authorities for the good of ordinary citizens;
- essential mechanism for reinforcement of supremacy of law;
- provider of informal methods to settle disputes that are free of any taxes, relatively short-term and inexpensive as compared to a court examination. An ombudsman does not replace court mechanisms, but rather supplements them with more quick and simple measures.

10　Cf. Kazakhstanskaya pravda, December 15, 1998.
11　Confidential interview with a Kazakhstani expert on human rights.
12　Unpublished draft law.

Beyond this, with regard to the drafting of a law, the following four critical aspects should be mentioned:

Appointment procedure. According to the principles of international institutions, there is no rigid uniform approach in appointing an ombudsman and his deputies. An important aspect in the appointment process, and which, according to international experts is crucial, is to ensure a maximum independence of the institution. Furthermore, it should ensure that reports are submitted to an authorized official or entity, which is comprised of several persons, and that the appointment does not result from a closed political process, which is non-transparent to the public. To ensure such an independence of the ombudsman or a human rights institution, it should be appointed by the parliament. However, such a precondition requires amendments to the constitution. Two main options exist: First, the president could propose one or several persons for the position of ombudsman, and the parliament would approve the decision. In addition, a special voting procedure could be established that requires a two-thirds majority of all parliamentary deputies, and not only of the session attendees. The officials appointed in this way would be more independent than those appointed by the president, even if such an appointment were made after some consultancy procedures with the parliamentary commissions. The second option would be that the candidates are selected and proposed by the parliament, but appointed by the president. This is another method of compliant with international standards of independence.

Independence. According to international experts, the law should ensure maximum independence of the assignee on human rights issues. Along with other conceptual aspects, this again requires amendments to the constitution and takes much more time. Therefore, the experts introduced additional proposals concerning the enhancement of independence beyond the necessity of constitutional changes. It was proposed to impose liability on any attempt to interfere with the national ombudsman's activities in order to influence his decision-making and to not fulfil the obligations envisaged by this law as well as other attempts to impede the activities of the ombudsman or his deputies.

Furthermore, the law should ensure that the ombudsman meets a wide range of credentials, which allow for efficiently realizing the remedial function. These credentials should include the capability of checking and initiating an investigation on the received complaints. Thus, for example, "a refusal to consider an application does not influence the ombudsman's right to initiate on its discretion a revision of actions that caused the application or any related actions".[13]

The experts participating in the development of the project considered that the law had to specify the types of complaints in relation to those which the ombudsman, on his discretion, decides to not accept or those he considers:

---

13   Unpublished draft law.

"The ombudsman, on his discretion, can take a decision not to consider or terminate the review of an application, in case that: (a) there is another efficient method to restore the violated right of the right of appeal, except for appeal via a court that could be used by the applicant irrelevant of the fact whether this was actually used by the applicant; (b) a violation that caused the application is of an inconsiderable degree or is of a bureaucratic character, (c) with consideration of all the application circumstances, further review is inappropriate or cannot be guaranteed; (d) the applicant had been aware of the actions that caused the application longer than twelve months and cannot explain the reasons of the delayed application for restoration of violated rights; (e) the facilities in the ombudsman's office are insufficient for an appropriate audit; (f) handling other applications is more urgent; (g) review of the application will not lead to essential results; (h) such (or similar) application was considered previously; (i) the applicants identification is not disclosed to the ombudsman".[14]

The other standard was concerned with the considerable period of limitation to arrange fact checks on civil right violations. "The ombudsman can proceed with the check of application even in case the applicant had known about the actions that caused the claim for more than twelve months, and cannot explain the reasons of the delayed application for restoration of violated rights, if such an audit is predetermined by public interest ... Refusal to consider an application does not influence the ombudsman's right on its discretion to initiate audit of the actions that caused the application or associated actions".[15]

A standard was proposed concerning the procedure for refusal to review or termination in the review of a claim. "If an ombudsman decides not to consider an application or suspend the review, the ombudsman shall notify the applicant about such a decision and explain the reasons. If an ombudsman decides not to consider an application, he can notify the relevant authorities accordingly. The notice envisaged by this clause can be made by the ombudsman verbally, however, substantiation of the refusal to handle the application shall be provided in writing".[16]

Another supplement refers to the delegation of authorities, should the ombudsman himself or his deputies face a conflict of interests. The ombudsman has the right to delegate in writing his obligations imposed by the law to the deputy ombudsman or another employee. The employees do not have the right to participate in the handling of claims, should they become interested, as this would create obstacles to fair and unbiased participation.

Confidentiality. In addition, the experts proposed to introduce in the draft law the following confidentiality stipulations. "The national ombudsman shall ensure non-disclosure of information concerning claims and inspections in-

---

14 Ibid.
15 Ibid.
16 Ibid.

cluding the applicants names and the inspection materials stored in the ombudsman's office, with exception of cases when the ombudsman considers such disclosure necessary for undertaking his obligations specified by this law or for preparation of reports envisaged by this law".[17] They also stipulated a regulation that would prevent the use of the confidentiality principle to the detriment of the transparency of the ombudsman's activities. "The national ombudsman can make and proclaim brief reports on confidential applications, results thereof, the procedure for relevant inspections and causes of refusal. Such a brief report can be stored in the office computer system and can be submitted by the ombudsman to provide assistance in governmental programs management, in replies to enquiries about the state bodies performance, in order to increase public awareness and provision the public with information about the ombudsman's activities. A short report prepared and circulated under this clause cannot disclose the applicant's name or other personal information."[18]

Finally, the developers proposed a regulation for the storage of materials dealing with complaints and inspections. "With relation to the materials on applications and inspections the legislation on government archives, periods of their storage and archiving does not apply. The ombudsman has the right to set rules regulating the materials on applications and other internal documents."[19]

Pluralism. The presence of more than one ombudsman and of four deputies – elected according to the same procedure as the ombudsman – is a recognized method of ensuring pluralism and diversity, as stipulated in the Paris Principles.

The development of the draft law

The development of the draft law was stipulated in the Kazakh government's drafting work of 2002 and approved by the resolution of 14 February 2002.[20] About eight versions of the draft law had been developed in joint efforts. The main stumbling block in achieving a compromise was the procedure for the ombudsman's appointment. In compliance with the draft law, the ombudsman has to be appointed by the president, in fact, by his administration. Thus, according to the experts' estimates and in compliance with the draft law under consideration, it would be difficult to avoid non-transparency and behind-

---

17   Ibid.
18   Ibid.
19   Ibid.
20   During the period when the draft was under review with relevant state authorities, I made an enquiry to the ministry of justice. Upon expiration of the period for the application's consideration, I received a response stating that "submission of this draft law is premature, in so far as the draft has not been approved by the government, and the final edition has not been determined". Confidential interview.

the-curtain actions, and moreover, rely on the appointed person's independence from the executive power. Finally, it was decided that the president would appoint the assignee after consultations with the parliamentary commissions, the list of which is also defined by the president. The president would also be charged with executing dismissals. Besides, the assignee can be appointed by the president to another position, which constitutes a basis for premature dismissal.

At that point in time, the experts were quite pessimistic in assessing the draft law and its efficiency, considering it as discreditable to the institute of an ombudsman. Certain concerns were expressed that, in the future, it will be more complicated to introduce amendments and additions to the existing law, as well as change critical clauses and raise them up to international standards. However, extended law-making work, discussions and consultations resulted in an individual presidential decree (signed on 19 September 2002) on the establishment of the position of an ombudsman. Thus, the ombudsman's position was established while ignoring the procedure of consideration in the Kazakh parliament. Control over the implementation of the decree is imposed on the presidential administration. The following essential aspects characterizing the legal framework of an ombudsman's activities have not been realized:

- The level of definition of the procedure for implementation of his powers is relatively low.
- Among the ombudsman's authorities are the right to enquiry, the right to be received by officials, the right to engage specialists and the right to enter and remain on the territory and in the premises of state bodies and organizations. However, in the Kazakh case, considerable exclusion clauses in the system of the ombudsman's credentials comprise restrictions on the list of officials, whose actions can be appealed. The assignee cannot handle complaints against actions and resolutions of the president, the parliament, its deputies, the government, the constitution, the general procurator, the central election commission nor the courts of the Republic of Kazakhstan.
- Meanwhile, there are certain standards of general character: The assignee has the right to take action to protect the people from having their rights and liberties violated. In procedural terms, the question remains in which way, and based on which facilities this function will be realized. Kazakh legislation does not provide the assignee with the right to be immediately received by the highest state officials, by heads of state institutions; the right to attend sessions of government, parliament and supreme court; the right to address the constitution board to obtain access to information that constitutes official, commercial and state secrets; the right to require assistance from officials, enterprises and institutions in conducting audits; the right to apply to the court for protection

of human rights and liberties; and the right to become familiar with criminal civil cases, etc. As per Kazakh legislation, the ombudsman is not empowered to control any authority in relation to cases on which a final resolution has been pronounced. The assignee for human rights in Kazakhstan does not have an absolute or partial right to carry out investigations on the violation of human rights and liberties by state institutions or officials.

- Pursuant to clause 3.23 of the decree, the ombudsman submits an annual report on his activities to the president. Based on the first year's results, the national human rights centre, which was established to ensure the assignee's activities, published a report on the ombudsman's activities.[21] This report shows reservation: "According to the Kazakhstani model, the assignee's report is submitted to the president of Kazakhstan and is not subject to governmental control."

According to experts who had had access to information on the latest version of the draft law, the document did not meet present-day challenges and did not essentially differ from the human rights commission under the president. Currently, this commission, the assignee on human rights, and the national centre on human rights (ensuring the functions of the latter) work parallel to each other, and their functions coincide by 90 per cent. The provision does not provide the assignee with a central and system-forming role. "The assignee in his activities supplements the existing tools of protecting rights and liberties of persons and citizens."[22] Furthermore, the experts have come to the conclusion that, in spite of long-term negotiations, there are some outstanding issues: insurance of independence, immunity, anticipatory termination of powers and extended credentials. The final version of the draft law does not outline the range of officials, who may become the focus of ombudsman's attention, nor those whose actions can be checked by the ombudsman. The document does not specify the ombudsman's powers, or the procedure for implementation thereof. A comparative analysis of the range of powers and the competence of the ombudsman in other countries of the Central Asian region (Kyrgyzstan, Uzbekistan) leads to the conclusion that the range of this institution's authorities in Kazakhstan can be regarded as restricted.

First results of the practical work of the Ombudsman

With regard to the ombudsman's short-term office, we can draw preliminary conclusions with respect to results and prospects of the functioning of this paramount remedial institute. Among the positive aspects are the following:

---

21   Report About the Activities of the Assignee on Human Rights 2004.
22   Confidential interview.

- An independent material and technical basis for the work of the assignee as well as the national centre on human rights in the form of a detached lodgement, an independent budgetary financing and the possibility of co-operation, probations and exchange of experiences with similar foreign institutes and international organizations etc. have been created.
- The consideration of citizens' complaints has increased.
- Awareness programmes and educational activities have been established.

Negative aspects of the current activities of the ombudsman are as follows:

- A pared-down mandate of powers does not allow in full the realization of the remedial potential of the ombudsman and leads to exclusions in the circle of public officers, whose activities cannot be the subject of inquiry.
- A too great diversity of important tasks for the incumbent assignee on human rights in countries with a developing democracy (a special role in the processes of democratization under the conditions of a reorganization of main political institutes);
- A lack of political will and practical resources in forming and realizing remedial infrastructure and strategy;
- Distancing from anti-corruption activity in the wide sense;
- Distancing from participation in the modification of the legal basis of the ombudsman's activities;
- An insufficient authority among officials and also a lack of power, which could strengthen the recommendation character of acts of response;
- A low level of citizens' awareness with respect to the activities of the ombudsman;
- A focus on a special "Kazakh pattern" of the ombudsman, characterized by a formal observance of the Paris Principles;
- A lack of a due system of accountability to the general public;
- The absence of the monitoring of the ombudsman's influence on the general situation regarding human rights and democratization in the country;
- A number of management deficits (inadequate personnel resources, lack of offices in regions, lack of information on the ombudsman in telephone directories; lack of equipment and proper facilities that can be accessed by citizens with limited capabilities etc.).

At the same time, the future prospects of the ombudsman institution are connected with two major problems at a higher level. The first one is common for most post-Soviet states. It is the problem of legislation implementation.

Here the paradox of law enforcement lies in the gap between de jure and de facto situations. The existence of democratic laws and constitutional declarations does not guarantee the performance and observance thereof. Thus, even though a legislative basis of the ombudsman's activity is perfect and the law passed by the parliament secures a sufficiently wide mandate and effective immunity for the assignee, establishing a powerful backbone for the independent institution remains to be seen.

The issue of implementation and introduction of new democratic institutions to out-dated political systems is closely related to another problem, which, during recent years, has become a subject of extended public discussions in Kazakhstan, namely, the necessity of political reform and reorganization. The focal points of these discussions are stagnation, non-transparency of political processes against the background of relatively stable economic growth, excessive power centralization, absence of strategy and tools for the decentralization thereof, absence of a system of checks and balances, an accountability system and, generally speaking, an absence of political will to form a transparent system of legal and political institutions.

Thus, the creation of truly independent and, at the same time, publicly accountable bodies and institutions directly depends on the political will and preparedness to implement a set of political reforms and introduce amendments to the current constitution. The complexity of establishing independent institutions in the country can be assessed by just viewing the example of the prolonged negotiations of the government and international institutions on the required institutionalization of the ombudsman, who is to be appointed by the parliament, accountable to the latter, and provided with a wide range of empowerments. However, the introduction of this institution required amendments to the constitution, which has traditionally been apprehended as an insurmountable obstacle. A similar situation has been observed in other spheres of public management; experts have, more than once, marked the necessity of creating a truly independent anti-corruption agency, office of the auditor general, an accounting commission, etc.

Evidently, the out-dated political system of Kazakhstan has exhausted its democratization potential and presently demonstrates what is at risk when there is negative regression. Under these circumstances, the assumptions made about a possible democratization of the political system through the introduction of certain political institutions are quite insubstantial. Such a move might bring about opposite outcomes: the new institutions are absorbed by the obsolete conformist political system and have thus become an integral part thereof. It is obvious that in Kazakhstan the administrative reforms have reached their utmost limit and entered a stagnation period. Only higher-level political reforms will be able to accentuate the activities of independent institutions including that of the ombudsman.

The ombudsman as an instrument of anti-corruption policy

In the world of established practice, the ombudsman institution is of special importance, as it is one of the most effective instruments against corruption. The international organization, Transparency International, features the ombudsman in the so-called national integrity system (NIS), which is "the sum total of the laws, institutions and practises in a country that maintain accountability and integrity of public, private and civil society organizations".[23] It is a system of independent institutes that work toward creating an efficient and effective government that works in the public's interest. Moreover, the ombudsman as an independent and authoritative institution, which provides citizens with the opportunity to address their complaints against administrative bodies, is not only a paramount element of the NIS, but also of the anti-corruption set of instruments represented by the UN Office for Drug Control and Crime Prevention (UNODC) in the framework of the Global Anti-Corruption Programme.

If a public authority or state employee becomes the subject of a complaint, an investigation must be conducted by an outside governmental body, which is free from factual or presumptive influence of the former. For example, it is unreasonable for an ombudsman to consider a citizen's complaint for financing by an organization, whose activity is under investigation in connection with the complaint. Under these circumstances, the objectivity of an ombudsman can be affected. True objectivity can only exist where complete independence is guaranteed.[24]

So-called administrative corruption at low and mid-level is perceived as deficient and as lacking accountability and transparency in the system of public management. In this case, corruption results from the inefficiency of the administrative system; and citizens fall victim to it. The powers of an ombudsman not only allow to effectively settle complaints of citizens regarding such matters, but also to make systematic recommendations with respect to issues of the improvement of public management. The opportunity to employ such a potential is especially important in transition economies at the stage of forming democratic institutions and a culture of the supremacy of law, given the absence of a developed and stable infrastructure for the protection of human rights and liberties in corrupt surroundings.

Administrative corruption in Kazakhstan is one of the acute problems which needs to be solved at the governmental level. According to the law "On Anti-corruption", all state structures and public officers – within the limits of their competence – have to take part in the cleaning-up of corruption. Unfortunately, today the ombudsman in Kazakhstan has not tasked him/herself with the prevention of administrative corruption, though this factor particularly

---

23   More information on the NIS is available onlineat http://www.transparency.org/activities/nat_integ_systems/country_studies.html#nis_concept.
24   Cf. UNODC 2001.

undermines the principles of due public management and the carrying out of transparent and effective activities by state authorities. Moreover, it is clear from conversations with employees of the national centre for human rights that the institution of the assignee has distanced itself from the mission in order to consider complaints connected with violations, which relate to corruption or official ethics, although the mandate of the assignee by no means prevents the realization of such a mission.

Basic conclusions and proposals

Based on the above analysis of legislation, and also on the data published in the first report of the assignee on human rights, it is possible to draw certain conclusions on the problems of the institutional establishment of the assignee on human rights and provide recommendations. In various countries, the institution of the ombudsman is in the development stage and is characterized by a diversity of models, whose features have not yet been clearly defined. Kazakh lawmakers, as well as the ombudsman himself, insist on the use of the Kazakh model of assignee's activities, which is institutionalized according to the executive model of national human rights institutions. In this respect, it should be noted that rigid adherence to a single model is not the target per se of an ombudsman's activities. The models for the efficient implementation of human rights and liberties protection are continuously being transformed. This is also predetermined by objective factors like the institutional establishment of the assignee on human rights on the global level and the idiosyncratic features of the Kazakh political and legal system.

The authorities and primarily the highest state official, who initiated the ombudsman institution and who is responsible for his appointment, as well as the society in the name of its relevant institutions and the ombudsman himself – while searching for an appropriate model – should be mainly guided by the general aim to protect human rights and liberties. In other words, the expected goals and results of the ombudsman's activities must follow a suitable form and model. Obviously, at present in Kazakhstan, there is no stable, effective, systematic infrastructure for human rights protection and there is no strategy for developing such an infrastructure.

It is the institution of the assignee on human rights that could take the responsibility of becoming a key entity in the formation and sustainability of a remedial infrastructure. Unfortunately, at present, the ombudsman institution cannot work as a system-forming element in its disintegrated structure of remedial entities and individual remedial actions.

The concept behind the ombudsman is the idea of an institution, which receives and considers complaints from citizens according to a simplified scheme without numerous bureaucratic procedures; which acts as a mediator/intermediary and a central person during negotiations for the settlement of disputes between a citizen and state structures; and which makes recommendations to state authorities and officials thereof. The ombudsman institution is based on the high moral prestige of the person exercising this task. Hence, the government should consider its citizens' high expectations when formulating recommendations on the character of the ombudsman. Forming an authority for the assignee on human rights and confidence, who is effective in his/her activities, has to become one of primary tasks for the ombudsman in Kazakhstan.

How state structures perceive the ombudsman has special significance. State employees as well as citizens must comprehend the goals and mission of the assignee on human rights and the importance of his/her recommendations. Unfortunately, it can hardly be said now that there is any cohesion in the activities of the ombudsman and related state structures.

Obviously, the ombudsman must become the main institution that determines policy in the sphere of human rights and democratization. The assignee on human rights should not only be able to make his/her recommendations to officers, but also determine a normative, legal and ethic basis for his/her own activities. One of the officers of the national centre on human rights in Kazakhstan spoke in an interview about the lack of power of the ombudsman.[25] At the same time, neither officials of the centre, nor the assignee intend to initiate any steps regarding the accretion of power. They are convinced that such proposals must originate from outside: either from members of parliament or from representatives of NGOs.

Bibliography

Documents

Constitution of the Republic of Kazakhstan, of 30 August 1995 (with amendments of 7 October 1998).

Law of the Kyrgyz Republic No. 136 of 31 July 2002 "About the Ombudsman (Kyrgyzs: akyikatchy) of the Kyrgyz Republic".

Law of the Republic of Uzbekistan of 24 April 1997 "About the assignee (Uzbek: oliy) of mazhilis for human rights (ombudsman)".

Principles concerning the status of national institutions engaged in human rights promotion and protection ("Paris principles"). Attachment to resolution 48/134 of the General Assembly of 20 December 1993.

Report About the Activities of the Assignee on Human Rights in the Republic of Kazakhstan 2003, Almaty, publishing house LEM, 2004.

Report of the Human Rights Commission under the President of the Republic of Kazakhstan about observance of human rights and liberties in the Republic of Kazakhstan for 1997.

Republic of Kazakhstan President's Decree No. 947 "On the Establishment of the Human Rights Assignee Position" with amendments introduced by decree No. 1474 of the President of the Republic of Kazakhstan's of 29. November 2004.

---

25   Confidential interview with an officer of the Centre on human rights in Almaty.

Republic of Kazakhstan President's Decree No. 1042 of 19 March 2003 "On the Human Rights Commission under the Republic of Kazakhstan's President" with amendments introduced by the President of the Republic of Kazakhstan's decree No.1325 of 30 March 2004.
Republic of Kazakhstan President's Decree No. 992 "On the Establishment of the National Human Rights Centre" of 10 December 2002.
Republic of Kazakhstan President's Decree No. 3470 of 22 April 1997 "On the Human Rights Commission under the President of the Republic of Kazakhstan" with amendments introduced by the President of the Republic of Kazakhstan's Decrees No. 3976 of 6. June 1998; No. 89 of 24. March 1999; No. 363 of 18. March 2000; No. 714 of 24. October 2001.
Republic of Kazakhstan President's Decree No. 3009 of 3 June 1996 "On Human Rights Commission under the President of the Republic of Kazakhstan.

Interviews

Confidential interviews with officials of the minsitry of justice of the Republic of Kazakhstan and of the national human rights centre, Almaty.
Bolat Baikadamov, head of the subdivision of the social and political department of the presidential administration, head of the secretariat of the human rights commission under the president.
Evgeny Zhovtis, director of the Kazakhstani bureau on human rights and legal compliance.
Leila Baishina, coordinator of ProUN project on human rights.
Ninel Fokina, director of the Almaty Helsinki Commission.

Secondary Literature

Gawanas, Bience. 2000. *The Role of the Ombudsman. Comprehensive Legal and Judicial Development. Toward an Agenda for a Just and Equitable Society in the 21 Century.* Washington.
Lindsnaes, Birgit/Lindholf, Lone/Yigen, Kristine 2000. (eds). *National Human Rights Institutions. Articles and Working papers.* The Danish Center for Human Rights, Copenhagen (quoted as: Lindsnaes/Lindholf/Yigen).
Vedel Kessing, Peter. 2000. *Implementation of the Western Ombudsman Model in Countries in Democratic Transition*, in: Lindsnaes/Lindholf/Yigen.
UN Office for Drug Control and Crime Prevention. 2001. (ed.), *Global Program against Corruption, Anti-corruption Tool Kits*, Vienna, online available at: http://www.unodc.org/pdf/crime/gpacpublications/manual.pdf
The World Bank 2000. (ed.). *Comprehensive Legal and Judicial Development. Toward an Agenda for a Just and Equitable Society in the 21 Century.* Washington.

Part IV:
Security through Democratization ?

Andrea Berg

All Eyes on Central Asia. Disintegration in Uzbekistan and Kyrgyzstan

After thousands of people had stormed the seat of government in the Kyrgyz capital of Bishkek on 24 March 2005, the then president Askar Akaev fled the country and signed his official resignation in Moscow on 4 April. Thereafter, the parliament announced re-elections for 10 July 2005. On this day, Kurmanbek Bakiev was elected the new president of Kyrgyzstan with barely 90 per cent of the votes. Thus, Kyrgyzstan is the first country in Central Asia where a post-Soviet change of power has taken place. In comparison with the turbulent developments, which have been characteristic for the first half of 2005 and have led to the fall of president Akaev, elections were unexpectedly quiet and unspectacular. None of the five other presidential candidates received a considerable amount of votes, so that protests by disappointed followers did not take place this time. Hence, it can be hoped that, in Kyrgyzstan, for the time being, political peace will come.

On 13 May 2005, the Uzbek governmental forces killed hundreds of civilians, who had participated in a demonstration in the city of Andijan in the Ferghana Valley. Despite international pressure, president Islam Karimov refuses, until today, to allow an independent international investigation team to work in the country. The situation in Uzbekistan appears at present quiet, but this quietude is deceptive. It is obvious to observers that the events in Andijan are not the last bloody conflicts between the government and the population, and opposition groups as well. Currently, the question put forth most frequently is whether and how long Karimov will stay in power.

Today, in Uzbekistan as well as in Kyrgyzstan, it is not always clear which individuals and political and economic groups are acting, nor with which motives; nor is it clear in which direction both countries will develop in the next couple of months and how much of an impact the events will have on the general security situation in Central Asia and Europe.

This article will contribute to a better understanding of both events as well as provide background information with regard to the respective causes of the present situation. Furthermore, in which direction(s) future developments are likely to go and what kind of task and challenges lay ahead of the international community will be discussed.

Kyrgyzstan

Course of events[1]

On 27 February and 13 March 2005, parliamentary elections in Kyrgyzstan took place. In the course of these elections, the amount of the seats in parliament was reduced from 105 to 75. The political mood in the country was already tense before, since the Central Election Commission had not admitted some applicants as candidates. The most prominent example was the former foreign minister, Roza Otunbaeva. Her candidacy was rejected in January with the reason that she had not lived in Kyrgyzstan in the last years. Her candidacy was probably rejected because she wanted to run for office in the same election districts as the daughter of the president, Bermet Akaeva. At meetings, which continued the whole of January and February, several non-governmental organizations and the opposition demanded free and fair elections.

In the first ballot on 27 February, only 31 of the 75 parliamentary seats were distributed, hardly one of the opposition candidates was successful. When it became clear that certain candidates would not get a seat in the parliament, already at this point in time, the population in southern Kyrgyzstan took to the streets to protest. After the second ballot on 13 March, 71 of the 75 parliamentary seats were distributed, five of them to opposition politicians. The population in the south demonstrated further.

A *Kurultai* (public gathering) in Jalal-Abad was organized for 15 March. At this meeting, a national coordination-council was elected; demands for a re-run of the elections and the resignation of Akaev were expressed. The opposition politician and former Prime Minister Kurmanbek Bakiev was one of the most important leading figures of the *Kurultai*. After ten-days of protests, on 18 March, an incensed crowd stormed the building of the provincial administration in Osh and conducted a *Kurultai*, there too, on 21 March. In the three days in between, governmental troops as well as demonstrators tried to capture and re-capture the buildings of the provincial administration respectively. On 20 March, demonstrators finally seized the building of the provincial administration in Jalal-Abad as well as the airport. A day later, demonstrators in Osh took hold of the building of the provincial administration, several police stations and the building of the secret service. Also in the northern provinces of Naryn and Talas more and more people took to the streets to protest. Until today, it is not quite clear whether the protests were organized, nor by whom. However, there is some evidence that influential local personalities supported the protest with financial means and logistics.

---

1   A short chronology of the events between January and March is available at IWPR's website (www.iwpr.org) entitled: Kyrgyzstan's "Tulip Revolution" Timeline. On 4 May 2005, the ICG published the report: Kyrgyzstan. After the Revolution.

On 22 March, the protests encroached on the capital of Bishkek. The arrival of more and more demonstrators from the southern provinces and Naryn gave the event a whole new dimension. While, on 22 March, a pro-governmental demonstration with more than 10,000 participants took place and the new parliament was inaugurated, on the next day, two huge anti-governmental organizations were held and many participants were detained.

Several opposition politicians, among them Bakiev and Otunbaeva, appealed to their followers to come to a big joint demonstration on the morning of 24 March in Bishkek. The protestors marched from two different sides toward the seat of the government in the White House uniting on the Ala Too central square. Later, on that same morning, a large group of protestors from Osh joined the meeting on Ala Too Square and started to attack the White House. Young people already present at the square supported them and together they were able to capture the White House within a very short time. Akaev and other members of the government had already left the building at that time.

The storming of the White House came as a surprise not only for the government, but also for opposition politicians. According to their statements, they had prepared themselves for a longer period of protests and negotiations. Although Bakiev and Feliks Kulov – who was freed from prison by his followers that same day – appealed to the population for collectedness and considerateness, lootings and plundering took place all over the city during the following days and nights. Especially shops belonging to the Akaev family and their political allies were attacked systematically. Only after several days was the interim-government able to establish law and order in Bishkek, at least during the day.

History of events

Kyrgyzstan became an independent nation in August 1991. Already in 1990, Askar Akaev had been named president of the Kyrgyz SSR and had become the international community's great white hope of liberalization and democratization. His reform policy made Kyrgyzstan the first Central Asian state to receive membership in the Word Trade Organization (WTO). Although these were considered political advancements, the Kyrgyz people experienced these reforms as shock therapy: the state – which had permeated all areas of life – suddenly bid farewell to the lives of its citizens. It withdrew the budget for welfare and pension plans and ceased to maintain any kind of welfare net for its people. The social costs for transformation were high; and poverty increased dramatically, especially in the south.

One important reason for this can be attributed to the structure of the Soviet economic system: the goal was not the self-sufficiency of each of the republics, but rather the specialization of certain economic areas. To Kyrgyzstan, this meant, above all, the development of electrical energy and agriculture in the mountainous areas located in the south. The kolkhozes there (collective farms) produced meat for the Soviet market and, in turn, were supplied – in part, directly from Moscow – with all provisions indispensable to life. The one-sided focus of production separated the people from their natural habitat and, as a result, caused them to forget how to live in the mountains independently. After their independence and in the course of economic reform, the factors affecting the mountainous environment suddenly became very acute again: no technology or organization that could cover their needs was available to them. They were forced to (re)learn how to provide for themselves again. Most people had to go through this learning process under unfavourable conditions and without any preparation. Poverty increased dramatically and a negative mood among the people was noticeably increasing. In addition to all of this, in the last years, clans from the north and the west of the country (*Ong*-Wing) have begun to dominate the southern clans (*Sol*-Wing and *Ichkilik*-Wing) with regard to economic and political issues and thus intensified the social differences between both regions. Akaev and his wife, who were both from the north, were able to ensure that their own clientele was provided with posts, while politicians from the south had very little influence in the capital.

In January 2002, when the popular politician from the south, Azimbek Beknazarov, was taken into custody, heavy protests broke out in the region, above all, in his home district Aksy. He was officially accused of abusing his former office as Prosecutor General. In effect, Beknazarov had criticized Akaev's power style time and time again; and he had, in particular, been outspoken against the Kyrgyz-Chinese border accords that would cede 95,000 hectares of Kyrgyz territory to its eastern neighbours. On 17 March, six people were killed when police troops fired at demonstrators in Aksy. The government was dissolved shortly after the former Premier Minister, Kurmanbek Bakiev, took responsibility and stepped down at the end of May 2002. The continuous unrest in the south, borne from the demand for more political participation, led Akaev to hold an uncertain referendum on 2 February 2003 that was to legitimize his claim on power until the end of his office in autumn of 2005. According to official statements, 78 per cent voted for his continuance in office. The OSCE declined to observe the referendum.[2] Although Akaev did not have any political solution, he was still able to secure a new legitimacy for himself and soothe the waters initially. The appearance of stability was, however, elusory and poverty has continued to grow. On the occasion of the city's anniversary in the summer of 2003, while those in the capital celebrated with fireworks and concerts, public service employees in the south were not receiving a salary. In less than two years, the pent-up displeasure would ultimately lead to the storming of the white house and the downfall of Akaev.

---

2   For more information on the referendum see ODIHR 2003.

Different from the change of power in Georgia and in the Ukraine – both had clear symbols and messages and a charismatic opposition leader – in Kyrgyzstan, there was great confusion about the coup d'état, a situation which was symptomatic for the distrust between the population and the opposition, as well as for the discord within the opposition, which broke up into more than 40 different parties. The political vision of the opposition was hardly known and its democratic reflections more than questionable. The opposition was more concerned with a change of power among the elite than with a real regime change.

Prominent opposition leaders such as Kurmanbek Bakiev und Rosa Otunbaeva took advantage of the population's displeasure and positioned themselves at the head of the protests in the south. Although both, and later also Felix Kulov, were presented in the international media as the new opposition leader, they were not unknown in their country; for a long time, they had belonged to the leadership of the country and, for a while, were very close to president Akaev. Bakiev, born in 1949 in the southern province of Jalal-Abad, was governor of the northern province of Chui and, from December 2000 until May 2002, prime minister. Because of the demonstrations in the southern Kyrgyz settlement of Aksy, where the militia shot seven civilians in 2002, Bakiev was forced to step down from his office. Bakiev is the leader of the "Peoples Movement of Kyrgyzstan", an electoral alliance comprised of nine parties. Kulov, born in 1948 in the northern city of Frunse (today Bishkek), was, among others, minister of interior, vice president and mayor of Bishkek. In March 2000, he was arrested, and in January 2001 was sentenced to 7 years of imprisonment on charges of abuse of office in order to prevent him from becoming a candidate in the presidential elections. Kulov has been the party leader of Ar-Namys since 1998. On 24 March 2005, he was freed from prison by his supporters and, in the mean time, has been rehabilitated by the court. Otunbaeva, born in 1950 in southern Osh, was, already under Akaev's rule, foreign minister of Kyrgyzstan and worked as ambassador in the US, Canada and Great Britain.

After having speculated for some time whether Bakiev or Kulov had any chances of running in the presidential elections and which one would be able to unite the north as well as the south, both candidates declared on 13 May that Kulov would not run in the elections, that instead he would be joining Bakievs electoral campaign team. Since then, Bakiev's victory in the elections has been considered more or less an arrangement – both by the population as well as by international observers.

Election campaign and security situation

When the official election campaign for the presidential election started on 14 June 2005, it was clearly dominated by Bakiev. Already one day after the Central Election Commission (CEC) had announced the registration of seven candidates – among them one woman – Bishkek was covered with billboards and flyers showing his portrait with slogans saying, "The future of our country is based on work and unity".

Especially the latter issue is of importance to the population. After the uprising in spring, the differences between the north and the south surfaced once more. Since then, the fragile security situation has made the population feel insecure, and international analysts are of the opinion that the state monopoly on the use of force is disintegrating and power is being relocated to the regional and local level. At these levels, politicians conducting non-transparent businesses dominate daily life and are fighting for the division of the political and economic vacuum that Akaev and his family left after they fled the country. During the weeks following the overturn of the government, violence and shootings resulted in many casualties and several dead persons. For instance, in the beginning of June, parliamentarian Jyralbek Surabaldiev was shot in Bishkek in broad daylight. In addition to his political activities, he was the owner of a market for second hand cars near Bishkek. Only last year, he strove vigorously to take this market from another person. Several days later, followers and opponents of another parliamentarian, Bayaman Erkinbaev, shot each other in Osh. One person died. Erkinbaev controls several markets in southern Kyrgyzstan, for example, the one in Kara-Suu at the Uzbek border.[3] During this same period of time, the election office of Bakiev in Bishkek was attacked and two guards were injured.

The violent incidents have not ceased. On 17 June, Urmat Baryktabasov, chairman of the movement "New Generation – Mekenim Kyrgyzstans" and his followers stormed the seat of the government in Bishkek again. His candidacy for the presidential elections had been refused by the CEC, because he has been holding Kazakh citizenship since 2002. It seems that the once summoned spirits cannot be quieted down anymore. Demonstrations, sit-ins and the storming of buildings have become routine in Kyrgyzstan since the end of March.

International organizations feared such a development and therefore have prepared a kind of written declaration of self-commitment on behalf of the candidates to be signed before elections. With their signature, they commit themselves to behave according to international standards and to the law, to keep their followers under control and to avoid any form of provocation and violence during the election campaign. The OSCE and UNDP invited the candidates to the noblest hotel of the capital, but only three of the seven candidates signed this "gentleman's agreement".

Further conflict potential in connection with the elections and the future unity of the country lies in the ethnic tensions embedded in southern Kyrgyzstan. In the provinces of Osh and Jalal-Abad, one quarter of the total population are Uzbeks. They are extremely anxious about the question of how their

---

3 Erkinbaev was shot dead on 21 September 2005 in Bishkek. He is the second member of parliament to be killed since March 2005.

interest will be represented in the future. No one has forgotten the bloody clashes between the Kyrgyzs and Uzbeks that took place in Osh and Uzgen in June 1990, when 300 persons lost their lives. One of the reasons for the outbreak of violence was tied to the demand to make Uzbek an official language in Kyrgyzstan. The Uzbek community knows of Bakiev; at least that he was born near Jalal-Abad and is thus familiar with life in the south, and that he has first hand experience with the co-existence of Kyrgyzs, Uzbeks and other ethnic groups. Furthermore, because of his Russian wife, he has a reputation for being an internationalist.

The increasing instability has led to the situation where the population wants peace and stability more than anything else. Many are afraid that their small-scale businesses will be destroyed or will collapse. In June 2005, many shops had slogans on their windows, such as "We are with the people" or "This shop is guarded by the people's patrol". Yet, it is questionable whether such measures will prevent looting in the case of new riots.

One of the candidates for the presidential elections seemed to also be worried about stability. On 23 June, the businessman and former governor of Jalal-Abad announced the resignation from his candidacy. According to him, a tandem made up of Bakiev as future president and Felix Kulov as future prime minister would be best to re-establish law and order in the country.

Whether the security situation will really stabilize in the time coming is not quite clear yet. We should probably prepare for a time without proper state control in Kyrgyzstan. The state may possibly remain as a façade without a core, and the real power will be relocated to the regional level. The state would loose its monopoly on the use of force on local patrons, for instance, on influential businessmen. Power would be personalized and the rule of law set aside.

Uzbekistan

Development of events

Up until now, the events that occurred in Andijan on the eve of 12 May 2005 have not been clearly understood. Various sources document that, on that night, the Uzbek secret service arrested relatives of a group of businessmen, who had participated in a protest in front of the court. It has also been repeatedly reported that an armed group attacked and seized a local police station and later a barrack, and that weapons stocked there were looted. Likewise, it has also been reported that, on that same night, some 50 to 100 armed men stormed into the jail in Andijan and freed 600 inmates. It is, however, unclear whether the same people carried out both raids. In addition, it is not yet known how the armed group(s) came together, nor whether family members of the accused businessmen were involved.

What is relatively certain, however, is that the armed men, who released the inmates, were informed about a protest that would take place on Babur-Place, the city's centre square. Thereafter, many of those released joined the group of armed men and headed toward the centre square and the local government building (*hokimiyat*). On the way there, an exchange of fire occurred involving the secret service building; 30 people are believed to have been killed. It is not clear whether the building was stormed in order to release the detained protesters, or whether the secret service first opened fire in order to stop the group from marching into the *hokimiyat*.

Come the break of dawn on Friday 13 May, more and more people – who had heard about the events or who had been mobilized – had begun to gather themselves on the Babur-Place in front of the *hokimiyat*. According to witnesses, on that day, some 5,000 civilians filled the square. The armed group had surrounded and occupied the *hokimiyat*. By the end of the day, they had taken about 30 hostage, among them the prosecutor general and the director of tax inspections. The people on the square used this opportunity to express their discontent with the situation in Andijan – high unemployment, lack of social security, excessive corruption of the local authorities and social repression – on a quickly improvised stage equipped with loud speakers. According to concurring statements, the armed group telephoned twice with the Uzbek Minister of Interior, Zokir Almatov, who refused to accept any negotiations. Around 4 o'clock in the afternoon, the government began with preparations to storm the *hokimiyat*. Although government troops kept firing at the people gathered at the square throughout the day – reports vary between 50 and 100 deaths – many persevered and remained on the square.

Eyewitnesses say that the main reason for their persistence was hope; the hope that President Karimov would show up in person and listen to their worries. Between 5 and 6 o'clock in the afternoon, the government troops began to attack and fire – from all sides – at the people gathered on the square from armoured track vehicles, lorries and military jeeps on which cannonry had been installed. This led to a mass panic. Two larger groups, each of which had taken hostages, fled from the square to one of the main streets (Cholpon Prospect). This resulted in a massacre in which about a hundred people – among them many women, children and youths – lost their lives. They were fired at from the doorway of homes, from rooftops and from behind barricades, where they had positioned themselves to shoot at their target mercilessly. Some survivors journeyed to the Kyrgyz border in a ten-hour march during the night only to encounter renewed firing. They were first able to cross the border after further negotiations. A camp was set up for the 500 refugees directly on the border; in early June it was moved inland to the Kyrgyz province of Jalal-Abad. In late July, all but fifteen of the asylum-seekers were evacuated to Romania. Another eleven were evacuated to Great Britain in mid-September

Background of events

The catalyst for the events in Andijan was the legal proceeding against 23 businessmen – entrepreneurs and trades people – that took place on 10 February of this year before the criminal court in Andijan. The defendants were accused of being members of a group called *Akromiya* and of preparing to overthrow the government. The name of this group – its existence and goals are highly speculative – has been traced to its alleged founder, Akrom Yuldoshev. In 1992, he composed a small booklet entitled "The Path to Faith" wherein he lays down his ideas about how to lead a life according to God. In the book, he also deals with questions pertaining to business life and the social responsibility of companies. In 1998, Yuldoshev was briefly imprisoned, sentenced and then granted amnesty; in 1999 – after the explosions in February in Tashkent – he was arrested again and sentenced to 17 years. The charges were described as follows: 1. Deliberate alteration of the constitution in an anti-constitutional way, public appeal to take over power; 2. Formation and leadership of criminal coalitions; 3. Deliberate preparation of information and materials that propagate religious extremism and fundamentalism.

From the very beginning, the process against the 23 businessmen in Andijan was accompanied by demonstrations. Family members, workers and neighbours gathered together in silence day after day before the courthouse. In interviews that were conducted in March and April, demonstrators explained that, with their silent protest, they were calling for justice for the defendants and that they did not believe the extremist group *Akromiya* existed. In fact, they were rather convinced that the business people had been accused, because they were successful and socially engaged. On 12 May, on the last day of the proceedings, over 2000 people gathered in front of the courthouse. The hearing for the proclamation of sentence was scheduled for 12 May; however, on this day it was postponed to an indefinite date. Furthermore, the protestors learned of the imprisonment of several young men who had participated in the demonstrations.

The extent of the blood bath in Andijan is shocking, yet the event itself did not come as a surprise and will probably not remain an isolated case. Andijan is the preliminary and tragic culmination of a socio-economic and political development that has grown more and more acute during the last years. The authoritarian president, Islam Karimov, former First Secretary to the Communist Party of the Uzbek Soviet Socialist Republic, rules the country with an iron fist. His position within the power apparatus is very dominant. Those human rights and freedoms proclaimed in the Constitution of 8 December 1992, such as the freedom of speech, freedom of assembly and the freedom of religion as well as political pluralism are not realized and are viewed as threats to the stability and internal security of the country. Political opponents of every kind are persecuted. In prisons, they are systematically tortured. Parliament is weak, and its members are exclusively from parties loyal to the government and the administration. The few opposition groups and movements that are not in parliament quarrel amongst themselves, and parts of their leadership are in exile.

Because of the forced political conformity of the secular parties in parliament and the fragmentation of the secular oppositional movements, most of the present-day opposition in Uzbekistan consists of illegal Islamist groups, such as the *Hizb-ut-Tahrir*. Sympathy for such organizations is not solely based on religious beliefs. Rather, concepts like the establishment of a Caliphate, in which lasting social problems, poverty and corruption are solved through the Islamic judicature, are very attractive and convincing in a state that hardly leaves its citizens with air to breathe. As shown in various interviews with members of the *Hizb-ut-Tahrir*, many young people see the organization as the only opportunity to make their views known politically and to voice their discontentment with the social conditions and the regime of Islam Karimov. The government keeps portraying both the *Hizb-ut-Tahrir* and other Islam(ist)ic groups as a bogey and symbol of Islamist terrorism and thus legitimizes its policies of repression by referring to the "conditions" in Tajikistan and Afghanistan.

Especially in the traditionally religious Ferghana Valley, the population began to suffer from such policies already in the 1990s. For instance, after the killing of several members of the police forces, the government blamed "Wahabist terrorists" and started a wave of arrests in 1997/1998 in Namangan and Andijan, where between 1,000 and 1,500 people were arrested. Another wave of arrests started following the Tashkent bomb attacks of 16 February 1999 aimed at the Uzbek president. On that day, six bombs went off killing 15 people and damaging several buildings. By 23 February, 30 people had been imprisoned after Karimov claimed that they all belonged to extremist religious groupings. Up until the beginning of March, between 200 and 500 more people shared the same fate. In June of 1999, 22 persons were accused of being connected to the attack, and following a mock trial, six of them were sentenced to death. The others were given prison sentences of up to ten to 20 years; none of them was acquitted. Furthermore, hundreds of people were arrested after distributing flyers in support of the accused at Tashkent markets and other public places.

In Uzbekistan, a total of several thousand were apprehended and detained because of their religious or political beliefs during the last years. Many of these are in the infamous forced-labour camp, *Jaslyk*, which has been set up by the Uzbek government in the desert southwest of the Aral Sea. The families only seldom receive news of the whereabouts of their relatives. Coffins are sent back nailed shut in order to hide the traces of torture. More and more often, people, most of them women, are demonstrating against the despotism of the government and the administration, and thereby risking persecution and violence.

The arbitrariness of the Uzbek government and the public authorities is not directed exclusively against religious and allegedly religious groups and individuals. Traders and small businesses also suffer from the lack of any kind of rule of law and the day-to-day abuses by the police. For example, the 2002 introduction of severe import restrictions meant forcing the population to only buy domestically produced goods. In October 2003 the government decided that small merchants should only be allowed to continue their sales in registered kiosks and shops, and that they were to use cash registers. These and other measures have ruined the standard of living of many merchants and their families. The rigorousness with which the police and the tax inspectors are enforcing the regulations and the sale of confiscated goods have led to more and more hatred and animosity, which more than once has led to strikes and protests of merchants and traders. Nearly comparable to hunger riots, the demonstrations at the beginning of November 2004 – where 5,000 and 10,000 people protested in Kokand only – show how dissatisfied the people are with the situation. Thus, the protests can be seen as symptomatic of the declining living standards in Uzbekistan, where many families only live from hand to mouth.

International reactions

The events in Andijan have attracted worldwide attention – at least in the short-term. At the same time, the access to information, to the town and to eyewitnesses was and is the most crucial problem with regard to reporting and analysing the events. In Uzbekistan, the most important websites, which were reporting on the events, have been blocked since 13 May. Regular television broadcasts no Russian news; cable television has been switched off completely. Only over satellite are all news stations available. In this way, the flow of information among the population has been stopped.
At the time of the demonstrations, a few journalists were in town, mostly waiting for the court decision in the trial against the 23 businessmen. In the meantime, the Uzbek government established a dense net of roadblocks on the road to the Ferghana Valley, as well as in and around Andijan and, in doing so, hindered journalists as well as representatives of international organizations to enter the town. Thus, many articles and analyses are based on interviews with refugees in neighbouring Kyrgyzstan.
The International Crisis Group (ICG) published the first report entitled "Uzbekistan: The Andijan Uprising" (20 pages) on 25 May. Human Rights Watch (HRW) followed with a 60-page report "Bullets were falling like rain" on 3 June. The Office for Democratic Institutions and Human Rights launched a 30-page report on the "Preliminary findings on the events in Andijan, Uzbekistan, 13 May 2005" on 20 June, and the Office of the High Commissioner for Human Rights published a "Report of the Mission to Kyrgyzstan by the Office of the High Commissioner for Human Rights

(OHCHR) Concerning the Killings in Andijan" on 12 July.[4] All four reports conclude that the government used indiscriminate and disproportional force against unarmed civilians and that the number of dead persons seems to be higher than stated by officials in Tashkent. In addition, all four organizations strongly recommend the establishment of an independent international investigation.

Shirin Akiner of the School of Oriental and African Studies (SOAS) in London has a completely different opinion: At the end of May, she travelled for one day to Andijan and – according to her own statements – she was able to talk to about 40 persons without any problem. On 29 May, back in Tashkent, she gave an interview on Uzbek state TV and published a 30-page report on 7 June titled "Violence in Andijan". Both the interview and the report coincide with the picture the Uzbek government has drawn of the events and, consequently, are used by the government for its own purposes. In the report, Akiner – who is working as an independent consultant for NATO and the FAST Programme of Swisspeace – underlines several times her attempts to report objectively and according to academic standards. At the same time, she does not take into account the ICG and HRW reports already published at that time, but condemns "sensationalist media reports" in general. If we take into account the immense pressure the Uzbek government has put on the inhabitants of Andijan since the event, and the fact that Akiner was accompanied by the governor of the province of Andijan, it seems evident that one should question the reliability of Akiner's sources.

On the inter-state level many governments expressed their concerns. In addition, international organizations such as the United Nations, the Organization for Security and Co-operation in Europe and the European Union commented on the events.

On 20 May 2005, the OSCE chairman in Office, Dimitrij Rupel, published a statement on the situation in Andijan and called the OSCE participating State Uzbekistan to allow an independent investigation into the events of 13 May. Simultaneously, he announced that the OSCE would work together closely in this affair with the United Nations and the European Union. Already, just a day before, on 19 May, the Luxemburg EU-chairmanship had issued a statement in the parliamentary assembly of the OSCE, in which the EU member states argued for an independent, international investigation and demanded unhindered access to Andijan for the representatives of the International Red Cross and the United Nations High Commissioner for Refugees (UNHCR). In a press statement on 23 May, the European Council voiced its support for the demands of the OSCE and the United Nations for a thorough clarification of the events. The NATO Council issued a press statement on 24 May condemning the "use of excessive and disproportionate force by the Uzbek security forces" and expressing its support for the United Nation's call for an

---

4   On 20 September 2005, Amnesty International as well as Human Rights Watch published new reports about the events and the aftermath.

independent international investigation. Simultaneously, Uzbekistan was reminded of its commitments in joining the NATO's Partnership for Peace Programme. On that same day, the United States government threatened to not pay Karimov financial support in the amount of 22 million USD, if no independent investigation of the incidents takes place. At the meeting of the EU foreign ministers on 13 June in Luxemburg, it was announced that the EU would discuss sanctions against Uzbekistan, should Karimov not allow an international investigation in the country.[5]

Whether the appeals and the announced pressure by the international community will have any effect on the government in Tashkent is doubtful for several reasons. On the one hand, up until now and especially after September 11, Karimov has been very successful in declaring his domestic problems with religious groups as anti-terror measures and, in doing so, has gained understanding and support from Western governments. Uzbekistan was the first state in Central Asia who became a member of the anti-terror coalition. Sanctions against Uzbekistan would possibly have the consequence that, among other things, the US and Germany would have to give up their military bases in the south of the country. On the other hand, Karimov does not depend on Western states – neither for his political legitimization nor for financial support. The great powers, Russia and China, support the attitude of Karimov and his thesis of Islamist terror without any reservations, as well as its neighbouring Kazakhstan, Kyrgyzstan and Tajikistan. Ten days after the events in Andijan, Karimov visited China. On the eve of his arrival, the Chinese Foreign Ministry announced that China supports Karimov's fight against "separatists, terrorists and extremists" wholeheartedly. At a meeting in June in Moscow, Karimov and the Russian president Putin discussed issues such as the international fight against terror and closer economic and military co-operation between both countries.

Future prospects

The events in Kyrgyzstan and Uzbekistan underline the effects of the lack of rule of law on the domestic level as well as the foreign security situation of both countries. President Karimov is only adding fuel to the flames by upholding his measures of repression. The pressure will keep on growing in the area with more and more minor bursts until one day the whole situation explodes into chaos and mayhem.

The Kyrgyz city Osh, one of the two places where the protests in Southern Kyrgyzstan began, is only 30 kilometres away from the Uzbek city of Andijan. In March, the population in the Uzbek side of the Ferghana Valley received an interesting lecture on what happens when people lay claim to the

---

5   They finally decided to impose sanctions on Uzbekistan on 3 October 2005 (see below).

street. They also had the opportunity to see that neither the administration, nor the police or the president are almighty. Yet, they were not aware of the fact that unless Akaev, Karimov was willing to use excessive and indiscriminate force against peaceful protestors.

Both countries are characterized by a fragile security situation for the coming period. In Kyrgyzstan, president Bakiev must re-gain the state monopoly one the use of force and guarantee stability at all levels and in all regions. In Uzbekistan, president Karimov wants to maintain power and is therefore looking for support from the two regional neighbours Russia and China. The sanctions of the EU[6] as well as the possible starting of the Moscow-mechanism by the OSCE will probably have no influence on the regime in Uzbekistan. In neighbouring Turkmenistan, president Sapamurat Niyazov has shown in the last years only too well that domestic power maintenance can also be realized without international co-operation if one disposes of sufficient resources. In Uzbekistan, the attempts to condition Western support are likely to be counterweighted by unconditional support from Russia and China. In addition, one should pay special attention to the fact that any attempts to isolate Uzbekistan politically and economically may lead the population to feel abandoned by the international community and to start to trust in promises of any kind from extremist groups.

International organizations should work toward implementing national laws and regulations at the local level. Only when the rule of law is guaranteed will the population start to believe in abstract concepts like democracy and their own right of participation in the political and economic system. Until this happens, their only option is to counter the abuse from above with illegal activities from below.

Bibliography

Akiner, Shirin. 2005. *Violence in Andijan, 13 May 2005: An Independent Assessment*. Washington/Uppsala. (online available at www.silkroadstudies.org).
Amnesty International. 2005. *Uzbekistan. Lifting the siege on the truth about Andizhan*. London. (online available at www.amnesty.org).
Human Rights Watch. 2005a. *Bullets were falling like rain. The Andijan Massacre, May 13, 2005*. New York. (online available at www.hrw.org).
Human Rights Watch.2005b. *Burying the Truth. Uzbekistan Rewrites the Story of the Andijan Massacre*. New York. (online available at www.hrw.org).
International Crisis Group. 2005. *Kyrgyzstan. After the Revolution*. Brussels, 4 May. (online available at www.crisiseb.org).
International Crisis Group. 2005 Uzbekistan. The Andijon Uprising. Brussels, 25 May. (online available at www.crisisweb.org).
ODIHR. 2003. *Kyrgyz Republic Constitutional Referendum 2 February 2003. Political Assessment Report*. Warsaw, 20 March. (online available at: www.osce.org/odihr/documents/reports/election_reports/kg).

---

6   The sanctions of the EU Council include visa bans for high-ranking officials involved in the massacre in Andijan and an arms embargo. In addition, EU aid programmes will be cut. The sanctions were decided on 3 October 2005.

ODIHR. 2005. *Preliminary Findings on the Events in Andijan, Uzbekistan, 13 May 2005.* Warsaw 20 June. (online available at www.osce.org/documents/odihr/2005/06/15233_en.pdf)
Office of the High Commissioner for Human Rights. 2005. Report of the Mission to Kyrgyzstan by the Office of the High Commissioner for Human Rights (OHCHR) Concerning the Killings in Andijan, Uzbekistan, 13-13 May 2005.

Anna Kreikemeyer

Instability in the Ferghana Valley: International Reactions

After the end of the civil war in Tajikistan (1992-1997), political change in Central Asia developed relatively peacefully. From time to time, speculations arose concerning stability in the Ferghana Valley. Scenarios were mostly related to violent clashes in the artificially separated, economically poor, densely populated and multi-ethnic region. Since the incursions of armed groups in South Kyrgyzstan in 1999 and 2000, threat perceptions have focussed on terrorism. Beyond this, the "coloured revolutions" in Georgia and Ukraine have raised the question of possible spillover effects into Central Asian states, where the issue of power change was on the agenda as well. Nevertheless, most observers were surprised about the sudden destabilizing events that took place in the heart of the Ferghana Valley in spring 2005. Both had their origin in popular discontent with the respective government, but they were solved by different means.[1]

After the parliamentary elections in Kyrgyzstan (27 February/13 March 2005), demonstrations in the southern part of the country spread to the capital and finally led to the ouster of president Askar Akayev on 24 March 2005. After a critical interim period, Kurmanbek Bakiyev, the former prime minister, who is from the south, was elected president in a legal and peaceful way on 10 July. Not far from the uprising in the Kyrgyz part of the Ferghana Valley, violence broke out on the Uzbek side. On the occasion of the trial against the 23 businessmen in May 2005, people gathered for a mass protest in the city of Andijan in the Uzbek part of the Ferghana Valley. President Islam Karimov gave orders to subdue the uprising. In the subsequent massacre, several hundred people, among them many women and children, were killed. More than 500 hundred participants of the demonstration fled to the neighbouring Kyrgyzstan.[2] While, in Kyrgyzstan, the new regime had difficulties in holding the state monopoly of power, in Uzbekistan, the old regime tried to keep the populace silent by implementing strong repressive measures. Thus, it can no longer be denied that the Ferghana Valley is destabilizing.

The focus of this article is on international reactions to this stability crisis in the Ferghana Valley. The key questions tackled here are the following: What are the reactions of neighbouring states, hegemonic powers, multilateral and

---

1 In case no other reference is made, information on the political development in general is taken from different news lines reporting on Central Asia. See the bibliography at the end of this article.
2 For more details on this event see the article by Berg in part IV of this volume as well as reports by the International Crisis Group 2005, Human Rights Watch 2005 and ODIHR 2005.

donor organizations as well as that of non-governmental organizations? What can we learn from their behaviour in this Central Asian crisis? What will be the consequences for future stability in this region?

My neighbour, my brother?

From the point of view of the Central Asian regimes, most of whom have friendship treaties,[3] common interests lie in good neighbourly relations that enable, first of all, the prevention of terrorism, of border conflicts, free trade and the management of water and energy flows. Co-operation in these policy fields is far from easy and much of the outcome depends on personal relations between presidents, regional leaders or businessmen.

In the neighbouring governments' reactions to the uprising in South Kyrgyzstan and to the power change in Bishkek, we can observe a common response. The presidents of the states bordering Kyrgyzstan quickly closed their borders, as they feared the scenario of a "coloured revolution". However, as soon as it became clear that the Kyrgyz interim government had gained control, they quickly recognized the new leadership, re-established good relations, welcomed first visits of the new government and offered economic co-operation. Of special interest was the reaction of Uzbekistan. Probably due to the large ethnic Uzbek population in neighbouring Kyrgyzstan, President Karimov most quickly established contacts, declared non-interference and sent humanitarian aid in order to help stabilize the situation. After an initial demonstration that he, of course, had preferred the previous regime, Kazakh president Nazarbayev showed his benevolence by lending economic support to Akaev's successor as well. His behaviour can be explained by the fact that Kazakhs and Kyrgyz perceive themselves as brotherly nations. With regard to a possible spillover of the Kyrgyz protest into other regions, both the Kazakh and the Tajik government quickly put more pressure on human rights activists. The Turkmen president did not react at all, but tried to hinder any information flow into the population and even closed the last interregional flight to Almaty.

Similar perceptions in the neighbouring countries' reactions to the events in Andijan can be observed. The Central Asian presidents instrumentalize "terrorist threats", when they are afraid that their power is being weakened. On 14 May 2005, even the Kyrgyz interim president, Bakiev, spoke of militant Islamists being responsible for the uprising in Andijan; and Tajik president Emomali Rakhmonov demanded that solidarity be shown with the common

---

3   Kazakhstan concluded friendship treaties with Tajikistan (13 January 1993), Turkmenistan (19 May 1993), Uzbekistan (24 June 2002) and Kyrgyzstan (26 December 2003), Uzbekistan with Kyrgyzstan (29 September 1992), Turkmenistan (16 January 1996) and Tajikistan (15 June 2000). On 10 January 1997, Kazakhstan, Kyrgyzstan and Uzbekistan signed a Permanent Friendship Treaty. See online http://www.atop.rice.edu/download/ATOPcand.pdf.

fight against terrorism by deploying rapid reaction troops. Due to the fact that ethnic Uzbek minorities inhabit Kyrgyzstan as well as Tajikistan, the governments of both countries have felt vulnerable to upheavals and the influx of refugees coming from Uzbekistan. The Kazakhs responded in a hesitant manner as its relationship to its southern neighbour had already been tense due to border disputes and the Uzbek reproach that terrorists were operating in Kazakh territory. Ongoing talks about a free trade zone were thus interrupted. Turkmenistan again did not keep the public informed about the events and made travelling to Uzbekistan difficult.

Due to the armed incursions in 1999/2000, time and time again, Kyrgyzstan had to hear from its neighbour that the terrorists operating in Uzbekistan come from the Kyrgyz territory. Furthermore, the new Kyrgyz government had to deal with the grave implications of the refugee crisis in the aftermath of the Uzbek crackdown in Andijan. On the one hand, Bishkek had an interest in good neighbourly relations with Tashkent, with whom it still had to solve territorial disputes, border demarcation, trade and customs problems, and from whom it receives the lion's share of its natural gas. On the other hand, shortly after the revolution, the interim government was confronted with strong pressure from the international community to not extradite the refugees from Andijan who had fled to Kyrgyzstan. A great number of them had already been stopped at the frontier by Kyrgyz border troops; a smaller number had been sent back to Uzbekistan between May and June 2005 by the Kyrgyz secret service. It was only after intense negotiations and high-level international pressure that, on 29 July 2005, 439 refugees could finally depart to third countries. On 16 September 2005, eleven remaining refugees, whom Tashkent had accused of having committed grave crimes and having escaped from the prison in Andijan, were airlifted to London by the Office of the UN High Commissioner for Refugees; four refugees remain in detention in Osh waiting out legal proceedings in Kyrgyzstan. This refugee policy, according to international standards, quickly led to Uzbek allegations that the terrorists, who were allegedly responsible for the outbreak of violence in Andijan, were trained in neighbouring Kyrgyzstan.

Competing hegemonies

What appeared at the horizon after the dissolution of the former Soviet Union first became clearly visible in Central Asia after September 11, 2001: in Central Asia, three hegemonic powers have since then been competing for influence.

The last bastion of Soviet power: Russia in Central Asia

Compared to relations with other former Soviet republics, Moscow's ties with the Central Asian regimes have remained more or less stable, both on the bilateral and on the multilateral level in the framework of the Commonwealth of Independent States (CIS). Relations are characterized by the growing importance of security relevant issues and energy economics. Furthermore, Russian policy towards the Central Asian region is influenced by a certain competition with the United States and by its rapprochement with China. As Moscow does not directly object to US military or economic activities in the region, it seems premature to talk about new "cold wars" and "great games". There are Russian experts as well who have expressed an interest in international partners helping stabilize the Central Asian region. However, the United States, Russia and China hold divergent assessments of the trends of democratization and possible "coloured revolutions".[4] Due to similar governance structures, the Russian and the Central Asian regimes share an interest in the stability of a more or less authoritarian power, which controls the transition of national economies and rejects interference into internal affairs. Thus, politically speaking, the regimes do not have to fear each other. To a greater or lower extent, they also share the strategic interest of preventing Islamist "extremism", be it in Chechnya, in the North Caucasus, in the Ferghana Valley or in Almaty.

Moscow has strategic partnership treaties with all Central Asian republics, except Turkmenistan. In addition to this, it is linked to its neighbours in the south through various treaties within the framework of the CIS (see below). Kazakhstan still seems to be the most stable neighbour for Moscow. On 18 January 2005, a border treaty for the longest international land frontier in the world (7,591 kilometres) was signed. The treaty can be seen as a formal renunciation of claims to the territories of Northern Kazakhstan, where many ethnic Russians live; but it can also be perceived as being related to the fear that Uzbek and Tajik drug traffickers and illegal migrants would enter Russia via Kazakhstan.[5] Nevertheless, Moscow is becoming increasingly concerned about Astana's intensifying pro-Western orientation in the energy and military sphere. While Russia is interested in production-sharing agreements and joint ventures, Kazakhstan is striving for an increased share in the Caspian Pipeline Consortium and is oriented towards laying pipelines on the Caspian seabed and opening it up to Western markets. That Kazakhstan's plans have been met with Russian disapproval can be explained by Russia's anger at

---

4   For the Russian Security Council Secretary Igor Ivanov, the political changes in Ukraine, Georgia, and Kyrgyzstan are "coups" (Russian: *perevoroty*) in which power changed hands in "unconstitutional" ways, with "violations of basic democratic principles". *Strategiya Rossii*, cited by Interfax, May 5, 2005. See also Torbakov 2005b.
5   The treaty is available at http://www.ln.mid.ru/nsrsngnsf/6bc38aceada6e44b432569e700419ef5/272e1fa8f21aae44c3256e4500537887?OpenDocument; see also Yermukanov 2005.

Kazakhstan for having built-up naval bases in the Caspian Sea and its intensified co-operation with the United States, Britain, Spain, Turkey and NATO. Kazakhstan also does not participate in the CIS joint air-defence exercises, nor does it support Russian plans for a joint naval force of the five Caspian bordering states.

As Turkmenistan president Saparmurat Nijazov regularly reassures the neutrality of his state, Russia does not need to fear a pro-Western security orientation. Moscow's traditional provider of natural gas has a 25-year treaty until 2028 to provide its neighbour with gas below world market prices and is still forced to make use of the existing ex-Soviet pipeline system through Russia. Nevertheless, as Russian Foreign Minister Lavrov's visit with Turkmenistan president Nijazov in October 2005 in Ashgabad illustrates, Moscow has to reassure its relationship with Turkmenistan by strategically beginning competition with the US, the Ukraine and Afghanistan-Pakistan in the energy field.

Despite an increasing number of visits from US ministers in the summer and autumn of 2005, this trend cannot be observed in Tajikistan, where especially military relations with Moscow are traditionally strong. While Tajik border protection is now finally under Tajik jurisdiction, Russia's 201st Motorized Infantry Division, which had been deployed in Tajikistan since the break-up of the Soviet Union, gained de jure status of a military base in September 2005.[6] For its part, Moscow had pressured Tajikistan on this issue by withholding an agreement on the legal status of Tajik labour migrants in Russia, whose remittances are critical to Tajikistan's economy.

Moscow's reaction to the regime change in Kyrgyzstan was to make quite clear that it would remain flexible as long as its basic interests were observed. By participating in the CIS election observation mission to the Kyrgyz parliamentary elections in February 2005, Moscow tried to demonstrate its support to the Akaev government, but it refused to intervene in favour of Akaev as soon as the strength of the successor became obvious. Like its regional neighbours, it quickly adjusted to the new circumstances as it became clear that the new regime was interested in good military relations with Moscow and the CIS. The new regime in Bishkek soon expressed that it wanted to keep the Russian air force base in Kant,[7] located 30 kilometres from the capital; and that it was interested in another Russian base in Osh, which was under the auspices of the Collective Security Treaty Organization (CSTO).

Contrary to centrifugal tendencies, between 1995 and 2003, Moscow's relations with Uzbekistan had already gained in intensity before the events in Andijan took place. In 2004, a strategic partnership treaty[8] was signed at the

---

6   The treaty is available at http://www.ln.mid.ru/nsrsng.nsf/6bc38aceada6e44b43256 9e700419ef5/432569d800221466c3257029002545f5?OpenDocument .
7   For more on the Kant Air Base see http://www.ln.mid.ru/nsrsng.nsf/6bc38aceada 6e44b4325 69e700419ef5/432569d80022146643256dc900313eb7?OpenDocument. ICG 2005: 19.
8   The treaty is available online at http://www.ln.mid.ru/nsrsng.nsf/6bc38aceada6e44b43 2569e700419ef5/432569d800221466c3256eb600317a9f?OpenDocument.

Shanghai Co-operation Organization's (SCO) summit in Tashkent. Within this framework, Russia upgraded its air defence facilities in Uzbekistan, modernized outdated Uzbek military equipment and supplied increased access to its military educational establishments for the training of Uzbek servicemen. Both sides granted each other the right to deploy military forces. In September 2005, for the first time since 1991, Uzbekistan hosted a joint military exercise with Russian troops that rehearsed an operation to destroy a terrorist detachment. After leaving the CIS Collective Security Treaty in 1999, Tashkent applied for membership in the Russian-dominated CSTO. In the energy economy, *Gazprom* and *Uzbekneftegaz* concluded a production sharing agreement on the Shakhpakty oilfield in April 2004; *Lukoil* and *Uzbekneftegaz* agreed on a production-sharing venture related to the Kandym oilfield. During the Andijan crisis, Karimov made use of the Kremlin's political interests. Furthermore, Moscow quickly echoed Uzbekistan's view of being a victim of extremism, and that its reactions to the demonstrations had to be accepted as an internal affair.[9]

Strong interests and principles: the United States in Central Asia

Contrary to Moscow, Washington's relations to the Central Asian republics were originally supposed to develop along the lines of US-American energy policy. Only after September 11, 2001 did relations intensify in the framework of the "Alliance against Terrorism". While economic interest remained, security policy became a main concern. The emphasis was rather put on air bases for the logistic support of US forces in Afghanistan; and common efforts for the fight against terrorism were undertaken as well. In its relationship toward other hegemons, Washington seems more concerned with its long-term strategic antagonism toward China than toward Russia. Contrary to Russia or China, domestic decision-making in the US is much more influenced by conflicting political, strategic and economic interests of different actors. While support for human rights, free elections and liberal economy is common sense, the US government is often divided on which security interests should gain priority. In the case of the Andijan events, this conflict can be observed very well .

It was already in the beginning of 2000 that Uzbekistan had been chosen as a key partner in the "Central Asian Border Security Initiative" when then-Secretary of State Madeleine Albright first visited Tashkent in April 2000.[10] In the aftermath of the September 11, 2001 terrorist attacks, bilateral relations intensified. Uzbekistan quickly became a member in the "Alliance against Terrorism" by allowing the use of its military airport and by offering an air

---

9 See Bigg 2005, Socor 2005d.
10 For more on the US Central Asia Border Security Initiative see http://www.eurasianet.org/departments/insight/articles/eav022201.shtml.

base in Karshi-Khanabad.[11] In 2002, the US and the Uzbek government concluded a strategic partnership agreement. Since then, Washington has shared intelligence on Islamist militants with Tashkent and has helped train and equip Uzbek forces.[12]

The Andijan events made manifest the conflict between political and strategic interests in the US government. While the State Department joined the Pentagon in the assessment that members of the Islamic Movement of Uzbekistan – designated a terrorist group by the US – may have been freed during the jailbreak, a controversy on the question of military support for the Karimov regime made their strong differences in foreign policy public.[13] Whereas State Department representatives advocated a stronger stance, the Defense Department officials kept a call for an independent international investigation out of a NATO communiqué.[14] Finally, due to domestic pressure from the Helsinki Commission in Congress and from well-known senators, who had visited Tashkent,[15] as well as that of NGOs, the State Department joined the appeals for an international investigation and pressed the Uzbek government to enact reforms.[16] On 14 June 2005, Secretary of State Condoleezza Rice wrote a letter to President Karimov stating her decision to recall US diplomats and, in a speech at the OSCE Parliamentary Assembly in Washington on 3 July 2005, she publicly condemned human rights violations in Uzbekistan.[17] This clear position quickly lead to the eviction of the US air base after Karimov had already suspended the landing of heavy transport planes as well as night flights for the US at Khanabad. After a last diplomatic effort to alter the decision in September, the US accepted the suspension and froze 20 billion USD of aid for Uzbekistan. The US Congress passed a resolution to accuse president Karimov before the International Criminal Court.

This political shift led to a quick re-orientation in security and political affairs. Secretary of Defense Donald Rumsfeld travelled to Kazakhstan, Kyrgyzstan and Tajikistan in August 2005 to reassure good relationships and

---

11 US Special Operations Forces, intelligence and reconnaissance missions, and air logistics flights all used the Karshi-Khanabad airfield in southeastern Uzbekistan. See Tully 2005a.
12 The Declaration on the Strategic Partnership and Cooperation Framework Between the United States of America and the Republic of Uzbekistan is available online at http://www.state.gov/p/eur/ rls/or/2002/11711.htm. US-trained military units might have participated in the Uzbekistan government's suppression of unrest in Andijan. See *New York Times* 20 June 2005.
13 For more on the threat assessment see http://www.state.gov/r/pa/prs/ps/2005/46637.htm. In 2004, the State Department suspended 18 million USD in aid to Uzbekistan because of Tashkent's poor human rights record, but soon the Pentagon restored this money and even added 3 million USD to the total – citing Karimov's co-operation with the US military. Only a few weeks later, the Pentagon gave even more money, 21 million USD to the Uzbek government to help neutralize its Soviet-era biological weapons. See Tully 2005b, Tyson/Wright 2005.
14 See *The Washington Post*. 14 June 2005.
15 See Tully 2005e; Pannier 2005.
16 See Tully 2005c; Tully 2005d; McMahon 2005.
17 See Dubnov 2005; Torbakov 2005a, Rice's remarks at the OSCE Parliamentary Assembly are available online at http://www.state.gov/secretary/rm/2005/48912.htm.

basing opportunities in Bishkek and Dushanbe. In October 2005, Secretary of State Rice orchestrated this shift politically by travelling again to these three states. During her tour, she praised Kazakhstan as the natural hegemon of the region while emphasizing the unprecedented opportunity for the country to lead Central Asia to democracy and to demonstrate their leadership skills in the upcoming democratic presidential elections in December 2005. Concerning Bishkek, the US agreed on new negotiations on a much higher price for the Ganci base and landing rights (see below). In Dushanbe, both Rumsfeld and Rice made clear that the US did not strive for a permanent military presence, but for military and technical co-operation in the fight against terrorism in Afghanistan. At the end of August 2005, a US general visited Ashgabad for talks with president Saparmurad Nijasov on border security and counter proliferation issues. In October 2005, a US undersecretary for arms control and international security travelled there as well.

In 2001, Kyrgyzstan had also become a member in the "Alliance against Terrorism" by opening an air base for the coalition forces at Ganci, close the main airport Manas near Bishkek. Due to these security political facts, Washington became concerned about the unrest in southern Kyrgyzstan and urged the government to practice restraint as well as condemn the use of force. Undersecretary for Political Affairs, Nicholas Burns, went to Bishkek on 22 March 2005 together with US Ambassador Steve Young and urged both the Kyrgyz government and the opposition to open a dialogue without preconditions and to lay the groundwork for free and fair presidential elections. At that time, the US was closely working with the OSCE and supporting the OSCE Representative for Central Asia, Alojz Peterle, in his efforts to facilitate a dialogue. The US also strongly endorsed the March 20th OSCE statement calling for non-violence and immediate dialogue. US officials have been in contact with both the government and opposition to reinforce this message.[18] The US government also provided humanitarian assistance and support to economic and political reforms.[19] During the Uzbek-Kyrgyz refugee crisis, after the massacre in Andijan, Secretary of State Rice underlined the importance of safeguarding Uzbek refugees and working closely with the UN High Commissioner for Refugees.[20] As a donor dependent country, Kyrgyzstan often has to meet such international demands. On the other hand, it has learned to make a virtue out of necessity. While president Bakiev quickly gave the US the reassurance that there would be no change in the status of the base,[21] the president, just as quickly, seized the opportunity to demand more money for the US base and its landing rights. This all occurred after the Declaration of the Shanghai Co-operation Organization concerning the closure of US bases in Central Asia (see below).

---

18 See online at http://www.state.gov/p/eur/ci/kg/c4493.htm.
19 A comprehensive overview of US assistance to Kyrgyzstan is available online at http://www.state.gov/p/eur/rls/fs/35990.htm. 2005/347.
20 See McMahon 2005.
21 See online at http://www.state.gov/p/eur/ci/kg/c4495.htm.

Opening up energy routes, but not to the "three evils": China in Central Asia

From a Central Asian perspective, China is a close neighbour. The economic take off of the People's Republic in the last couple of years has reinforced its economic interests and opened it up to its neighbours and the global economy. From a global perspective, China is on its way to becoming a hegemonic power in the Far East. On the one hand, Beijing is eager to search for reliable energy sources close to its borders. On the other hand, this opening up and quick modernization bears the risks of democratization, be it on a political-ideological, or a religious or national level. Therefore, in its co-operation with Central Asian neighbours, China wants to find partners in its fight against the so-called "three evils" (separatism, extremism, terrorism). One very concrete evil, for example, would be democratic spillover effects and any kind of separatism, or Muslim insurgency, particularly in areas neighbouring its restive province Xinjiang.[22] Closely related to these political and security interests is the strategic goal to keep the US from increasing its support for democratization close to its border. This perspective brought Beijing closer to its neighbour Russia with whom it shares these interests. The foundation of the Shanghai Co-operation Organization (SCO, see below) can be seen as the first expression of China's regional ambitions in Central Asia.

Also, China can best develop its energy interests with Kazakhstan. In July 2005, plans for an oil pipeline through Kazakhstan were discussed between presidents Nazarbayev and Hu Jintao in Astana. A trans-Kazakhstani railroad line from the shore of the Caspian Sea to West China is another promising project. This has to be seen in conjunction with the controversial acquisition by China National Petroleum Corporation (CNPC) in October 2005 of PetroKazakhstan, a Canadian-owned Kazakh oil company. These developments indicate that Beijing's moving into the region's energy industry with a more aggressive policy aimed at securing access to fuel resources. This inevitably leads to corresponding struggle for political influence in Central Asia.[23]

Turkmen and Chinese bilateral economic ties have been growing since the 1990s. Constructing a gaz pipeline from China to Turkmenistan through Kazakh territory, or through Afghanistan and Tajikistan to Pakistan would be beneficial for all countries.[24] Agreements with Uzbekistan include a 600-million USD oil joint venture for investment in Uzbekistan's oil and gas fields, and president Karimov hopes to attract 1.5 billion USD in Chinese investments over the next couple of years.[25]

---

22   See Blank 2005.
23   See Peimani 2005, *Almaty Herald* 3 November 2005.
24   In July 2005, China and Turkmenistan signed agreements on technical and economic co-operation, as well as loan agreements and a co-operation deal in the oil and gas sector. See Blagov 2005.
25   The joint venture was concluded between the China National Petroleum Corporation (CNPC) and Uzbekneftgaz. China will provide technology to develop 23 fields in the rela-

Beijing's reactions to the revolution in Kyrgyzstan and to the massacre in Andijan can be seen as outward demonstrations of a both military and authoritarian course. Recalling the demonstrations on Tiananmen Square (1989), the uprisings in South Kyrgyzstan alarmed Beijing's rulers. Even though it has been 15 years since China has been able to offer anything more than a military answer to its Kyrgyz neighbour, Beijing has offered the possibility of Chinese military deployment under the aegis of the CSTO or the SCO to Kyrgyzstan. President Bakiev had nothing against to balance still this proposal with the two other Russian and American bases on his territory.[26] In this context, the Chinese reaction to the Uzbek policy during the Andijan events seems only consequent. In an atmosphere of public outrage toward the Uzbek government, both presidents, Karimov and Hu Jintao demonstratively signed a Friendly Partnership Treaty and ten co-operation agreements on 25-27 May 2005.[27] The Chinese president expressed his appreciation of the way the Uzbek people had chosen to develop their country in light of their own reality as well as their efforts in safeguarding national independence, sovereignty and territorial integrity.[28]

Post-Soviet, multi-vector and weak multilateralism

After the break-up of the former Soviet Union, we can observe various forms of multilateral co-operation between the Central Asian states: the post-Soviet type in the framework of the CIS, the multi-vector one in the framework of the SCO and the weak type in the framework of the OSCE. With regard to destabilization in the Ferghana Valley, it is characteristic that these organizations can hardly offer proper stabilizing initiatives. The way in which these organizations could become effective very much depends on the role the three hegemons play.

A vehicle of "civilized divorce": The Commonwealth of Independent States

Looking back, Russian president Vladimir Putin described the Commonwealth of Independent States (CIS) as a vehicle of "civilized divorce"[29] and indeed, despite Moscow's leading position since 1992, the centrifugal tendencies in the CIS development have always been stronger than centripetal ones. Even the characteristic Potemkin way of keeping up a declaratory for-

---

tively inaccessible Bukhara-Khiva region and produce some one million tons of oil annually as well as gas condensate when it reaches capacity.
26 On the possible establishment of a Chinese military base in Kyrgyzstan see *Huanqiu Shibao* 31 May 2005.
27 The respective documents are available online at http://www.fmprc.gov.cn/eng/wjb/zzjg/dozys/gjlb/3255/3257/t197389.htm.
28 See McDermott 2005.
29 Lukianov 2005.

mal behaviour, despite informal decision-making tactics, could not cover this fragmentation.[30] Since the CIS summit in June 2005, it has become clear that Russia now has more interest in shifting its emphasis to an integrated Collective Security Treaty Organization (CSTO).[31] This can be interpreted as a fall back position on the "core" group of the CIS – Belarus and the Central Asian states. With most of these often being dependant neighbours, Russia could continue its post-Soviet manner of integration under the de facto direction of Moscow. Some examples in the field of military security, just to name a few are the anti-terrorist centre in December 2000 and, in August 2001, the collective rapid reaction forces which were created in Bishkek; a central united air defence system and a second Russian military base in Kyrgyzstan are in the making. The CSTO members agreed to lift their trade barriers against the Russian arms industry in return for low pricing.[32]

While the contemporary circumstances for international relations in Central Asia have considerably changed since the break-up of the Soviet Union, Moscow has not yet learned much from its failing post-Soviet form of integration in the CIS framework. In the footsteps of Boris Jelzin, who already tried in 1994, President Putin today again aims at an "international recognition of the Russian-led CSTO as a regional security organization, part of a global security system in which Russia would enjoy a sphere of influence and bloc-leader status"[33] in security matters within Central Asia. However, the expected shift of US and NATO strategies in the region, on which he counts, has not taken place. Again, he has underestimated the continuing centrifugal trends of shifting and multi-vector integration of his Central Asian neighbours and their different power interests.[34]

Another paper tiger? The Shanghai Cooperation Organization

In the Shanghai Cooperation Organization's (SCO)[35] reaction to the events in Kyrgyzstan and Uzbekistan, we can recognize some of the main characteris-

---

30 "Since the foundation of the CIS more than 1,000 different agreements were adopted and more than 50 institutions were created, only 7-10 per cent of all agreements have been implemented." Kropatcheva 2005. "It was the familiar CIS method of adopting pro forma an unsatisfactory document, commissioning in the same motion improvements to the 'adopted' document, albeit without expecting any significant improvements to be made, and calling for another debate on the issue some day, only to repeat the cycle." Socor 3 June 2005. Compare also Kreikemeyer/Zagorskij 1995.
31 The members of the CSTO are Russia, Belarus, Armenia, Kazakhstan, Kyrgyzstan and Tajikistan. The Charter of the CSTO is available online at http://www.dkb.gov.ru/start/in dex.htm; for more on the CIS summit see online http://www.dw-world.de/dw/article/ 0,1609626,00. html?maca=de-newsletter_ostfokus-643-html.
32 See McDermott 2005.
33 Socor 2005b see also Socor 2005c.
34 See McDermott 2005.
35 The SCO is an intergovernmental, international organization founded in Shanghai on 15 June 2001 by Russia, China, Uzbekistan, Kyrgyzstan, Kazakhstan and Tajikistan. It aims at strengthening confidence-building and disarmament in the border regions of its mem-

tics of this organization's international behaviour. At their summit in Astana on 5 July 2005, the SCO leaders signed a joint declaration and a concept on the "SCO Cooperation against Terrorism, Separatism, and Extremism" as well as a bilateral Russo-Chinese declaration on "World Order in the 21st Century". Taken together, both documents demonstrate the SCO's understanding of mutually beneficial co-operation guided by the principles of respect for each other's independence, sovereignty and territorial integrity and, above all, for non-interference in each other's internal affairs. The organization also demonstrated that it perceives Central Asia as its sphere of influence; it sees it as an area where it wants to minimize international pressure and influence, particularly that of the US. This is why in the summit's final declaration, the SCO asked the forces in the US-led coalition in Afghanistan to clarify a timeframe for withdrawal from US bases in Uzbekistan and Kyrgyzstan. The SCO leaders would rather fill the vacuum themselves.[36]

In the following weeks, however, both on the US and on the Central Asian side, it became clear that the scope of this kind of multilateralism in the Far East quickly finds its limits in national interests. The United States rejected the SCO's above-mentioned call to set a date for the withdrawal of their forces from bases in Central Asia, arguing that their presence in the region is determined by bilateral agreements. The Central Asian SCO member Kyrgyzstan, who had just signed the above-mentioned final SCO declaration also rediscovered its national interest in the prolongation of a bilateral agreement with the US on the Ganci air base near Manas airport. On 23 August 2005, the Kazakh foreign minister confirmed that, given the growing strategic importance of Central Asia, he understands the renaissance of "great game" power constellations in the region, but he also pledged his country's support for US military operations in Central Asia and said his country worked to water down neighbouring countries' efforts to evict American troops from the region.

Given this kind of contradiction between multilateralism and national interests, it becomes clear that this recent Chinese-Russian integration effort shares the fate of post-Soviet multilateralism in the framework of the CIS: it mostly remains of declaratory character, which seems to be sufficient for members' goals.[37] The purpose of the SCO is not yet to become a supranational multilateral security body, affecting the national interests of its members and offering valuable assistance in times of trouble. While the Tashkent SCO summit in 2004 formally had decided to strengthen the multilateral co-operation between member states, the SCO anti-terrorist centre, already

---

bers. The president of Uzbekistan had been invited to the 2000 Dushanbe Summit as a guest of the host state.

36 See Blagov 2005c, Socor 2005d, McDermott 2005.
37 "Indeed the SCO itself has produced numerous statements from its previous meetings, promoting the SCO's security credentials within the region, amounting to little more than a mantra against "terrorism, separatism, extremism, and drug trafficking." McDermott 2005.

based in Tashkent, did not even have any practical effect on the Andijan crisis. The SCO-Afghanistan Contact Group to support anti-drug efforts and the agreement on mutual assistance in emergency situations appears to be of declaratory character as well. It seems that the proposal to create SCO rapid-deployment forces, or the plan to sign an agreement on a nuclear-free zone in Central Asia will have the same fate. Even increasing interaction with other international organizations, with the Association of Southeast Asian Nations (ASEAN), or with observers in Iran, India, Pakistan and Mongolia, or even NATO will not increase multilateralism in Central Asia. As long as neo-patrimonial rule persists in Central Asia, every single president will have to look for ways to stay in power and how to instrumentalize foreign policy for this purpose. Substantive regional co-operation is not in the president's interest, as this would mean surrendering the badly needed control and resources to an international or even supranational body.[38]

Unique possibilities but also strong provisos: The OSCE

While the Central Asian states joined the OSCE shortly after their independence, the Organization really began working in each participating State of the region only in 1999. Thus, it needed some time to develop both conceptual and practical policies towards its Central Asian participating States.[39] Among the security relevant international organizations, except for the UN, the OSCE plays a unique role in the region, as the Central Asian host countries are equal members. The Office for Democratic Institutions and Human Rights (ODIHR) carried out election observations in all countries except Turkmenistan; the High Commissioner on National Minorities, the Representative on Freedom of the Media and the Parliamentary Assembly are active as well.

In Kyrgyzstan, already before the February 2005 elections and the subsequent uprising, the preconditions for the work of the OSCE Centre in Bishkek is better than in neighbouring Uzbekistan. This is why the Organization was able to maintain channels of communication and was prepared to mediate and support a dialogue. In the acute crisis, some difficulties had to be overcome. After some time, the Centre in Bishkek and the Vienna-based OSCE institutions (Special Representative on Central Asia, Chairman in Office, Secretary General) finally started working together in crisis prevention, conflict management and stabilization with the respective Kyrgyz authorities. They urged the observation of the country's laws, the need for national unity, a peaceful resolution of conflicts and democracy based on economic development. A joint Kyrgyz-OSCE work plan, developed after the 24

---

38   On the concept of neo-patrimonial rule in Central Asia see the article of Geiss in this volume.

39   On the state and development of OSCE-Central Asian relations see the article of Kreikemeyer in this volume.

March events, was designed to support stability and security.[40] Various assistance projects were launched especially for the south of the country: a media centre in Batken,[41] the promotion of investment and employment opportunities as well as an information centre for the fight against transborder threats in Bishkek. The new Kyrgyz leadership acted co-operatively; interim president Bakiev addressed an OSCE Permanent Council meeting in Vienna and signed a politically binding code of conduct (Charter of Accord) for the 10 July elections.[42] However, during the refugee crisis, both UNHCR and OSCE had to realize that, with their human rights standards, they had to compete with tough Kyrgyz interests in its neighbourhood policy as well.[43]

In Uzbekistan, the OSCE could hardly cope with this kind of tough power interests of the leadership. While the Karimov regime showed very restrictive behaviour toward international organizations, who touched upon the human rights standards in the country, its attitude towards them worsened to deep mistrust and hostility in line with the Andijan events. The OSCE Centre in Tashkent had to balance very carefully between OSCE commitments and its fragile stand on the ground. An early offer by the OSCE Centre to assist in the examination of the deeper causes of the unrest and an appeal to the Uzbek government to allow international involvement in the investigation were rejected. From 16-18 May 2005, the Centre deployed a two-man fact-finding team to the Andijan region and the Eastern Ferghana Valley, and the head of centre went to Andijan together with other diplomats and journalists at the government's invitation on 18 May 2005. Furthermore, representatives of the OSCE and the UN met for investigation purposes at the Kyrgyz-Uzbek border. In Tashkent itself, the Centre had to cope with a rally in front of the OSCE office, which the authorities tried to disrupt. Other OSCE institutions became active as well. The ODIHR issued a report on events in Andijan based on in-depth interviews conducted with residents who had fled to Kyrgyzstan; the OSCE Representative on Freedom of the Media informed on cases of human rights violations[44] and the Chairman-in-Office demanded an international investigation. The OSCE Parliamentary Assembly, in its Washington Declaration, threatened to apply the Moscow Mechanism.[45] On 29 July 2005, OSCE Secretary General Marc Perrin de Brichambaut held talks with Uzbek president Karimov and foreign minister Ganiyev as well as with civil society representatives. While he raised again the call for an independ-

---

40 See online http://www.osce.org/pc/item_1_14639.html.
41 See online http://www.osce.org/bishkek/item_1_14096.html; http://centrasia.org/newsA.php4?st=1117744380.
42 Four of the seven presidential candidates refused to sign. See Saralaeva 2005 and the article by Berg in Part IV of this volume.
43 On 30 May 2005, the OSCE appealed to Kyrgyzstan to not repatriate refugees from neighbouring Uzbekistan; on 14 June 2005, the OSCE Chairman-in-Office expressed concern about four deported Uzbek asylum-seekers. http://www.osce.org/bishkek /item_1_1534 9. html.
44 See online at http:/www.osce.org/fom.
45 See online at http://www.oscepa.org/admin/getbinary.asp?FileID=1069.

ent international investigation on the events in Andijan, he stressed the OSCE's interest in a balanced co-operation in all three dimensions, especially assistance in Uzbekistan's capacity to uphold its OSCE commitments.

Donors and critics: The examples of the European Union, the European Bank for Recovery and Development, and human rights organizations

Beyond those multilateral organizations in which the Central Asian states are equal members themselves, for the most part, Western international organizations with political or economic interests are active in the region. The European Union has an interest in developing economic relations with the states, that is, in building a bridge to the Far East; the diversification of access to energy resources and a respective infrastructure is especially important. This is also the reason why the EU supports conflict prevention and stabilization in the Central Asian region. While still far less influential than the hegemons, the EU has negotiated partnership and co-operation agreements (PCA) with the single states, and offers technical and humanitarian aid according to its Strategy for Central Asia for 2002-2006.[46] The PCA's are aimed at the facilitation of trade and investment as well as reforms in the fields of justice and home affairs. Through the PCA, a country is committed to democratic norms and encouraged to engage in regional co-operation.[47] As regards ODIHR reports on election monitoring, the EU Council of Ministers can issue declarations on elections, for example, on the parliamentary elections in Uzbekistan in December 2004, which did not conform with OSCE commitments and international standards.[48]

In recent years, the EU intensified its activities in Central Asia through the delegation of the European Commission in Almaty and respective offices in Bishkek and Dushanbe. The Commission has tried to strengthen its visibility in the region, namely through a visit of the external relations commissioner, Chris Patten, who especially emphasizes co-operation interests in the fields of fight against oder prevention of drug trafficking and antiterrorism. The head of the EU delegation in Almaty, Adrian van der Meer finds that it is vital that knowledge of European integration be increased as an example of successful regional co-operation, which he believes is still necessary for Central Asia.[49]

---

46 The PCA between the EU and Uzbekistan was signed on 1 July 1999. The Commission's Strategy Paper is available online at http://www.europe.eu.int/comm/external_relations/ceeca/rsp2/index.htm. See Lobjakas 2005a.
47 See online at http://europa.eu.int/comm/external_relations/uzbekistan/intro/ index.htm#rels.
48 See online at http://europa.eu.int/rapid/pressReleasesAction.do?reference=PESC/05/2&format= HTML&aged= 1&language=DE&guiLanguage=en.
49 See *Almaty Herald* 3 November 2005.

During the power change in Kyrgyzstan, the EU acted in line with the OSCE. It showed its interest in security and stability and appealed to the newly appointed leaders to restore public order as soon as possible. Given these preconditions for a dialogue with all political forces – for example, the implementation of a policy of national reconciliation and respect for democratic values and human rights – the EU assured its willingness to further cooperate. With regard to the deterioration of political control in Kyrgyzstan and the threatening energy crisis in Winter 2005, the EU put emphasis on the rule of law and on improvement of the energy sector in the country. With regard to Tajikistan, the main activities of the EU are still directed toward humanitarian aid.

In its reaction to the events in Andijan, the European Commission expressed its "deep concern" about the violence, called on the Uzbek government not to use force and urged it to abide by the provisions of the PCA. The EU presidency, Luxembourg, the EU foreign ministers, the High Representative for Common Foreign and Security Policy, Javier Solana and the European Parliament also expressed their concern in various forms. Together with the UN, the European Commission called for an independent international inquiry into the Andijan events and gave Uzbekistan until the end of June to change its mind, or face possible consequences.[50] Tashkent did not agree, and refused to grant an entry visa to Solana's human rights representative, ignored his letter of protest and rejected the resolution of the EU parliament. On 9 September Solana's newly appointed Special Representative for Central Asia, Jan Kubis, visited president Karimov and on 3 October 2005, the EU council of ministers passed sanctions according to which the PCA with Uzbekistan was suspended, an arms embargo was decreed and visas were denied. There were also signals that the possibility of a further dialogue with Tashkent should not be excluded.

With regard to conditionality, the European Bank for Development and Reconstruction (EBRD) had already adjusted its loans to basic requirements in the field of human rights and democratization. In some cases, it suspended its programmes because benchmarks were not met. Already in May 2003, it declared conditionality for credits due to the UN Special Representative for the torture report on "systematic torture" in Uzbekistan, and suspended the lion's share of its loans, since conditions had not been met.[51] With respect to the events in Andijan, EBRD president Jean Lemierre worte a letter to president Karimov expressing his serious concern. While announcing to follow

---

50   On the reaction of the EU Commission see online at http://www.rferl.org/featuresarticle/2005/6/7339BF0A-0E78-4D50-BE26-2767280B722D.html; on the reaction of the European Parliament see online at http://www.europarl.eu.inthttp://www.rferl.org/ featuresarticle/2005/06/2a3fb273-fd0a-448b-8504-e44dced0c0c7.html; see also Lobjakas 2005b, on the ultimatum of the European Commission on 14 June 2005 see online at http://www.cacianalyst. org/news.php.

51   See online at www.ebrd.com; Lobjakas 2005c; Katargin 2005; Donovan 2005; ICG 2004; MacFarlane 2003.

closely the reform process in Usbekistan the bank remains committed to maintaining a dialogue, but it also annouced that it will limit its private sector projects and will not initiate public sector projects.[52]

Conditionality can be a strong instrument to prevent the misuse of donor's aid. However, the influence of donor organizations is limited to their ability to engage the host state in negotiations based on its own conditions. International non-governmental organization in the human rights field[53] are much more flexible in criticizing from the outside, as they usually have no proper interests in co-operation with the respective states, and can easily refrain from their engagement in authoritarian countries. Thus, they are able to protect human rights and rule of law by denouncing regimes that commit respective violations and by putting pressure, not only on governments in Central Asia, but also on the international community. In the aftermath of the Andijan, events these NGOs were very active. While they had already denounced detentions and persecutions, the International Red Cross was the first to (unsuccessfully) demand access to the victims. Human Rights Watch quickly issued a report on the massacre and put strong pressure on US policy.[54] Together with others, it put strong emphasis on an international investigation by setting up a fact-finding mission. Freedom House emphasized more freedom for the press, and the International League for Human Rights, along with the OSCE Parliamentary Assembly, demanded that the Moscow Mechanism be implemented. In line with other states and organizations such as the US, UNDP and OSCE, the League also appealed to the Kyrgyz government to a carefully review the Uzbek refugees' asylum claims in accordance with international humanitarian law and to provide the necessary assistance. While the Uzbek government ignored the demands of states and international organizations, it put pressure not only on local but also on international NGOs by refusing visas and by controlling registration and budgets.[55]

Conclusions

Summarizing the reactions of neighbouring states, hegemonic powers, multilateral, donor and non-governmental organizations, we can observe that every

---

52 Lemierre's letter is online available at http://www.ebrd.com/about/strategy/country/uzbe/letter.pdf.
53 Among the biggest NGOs are the International Committee of the Red Cross (http://www.icrc.org), Amnesty International (http://www.amnesty.org), Human Rights Watch (http://www.hrw.org), International League for Human Rights (http://www.ilhr.org), International Helsinki Federation (http://www.ihf-hr.org), Freedom House (http://www.freedomhouse.org), Forum 18 (http://www.forum18.org).
54 Cf. http://www.forum18.org/Archive.php?article_id=170.
55 From mid 2004 onward, the activities of the the Soros Foundation, of Internews, of the American Institute of Democratic Freedoms, of Freedom House, of the International Republican Institute and of Soros' Open Society Institute were suspended. See Rubleva/Mukhamedjarova 2005.

actor is interested in stability; however, the definition of stability and the means of reaching it differ considerably. Concerning the understanding of stability, we can distinguish four groups:

First, we have the regimes of the Central Asian region and the hegemonic powers of Russia and China, who support them by bilateral and multilateral (CIS, SCO) means. Their perception of stability is mainly characterized by the goal of staying in power and therefore by the interest of non-interference in internal affairs and, last but not least, by the readiness to use violence in cases where this understanding of stability is endangered. This basis is endangered as soon as other groups in the respective societies join their efforts in gaining influence to change the respective power structures. Since the first "coloured revolution" in Central Asia took place in Kyrgyzstan, every election campaign thereafter has become a potential threat to stability.

Second, there is the United States, who follows hegemonic goals in the region by trying to secure energy resources and transport, as well as possibilities to combat terrorism in the region and especially beyond. These goals have already led to a certain competition with Russia and China. Concerning stability, the internal affairs of a Central Asian state only become important in Washington when a certain extent of authoritarianism leads to human rights violations in these countries. At such a point, the US economy and its security interests can be superimposed by the goal of securing freedom and democracy, and national values that traditionally have strong support. The massive human rights violations during the massacre in Andijan led exactly to this conflict between US foreign political goals. The final decision to insist on freedom and democracy with regard to Uzbekistan, without giving up the economic and security political interests throughout the region, increased the competition for influence between Russia and China.

Third, the OSCE and, to a certain extent, also international donor organizations such as the EU and the EBRD, who combine their engagement for common security, or for partnership and co-operation with a normative approach, are active in the region strengthening stability by trying to support transition processes on the ground. This goal leads to certain limitations on their action on the ground, since, on the one hand, their values do not necessarily contribute to the power of the authoritarian regimes, nor to the growing influence of their supporters, Russia and China. On the other hand, the realization of their goals cannot be underscored by the stationing and financing of military bases as is the case with the US.

Fourth, the international non-governmental human rights organizations, who try to prevent human rights violations with both activities on the ground and from the outside, have already made clear that, in their self understanding, human rights and fundamental freedoms are prerequisites for stability. Given the current state of political and individual liberty in the different Central Asian states, these organizations will have to continue their struggle for a long time, sometimes only having the possibility to criticize from the outside.

The political developments in Kyrgyzstan since spring 2005, and the massacre in Andijan as the latest and utmost expression of repression in Uzbekistan, are clear indicators of destabilization. In Tajikistan, most of the population lives below minimal living standards; in Turkmenistan the great majority of the population has no other choice than to tolerate an anachronistic dictatorship. And in Kazakhstan, many people have to live with the massive corruption of the country's nouveau riche oil elite. Thus, the consequences for future stability in this region can only be called negative and disquieting.

Bibliography

Newslines

http://www.akipress.com
http://www.eurasianet.org
http://www.ferghana.ru
http://www.gazeta.ru
http://www.iwpr.net
http://www.ng.ru/
http://www.regnum.ru
http://www.rferl.org

Articles

Bigg, Claire. 2005. Uzbekistan: Karimov, Putin say Andijan violence was planned abroad. Moscow. In: *Radio Free Europe/Radio Liberty. Central Asia Report*, 29 June.

Blagov, Sergei. 2005a. Shanghai Cooperation Organization Summit suggests new Russia-China links. In: *Eurasia Daily Monitor*, 2 (130), 6 July.

Blagov, Sergei.2005b. Turkmenistan explores export alternatives for its natural gas. In: *Eurasia Daily Monitor*, 2 (152), 4 August.

Blank, Stephen. 2005. Turns in Chinese policy towards Central Asia. In: *Central Asia- Caucasus Analyst*, 15 June.

Chivers, C.J./Thom Shanker. 2005. Uzbek ministries in crackdown received US aid. In: *The New York Times*, 20 June.

Donovan, Jeffrey. 2005. Uzbekistan: UN, EU calls for international probe into violence. In: *Radio Free Europe/Radio Liberty. Central Asia Report*, 19 May.

Dubnov, Arkady. 2005. The first indications of nervousness in Tashkent appear three weeks after the Andizhan tragedy. In: *Vremya Novostei*, 7 June.

Human Rights Watch. 2005a. *Bullets were falling like rain. The Andijan Massacre, May 13, 2005.* New York. (online available at www.hrw.org).

Human Rights Watch.2005b. *Burying the Truth. Uzbekistan Rewrites the Story of the Andijan Massacre.* New York. (online available at www.hrw.org).

International Crisis Group. 2005. *Kyrgyzstan. After the Revolution.* Brussels, 4 May. (online available at www.crisiseb.org).

International Crisis Group. 2005 *Uzbekistan. The Andijon Uprising.* Brussels, 25 May. (online available at www.crisisweb.org).

International Crisis Group. 2004. The failure of reform in Uzbekistan: Ways forwards for the international community. Asia Report, Nr. 76, 11 March.

Lobjakas, Ahto. 2005a. Uzbekistan: EU urges Tashkent to refrain from further use of force. Washington. In: *Radio Free Europe/Radio Liberty. Central Asia Report*, 17 May.

Lobjakas, Ahto. 2005b. Uzbekistan/EU: EU Foreign Ministers condemn Uzbek authorities for Andijon killings. In: *Radio Free Europe/Radio Liberty. Central Asia Report*, 23 May.

Lobjakas, Ahto. 2005c. Uzbekistan: EU, Uzbek relations heading for showdown over Andijan, Brussels. In: *Radio Free Europe/Radio Liberty. Central Asia Report,* 7 June.
Lukianov, Fedor. 2005. Casting the peelings aside. Russia has recognized the impossibility of integration within the CIS. In: David Johnson's Russia List 9103.
McMahon, Robert. 2005a. US renews calls for inquiry into Uzbek events. Washington. In: *Radio Free Europe/Radio Liberty. Central Asia Report,* 25 May.
McMahon, Robert. 2005b. Uzbekistan: Report cites evidence of government 'Massacre' in Andijan. In: *Radio Free Europe/Radio Liberty. Central Asia Report,* 7 June.
McMahon, Robert. 2005c. Uzbekistan: US denies divisions on policy, renews inquiry call. Washington. In: *Radio Free Europe/Radio Liberty. Central Asia Report,* 15 June.
McDermott, Roger N. 2002. Russia's Security Agenda in Central Asia. In: *Central Asia and the Caucasus (CAC),* 2 (14), pp. 16-22.
McDermott, Roger N. 2005. Andijan's aftermath raises security stakes in Kyrgyzstan. In: *Jamestown Foundation. Eurasia Daily Monitor,* 2 (101), 24 May.
ODIHR. 2005. *Preliminary Findings on the Events in Andijan, Uzbekistan, 13 May 2005.* Warsaw 20 June. (online available at www.osce.org/documents/odihr/2005/06/15233_en. pdf).
Pannier, Bruce. 2005. Uzbekistan: Officials refuse to meet with US Senate delegation. Prague. In: *Radio Free Europe/Radio Liberty. Central Asia Report,* 30 May.
Peimani, Hooman. 2005. China's acquisition of Petrokazakhstan: A blessing or a curse? In: *Central Asia – Caucasus Analyst.* 7 September, online available at http://www.cacianalyst.org/vi ew_article.php?articleid=3629.
Poletaev, Eduard/Zamir Karajanov. 2005. Kazak border treaty signed. In: *IWPR, Reporting Central Asia,* Nr. 343, 26 January.
Rubleva, Tatiana/Liliya Mukhamedjarova. 2005. The authorities of Uzbekistan get rid of the organizations involved in rosy and orange revolutions. In: *Nezavisimaya Gazeta,* 08 April.
Saralaeva, Leila. 2005. Kyrgyzstan: OSCE election charter "Patronising". In: *IWPR'S reporting Central Asia,* No. 388, 17 June.
Socor, Vladimir. 2005a. CIS collective security treaty organisation holds summit. In: *Jamestown Foundation. Eurasia Daily Monitor,* 2 (123), 24 June.
Socor, Vladimir. 2005b. From CIS to CSTO: Can a core be preserved? In: *Jamestown Foundation. Eurasia Daily Monitor,* 2 (125), 28 June.
Socor, Vladimir. 2005c. SCO asks Washington to set date for withdrawal of forces. In: *Jamestown Foundation. Eurasia Daily Monitor,* 2 (130), 6 July.
Socor, Vladimir. 2005d. Unprecedented Uzbek-Russian Joint Military Exercise held. In: *Jamestown Foundation. Eurasia Daily Monitor,* 2 (179), 27 September.
Tully, Andrew. 2005a. US urges restraint in Uzbekistan. Washington. In: *Radio Free Europe/Radio Liberty. Central Asia Report,* 13 May.
Tully, Andrew. 2005b. Uzbekistan: Rights groups urge stronger US pressure on Karimov. Washington. In: *Radio Free Europe/Radio Liberty. Central Asia Report,* 18 May.
Tully, Andrew. 2005c. Is Washington able to help opposition in Uzbekistan and Azerbaijan? In: *Radio Free Europe/Radio Liberty. Central Asia Report,* 20 May.
Tully, Andrew. 2005d. Uzbekistan: Bush allies seek harsher US treatment of Karimov. Washington. In: *Radio Free Europe/Radio Liberty. Central Asia Report,* 3 June.
Tully, Andrew. 2005e. Uzbekistan: U.S. sharpens call for independent probe of Andijon bloodshed, while Russia objects. Washington. In: *Radio Free Europe/Radio Liberty. Central Asia Report,* 10 June.
Tyson, Ann Scott/Robin Wright. 2005. Crackdown muddies U.S.-Uzbek relations. Washington in Talks on Long- Term Use of Base. In: *Washington Post,* 4 June.
Torbakov, Igor. 2005a. Moscow and Washington pursue diverging policies in Uzbekistan, Central Asia. In: *Jamestown Foundation. Eurasia Daily Monitor,* 2 (118), 17 June.
Torbakov, Igor. 2005b. Russian Foreign Policy Experts Debate Interaction with America in Greater Central Asia. In: *Jamestown Foundation. Eurasia Daily Monitor,* 2 (196), 21 October.
Yermukanov, Marat. 2005. Russian- Kazakh border agreement sparks nationalist reaction. In: *Jamestown Foundation. Eurasia Daily Monitor,* 2 (19), 27 January.

Appendix

John Myraunet/Fausta Šimaitytė

Relations Between Central Asian States and Multilateral Organizations. A Chronology

21 December 1991	The heads of eleven of the former Soviet republics, Azerbaijan, Armenia, Belarus, Kazakhstan, Kyrgyzstan, Moldova, Russia, Tajikistan, Turkmenistan, Uzbekistan and Ukraine, adopt the Alma-Ata Declaration and sign the Protocol to the agreement on the establishment of the Commonwealth of Independent States (CIS).[1]
30 December 1991	CIS council of heads of state in Minsk: agreement on strategic and armed forces, and border troops
30 January 1992	Kazakhstan, Kyrgyzstan, Tajikistan, Turkmenistan and Uzbekistan are admitted to the CSCE at the meeting of the Council of Ministers in Prague.
14 February 1992	CIS council of heads of state and government in Minsk
26 February 1992	Tajikistan and Uzbekistan sign the Helsinki Final Act.
2 March 1992	Kazakhstan, Kyrgyzstan, Tajikistan, Turkmenistan and Uzbekistan are admitted to the United Nations.
20 March 1992	The council of heads of state of the CIS discusses military-related issues in Kiev.
15 May 1992	CIS council of heads of state and government in Tashkent, signature of the treaty on collective security
8 July 1992	Kazakhstan, Kyrgyzstan and Turkmenistan sign the Helsinki Final Act.
13-23 September 1992	UN Secretary-General, Boutros Boutros-Ghali, dispatches a fact-finding mission to Uzbekistan and Tajikistan.
23 Sept. 1992	Kazakhstan signs the CSCE Charter of Paris.
9 October 1992	CIS council of heads of state and government in Bishkek on a single monetary system and coordination of fiscal, credit and monetary policy of the states-parties in the ruble zone
1-5 November 1992	Secretary General of NATO, Manfred Woerner, visits Kazakhstan and Kyrgyzstan.
28 November 1992	Kazakhstan, Kyrgyzstan, Tajikistan, Turkmenistan and Uzbekistan join the Economic Cooperation Organization (ECO) after their formal accession to the Treaty of Izmir at an extraordinary meeting of the ECO council of ministers held in Islamabad on 28 November 1992.

---

1   Georgia joins the CIS after signing the documents on 9 December 1993.

November 1992	UN Secretary-General, Boutros-Ghali, sends a UN good offices mission to Tajikistan.
1992	Kyrgyzstan, Tajikistan and Turkmenistan join the Organization of the Islamic Conference (OIC).
21 January 1993	A small UN unit of political, military and humanitarian officers is dispatched to monitor the situation in Tajikistan.
22 January 1993	The CIS Charter is adopted at a joint meeting of the CIS council of heads of state and government in Minsk.
1 February 1993	The president of Kazakhstan, Nursultan Nazarbayev, meets with NATO Secretary General, Manfred Woerner, at NATO Headquarters.
16 April 1993	Extraordinary meeting of the CIS heads of state in Minsk on a proposal by Boris Yeltsin and Nursultan Nazarbayev on strengthening the CIS .
26 April 1993	UN Secretary-General, Boutros-Ghali, appoints Ismat Kittani from Iraq as his special envoy for Tajikistan.
April 1993	The CSCE Chairman in Office (CiO), accompanied by a team of CSCE experts, visits the Central Asian states.
29 September 1993	The president of Turkmenistan, Saparmurad Niyazov, makes an official visit to NATO headquarters.
24 September 1993	CIS council of heads of state and government in Moscow: signature of a treaty on the establishment of the Economic Union. Kazakhstan, Kyrgyzstan, Russia, Tajikistan and Uzbekistan decide to establish the CIS Collective Peacekeeping Forces in Tajikistan
27 October 1993	Uzbekistan signs the CSCE Charter of Paris.
1 December 1993	OSCE Council of Ministers in Rome establishes the CSCE Mission to Tajikistan.
23-24 December 1993	CIS council of heads of state and government in Ashgabad: Turkmenistan joins the Economic Union
December 1993	UN Secretary-General, Boutros-Ghali, appoints Ramiro Píriz-Ballón from Uruguay as his special envoy for Tajikistan.
10-11 January 1994	Heads of state and government of NATO countries launch the Partnership for Peace Programme (PfP) at the Brussels Summit.
21 February – 1 March 1994	The Secretary General of CSCE visits all five CSCE participating States in Central Asia.
15 April 1994	CIS council of heads of state in Moscow: all the CIS states sign the agreement on establishment of a free trade zone
April 1994	The CSCE High Commissioner on National Minorities (HCNM), Max van der Stoel, makes his first visit to the

	Central Asian part of the CSCE area (Almaty and Bishkek). In Kazakhstan, the HCNM presents recommendations on the use of the Russian language, on the ethnic balance among public officials, and on mechanisms to address complaints regarding ethnic discrimination.
10 May 1994	Deputy prime minister of Turkmenistan, Boris Shikmuradov, signs the PfP framework document.
27 May 1994	The foreign minister of Kazakhstan, Kanet Saudabaev, signs the PfP framework document.
1 June 1994	The president of Kyrgyzstan, Askar Akayev, signs the PfP framework document.
3 June 1994	Kyrgyzstan signs the CSCE Charter of Paris.
13 July 1994	The foreign minister of Uzbekistan, Saidmukhtar Saidkasimov, and defence minister Rustam Ahmedov sign the PfP framework document.
September 1994	Signature of the Teheran agreement on a temporary ceasefire and the cessation of other hostile acts on the Tajik-Afghan border and within the country for the duration of the talks.
October 1994	A UN technical survey team visits Tajikistan and 15 military observers are deployed in Dushanbe, Garm, Kurgan-Tube and Pyanj.
20 October 1994	The ceasefire in Tajikistan comes into effect following a public announcement by the head of the United Nations office in Dushanbe, Liviu Bota.
21 October 1994	CIS council of heads of state and government in Moscow on further integration
16 December 1994	The UN Security Council decides to set up the UN Mission of Observers in Tajikistan (UNMOT).
1994	Kazakhstan, Uzbekistan and Kyrgyzstan create the Central Asian Economic Community (CAEC).
7-9 January 1995	The Secretary General of the OSCE, Wilhelm Höynck, visits Tajikistan.
23 January 1995	The Partnership and Cooperation Agreement (PCA) between the EU and Kazakhstan is signed.
9 February 1995	The PCA between the EU and Kyrgyzstan is signed.
10 February 1995	CIS council of heads of state and government in Almaty on security and defence issues
March 1995	New head of UNMOT is Darko Silovic from Croatia.
16 March 1995	The OSCE liaison office in Central Asia is established in Tashkent.
May 1995	The HCNM makes his second visit to Central Asia.

26 May 1995	CIS council of heads of state and government in Minsk: the term of presence of the CIS peace-keeping forces in Tajikistan is prolonged to the end of 1995
6 July 1995	The OSCE Permanent Council decides to provide for the opening of three field offices of the OSCE Mission to Tajikistan in Kurgan-Turbe, Shartuz and Dusti.
10 October 1995	The field offices of the OSCE Mission to Tajikistan in Kurgan-Tube, Shartuz and Dusti are officially opened.
1995	An agreement on the deepening of integration in economic and humanitarian field is signed within the framework of CIS by Belarus, Kazakhstan, Kyrgyzstan and Russia.
1995	Kazakhstan joins the OIC.
19 January 1996	CIS council of heads of state in Moscow on the further development of the CIS in the field of economics and, in particular, of the formation of the customs and payments union
April 1996	The OSCE HCNM visits Kyrgyzstan and meets with government officials in Bishkek and officials in Osh and Djalal Abad.
May 1996	UN Secretary-General, Boutros-Ghali, appoints Gerd Merrem from Germany as a resident Special Representative and Head of Mission of UNMOT.
9-13 September 1996	The OSCE Troika visits Central-Asia to promote more active participation of the countries in the region in the OSCE.
13 November 1996	The president of Uzbekistan, Islam Karimov, visits the NATO headquarters.
1996	Uzbekistan joins the OIC.
1996	The heads of state of China, Russia, Kazakhstan, Kyrgyzstan and Tajikistan come together in Shanghai to discuss and sign agreements on the strengthening of confidence-building and disarmament in the border regions. They agree to meet every year under the so-called Shanghai Five mechanism.
10-15 March 1997	The Secretary General of NATO, Javier Solana, visits the four PfP members in Central Asia, Kazakhstan, Kyrgyzstan, Uzbekistan and Turkmenistan.
27-28 March 1997	CIS council of heads of state and government in Moscow on economic integration and the prolongation of the term of presence of the collective peace-keeping forces in Tajikistan.

3-5 June 1997	The OSCE HCNM visits Kazakhstan to familiarize himself with the current state of inter-ethnic relations in the country.
5 June 1997	The OSCE Permanent Council decides to provide for the opening of two field offices to the OSCE Mission to Tajikistan in Garm and Khujand.
6-8 June 1997	The OSCE HCNM visits Kyrgyzstan, where he meets with members of the government and attends a workshop on inter-ethnic tolerance in the Osh region.
27 June 1997	The general agreement on the establishment of peace and national accord in Tajikistan is signed. The parties request the United Nations assistance in the implementation of the agreement. The OSCE Mission to Tajikistan becomes a signatory to the protocol on the guarantees of implementation of the agreement.
12 September 1997	The UN Security Council takes the decision to expand the size of UNMOT.
16 October 1997	ODIHR signs a memorandum of understanding with the government of Uzbekistan, which includes a commitment to implement several projects in the field of democratization and human rights.
23 October 1997	CIS council of heads of state and government in Chisinau on a draft agreement on a common agrarian market
February 1998	The OSCE Mission to Tajikistan becomes an adviser to the Commission for National Reconciliation (CNR).
23 February 1998	The President of Turkmenistan, Saparmurat Niyazov, visits NATO headquarters.
April 1998	The OSCE CiO, Bronisław Geremek, visits all five Central Asian States.
29 April 1998	CIS council of heads of state in Moscow on improvement of the CIS's activity and military co-operation
May 1998	UN Secretary-General, Kofi Annan, appoints Jan Kubiš from Slovakia as a resident Special Representative and Head of Mission of UNMOT.
May 1998	The PCA between the EU and Turkmenistan is signed.
1-2 June 1998	The OSCE HCNM visits Uzbekistan.
20 July 1998	Four members of UNMOT are murdered.
23 July 1998	The Permanent Council establishes the OSCE Centres in Almaty, Ashgabad and Bishkek.
September 1998	OSCE Secretary General, Giancarlo Aragona, visits Uzbekistan.
16-21 November 1998	An ODIHR needs assessment mission visits Kazakhstan to assess the conditions and level of preparation for the presidential election scheduled for 10 January 1999. The

	mission concludes that Kazakhstan does not meet OSCE election related commitments in the pre-election process and, based on these findings, the ODIHR decides not to launch a full-scale election observation mission, but rather a limited election assessment mission.
1998	Tajikistan joins the CAEU.
10 January 1999	An election assessment mission, consisting of 15 experts, observes the presidential election in Kazakhstan to give a general evaluation of the election. The mission finds that the election process falls far short of the standards to which Kazakhstan, as an OSCE participating State, has committed itself.
28 January 1999	The president of the Kyrgyzstan, Askar Akaev, gives an address to the Permanent Council of the OSCE.
January 1999	The OSCE Centres in Almaty, Ashgabat and Bishkek start their work.
February 1999	A decision of the Interstate Council of Belarus, Kazakhstan, Kyrgyzstan and Russia, within the CIS framework, recognizes Tajikistan as a participant of the customs union.
12-20 February 1999	Helle Degn, President of the OSCE PA, visits Kazakhstan, Kyrgyzstan, Uzbekistan and Turkmenistan.
1 July 1999	The PCAs between the EU and Kazakhstan, Kyrgyzstan and Uzbekistan enter into force.
8 July 1999	The minister for foreign affairs of Uzbekistan, Abdulaziz Kamilov, gives an address to the Permanent Council of the OSCE.
28 September – 4 October 1999	OSCE CiO, Knut Vollebaek, visits the Central Asian OSCE states, Turkmenistan, Uzbekistan, Tajikistan, Kyrgyzstan and Kazakhstan.
September 1999	UN Secretary-General, Kofi Annan, appoints Ivo Petrov from Bulgaria as a resident Special Representative and Head of Mission of UNMOT.
1 September 1999	An ODIHR election observation mission is established to monitor the pre-election preparations, the election campaign, and the media before the 10 October parliamentary elections in Kazakhstan. Linda Edgeworth is head of the long-term election observation mission.
14 October 1999	The foreign minister of Tajikistan, Talbak Nazarov, addresses the OSCE Permanent Council.
10 October 1999	The parliamentary elections in Kazakhstan are observed by the ODIHR and OSCE PA. The election observation mission concludes that the elections constitute a tentative step towards international standards, but fall short

	of the OSCE Copenhagen commitments. Ihor Ostash, Vice-President of the OSCE PA, leads the short-term observers as Special Representative of the OSCE CiO.
24 October 1999	The second round of parliamentary elections in Kazakhstan is observed by the ODIHR with a reduced number of observers compared to the first round. The election observation mission concludes that the elections constitute a tentative step towards international standards, but fall short of the OSCE commitments.
November 1999	ODIHR decides not to establish a regular election observation mission for the parliamentary elections in Uzbekistan scheduled for 5 December 1999. Instead, the ODIHR deploys a limited assessment mission of election experts. The assessment mission is headed by Ambassador Madeleine Wilkens of Sweden.
5 December 1999	The ODIHR limited election assessment mission evaluates that the parliamentary elections in Uzbekistan fall short of the OSCE Copenhagen commitments.
December 1999	ODIHR decides not to deploy an observation or limited assessment mission to Turkmenistan for the parliamentary elections scheduled for 12 December 1999. This decision is taken due to grave concerns that the broad electoral framework in Turkmenistan falls far short of the OSCE Copenhagen commitments.
25 January 2000	CIS council of heads of state and government in Moscow: a decision on counteracting international terrorism in the light of the OSCE Istanbul summit is adopted
February 2000	The field office to the OSCE Mission to Tajikistan in Khujand starts operating.
10 February 2000	The OSCE Permanent Council decides to establish an OSCE Field Office in Osh, Kyrgyzstan.
20 February 2000	An ODIHR election observation mission observes the parliamentary election in Kyrgyzstan. It concludes that the elections not are in full compliance with OSCE commitments.
24 February 2000	The President of the Republic of Kazakhstan Nursultan Nazarbayev gives an address to the Permanent Council of the OSCE.
27 February 2000	The United Nations and OSCE deploye a joint electoral observation mission (JEOM) to observe parliamentary elections in Tajikistan. Ambassador Zenon Kuchciak, Poland, heads the JEOMT. The mission notes the significance of the inclusion of former warring parties and others in the electoral process and the fact that Tajiki-

	stan had held its first multi-party election in an atmosphere free of violence. However, it also points out that the election did not meet minimum standards.
12 March 2000	An ODIHR election observation mission observes the second round of parliamentary election in Kyrgyzstan. It concludes that the elections not are in full compliance with OSCE commitments.
23 March 2000	The foreign minister of Kyrgyzstan Muratbek Imanaliew gives an address to the Permanent Council of the OSCE.
April 2000	The OSCE Field Office in Osh, Kyrgyzstan, starts its work.
April 2000	The CAEU member states, Kazakhstan, Uzbekistan, Kyrgyzstan and Tajikistan sign an agreement on co-operation in fighting terrorism, extremism and trans-border organized crime.
15 May 2000	UNMOT withdraws from Tajikistan.
20-21 June 2000	CIS council of heads of state and government in Moscow on joint efforts in the field of the struggle against international terrorism, other kinds of extremism, security and stability. A decision on the establishment of an Anti-terrorism Centre in Bishkek is adopted. After an appeal by Tajikistan, a decision is taken to cease functioning of the collective peace-keeping forces in this country and to launch their disband.
27 June 2000	The president of Kazakhstan, Nursultan Nazarbayev, visits NATO headquarters.
29 October 2000	An ODIHR election observation mission observes the presidential elections in Kyrgyzstan. It concludes that the election failed to comply with OSCE commitments.
30 November – 1 December 2000	CIS council of heads of state and government in Minsk takes a final decision on launching a full-range activity of the CIS Anti-terrorist Centre in Bishkek.
Datum? 2000	The Dushanbe Summit of the Shanghai Five is held.
25-26 April 2001	The OSCE Secretary General Kubiš visits Tajikistan.
29 April – 4 May 2001	The president of the OSCE Parliamentary Assembly (PA), Adrian Severin, visits Tajikistan, Kazakhstan and Kyrgyzstan. He presents a new OSCE PA initiative on a Trans-Asian Parliamentary Forum. Such a forum, which would be organized in the framework of the OSCE PA, is designed to bring together parliamentarians in the OSCE region, as well as those from the Asian partners for co-operation, in order to discuss various developments in Central Asia.

31 May – 1 June 2001	CIS council of heads of state and government in Minsk
4-8 June 2001	The OSCE CiO, Mircea Dan Geoana, visits Kazakhstan, Kyrgyzstan, Tajikistan and Turkmenistan. He stresses the importance of a regional approach to tackle the problems of extremism, trafficking in drugs, weapons, human beings, and the growth of extremist movements.
14 June 2001	The OSCE CiO announces the appointment of Wilhelm Höynck, as his Personal Representative for Central Asia.
15 June 2001	On the fifth anniversary of the Shanghai Five, the heads of state of its members and the president of Uzbekistan meet in Shanghai, and sign a joint declaration admitting Uzbekistan as member of the Shanghai Five mechanism and issuing the founding declaration on the establishment of the Shanghai Cooperation Organization (SCO). They also sign the Shanghai convention against terrorism, separatism and extremism.
17-28 June 2001	Ambassador Wilhelm Höynck, Personal Representative of the OSCE CiO for Central Asia visits the region.
14 September 2001	SCO heads of government hold a meeting in Almaty to discuss regional economic co-operation and sign a memorandum on the basic objectives and orientation of regional economic co-operation.
19 October 2001	The minister for foreign affairs of Tajikistan, Nazarov, addresses the Permanent Council of OSCE.
22 October 2001	The OSCE CiO, Geoana, visits Uzbekistan.
29-30 November 2001	The 10th anniversary jubilee summit of the CIS is held in Moscow.
13-14 December 2001	The "Bishkek international conference on enhancing security and stability in Central Asia: strengthening comprehensive efforts to counter terrorism" is held in Kyrgyzstan. The conference is organized by the OSCE and the United Nations Office for Drug Control and Crime Prevention. It adopts a declaration and a programme of action.
7 January 2002	The ministers of foreign affairs of the member states of the SCO meet in Beijing.
28 February 2002	An agreement between Kazakhstan, Kyrgyzstan, Tajikistan and Uzbekistan establishes the Central Asia Cooperation Organization (CACO).
7 June 2002	The Heads of SCO member states meet in St. Petersburg and sign the SCO Charter, as well as the agreement on a counter-terrorism regional structure.

17-18 June 2002	OSCE Secretary General, Kubiš, visits Tajikistan.
8-9July 2002	The OSCE CiO, Antonio Martins da Cruz, visits Kyrgyzstan and Tajikistan.
October 2002	China and Kyrgyzstan conduct a bilateral joint anti-terrorism military exercise within the SCO framework.
29 October – 1 November 2002	The CiO of the OSCE, Martins da Cruz, visits Kazakhstan, Uzbekistan and Turkmenistan
31 October 2002	The OSCE Permanent Council renames the Mission to Tajikistan "OSCE Centre in Dushanbe".
6-7 October 2002	CIS council of heads of state and government and CIS council of foreign ministers in Chisinau
17 December 2002	The OSCE Academy in Bishkek is inaugurated in Kyrgyzstan.
December 2002	In view of conflicting reports on the circumstances surrounding the 25 November assassination attempt on Turkmenistan's President, Saparmurat Niyazov, and the way the investigation was being conducted, a group of ten OSCE States invoked the Organization's Moscow Mechanism. Ten States appoint Emmanuel Decaux, professor of international law at the university of Paris, to look into all human dimension matters relating to the conduct of the Turkmenistan investigations following the assassination attempt and the circumstances surrounding it.
February 2003	An international fact-finding mission established in December 2002 by the Moscow Mechanism to examine the investigations by the Turkmen authorities of the assassination attempt on President Niyazov begins its work.
13 March 2003	The OSCE CiO, Jaap de Hoop Scheffer, formally announces the appointment of Martti Ahtisaari as his Personal Envoy for Central Asia.
22-24 March 2003	The Personal Envoy of the OSCE CiO for Central Asia, Ahtisaari, visits Kyrgyzstan and Tajikistan.
29 April 2003	SCO council of ministers of foreign affairs in Almaty
April 2003	The OSCE HCNM, Rolf Ekeus, visits Kyrgyzstan
18-29 May 2003	The OSCE CiO's Personal Envoy for Central-Asia, Ahtisaari, visits Kyrgyzstan, Uzbekistan, Tajikistan and Turkmenistan.
May 2003	The permanent representatives to the OSCE of Bulgaria, France, Ireland, Norway and Sweden visit Kyrgyzstan, Kazakhstan and Tajikistan.
7-9 June 2003	The president of the OSCE PA, Bruce George, visits Kazakhstan, where he chairs the first Trans-Asian Par-

	liamentary Forum. More than 90 parliamentarians from 25 OSCE participating States take part in the two day forum on "The Trans-Asian Dimension of the OSCE: a Vital Security Link".
7-10 June 2003	The director of ODIHR, Christian Strohal, visits Kazakhstan and Kyrgyzstan. In Kazakhstan, he addresses the Trans-Asian Parliamentary Forum. Strohal also visits Sergei Duvanov, a Kazakh journalist and human rights defender who was sentenced to several years in prison, earlier that year, following a trial that was characterized as seriously flawed by observers.
9-10 June 2003	The president of the OSCE PA, Bruce George, visits Kyrgyzstan.
7-11 July 2003	The OSCE CiO, de Hoop Scheffer, visits Kazakhstan, Uzbekistan, Kyrgyzstan and Tajikistan.
18 September 2003	The OSCE CiOmeets with the deputy prime minister and foreign minister of Turkmenistan, Rashid Meredov, at UN headquarters in New York. Human rights, exit travel legislation, and full access by the International Committee of the Red Cross to Turkmen prisons are among the issues discussed.
18-19 September 2003	CIS council of heads of state and government and CIS council of foreign ministers in Yalta
23 September 2003	SCO council of heads of government in Beijing adopts a plan for multilateral economic and trade cooperation of the SCO member states
16 December 2003	The European Commission opens negotiations with Tajikistan for a PCA.
15-19 March 2004	EU Commissioner Chris Patten visits Kazakhstan, Tajikistan, Kyrgyzstan and Uzbekistan.
5-9 April 2004	The OSCE CiO, Solomon Passy, visits all five Central Asian republics.
10-13 May 2004	The Personal Envoy of the OSCE CiO for Central Asia, Ahtisaari, visits Tajikistan. At his meeting with president Rahmonov, one of the issues discussed is the 2005 parliamentary elections in Tajikistan.
10-12 June 2004	The OSCE CiO's Personal Envoy for Central Asia, Ahtisaari, visits Kyrgyzstan and Turkmenistan.
21-24 June 2004	ODIHR undertakes a needs assessment mission (NAM) to Kazakhstan to assess the conditions and level of preparation for the parliamentary elections scheduled for 19 September 2004 and to advise on modalities for the establishment of an EOM. The NAM recommends that an EOM be established.

6-7 September 2004	The OSCE Secretary General Kubiš visits Tajikistan, Uzbekistan
19 September 2004	An EOM consisting of ODIHR, OSCE PA and the Parliamentary Assembly of the Council of Europe observes the parliamentary elections in Kazakhstan. US Ambassador Robert Barry is head of the ODIHR EOM. The Mission reports serious shortcomings and states that the election process falls short of the OSCE commitments and other international standards for democratic elections in many respects.
22 September 2004	An ODIHR NAM visits Uzbekistan before the legislative chamber elections of 26 December are published. The NAM recommends that a limited election observation mission be established to observe the elections.
18 October 2004	CACO council of heads of states in Dushanbe admitts Russia to the organization
24-25 November 2004	Rolf Ekeus, the OSCE HCNM, visits Tajikistan. During the visit he focuses on issues such as language, education and representation in the public life of the country.
29-30 November 2004	The OSCE CiO's Personal Envoy for Central Asia, Ahtisaari, visits Kyrgyzstan.
13-15 December 2004	The OSCE HCNM, visits Turkmenistan. He discusses a possible assessment of the living conditions of the national minorities in the country, education as a means of integration into society and comprehensive development of the dialogue between the OSCE and Turkmenistan with government officials.
3 February 2005	The OSCE CiO, Slovenian foreign minister Dimitrij Rupel, appoints seven members of a Panel of Eminent Persons. At the Ministerial Council in Sofia, the foreign ministers of the OSCE participating States agreed to appoint such a Panel to review the effectiveness of the Organization, its bodies and structures and provide an assessment in view of the challenges ahead. One of the members of the Panel is Kuanysh Sultanov from Kazakhstan.
15-16 February 2005	The OSCE CiO visits Kazakhstan and Uzbekistan.
22 February 2005	The OSCE CiO appoints Alojz Peterle as his Personal Representative for Central Asia.
27 February 2005	An EOM from ODIHR observes the parliamentary elections in Tajikistan. It is headed by Peter Eicher of the United States and concludes that the election fails to meet many OSCE commitments.

27 February 2005	An EOM from ODIHR, OSCE PA and the European Parliament observes the parliamentary elections in Kyrgyzstan. It concludes that the election falls short of OSCE commitments.
9 March 2005	Robert Simmons, the NATO Secretary General's Special Representative for the Caucasus and Central Asia, visits Kazakhstan and Uzbekistan.
15-19 March 2005	EU external relations commissioner, Chris Patton, travels to Central Asia and meets with the representatives of the governments of Kazakhstan, Tajikistan, Kyrgyzstan and Uzbekistan.
17 March 2005	The OSCE CiO discusses the Organization's role in Central Asia with the president of Uzbekistan, Karimov.
21 March 2005	The OSCE CiO, Rupel, urges all sides to engage in a dialogue to defuse the tension over the post-election situation in Kyrgyzstan.
21 March 2005	UN Secretary General, Kofi Annan, expresses concern over escalation in Southern Kyrgyzstan.
22 March 2005	The OSCE CiO offers the Organization's assistance in ending tension to the president of Kyrgyzstan, Akayev.
23 March 2005	OSCE Troika urges parties in Kyrgyzstan to refrain from violence.
24 March 2005	The OSCE CiO's Personal Representative for Central Asia, Peterle, arrives in Bishkek for talks with government and opposition leaders, which he hopes will help achieve an easing of political tensions.
25 March 2005	EU High Representative for the Common Foreign and Security Policy, Javier Solana, expresses support to the OSCE mission in Bishkek and OSCE CiO's Special Representative for Central Asia.
29 March 2005	The EU commissioner for external relations and European neighbourhood policy, Ferrero-Waldner, makes a statement on the political situation in Kyrgyzstan in which she appeals to all parties of the conflict to respect the fundamental principles of the EU-Kyrgyz PCA.
30 March 2005	The EU Council of Ministers makes a declaration on the political situation in Kyrgyzstan in which it calls on the new leadership to restore public order and welcomes the decision of the Kyrgyz parliament to organize presidential elections within the next three months and parliamentary elections within six months.
18 April 2005	The new political leadership in Kyrgyzstan discusses with the visiting OSCE CiO a joint OSCE-Kyrgyz work plan to help the country maintain stability.

20 April 2005	The OSCE CiO offers the Turkmen leadership help in boosting its participation in the Organization.
5 May 2005	Uzbekistan gives official notice of withdrawal from the organization GUUAM
8-9 May 2005	CIS summit in Moscow: the recent political changes in Ukraine, Georgia, and Kyrgyzstan are described as "coups"
14 May 2005	NATO Secretary General de Hoop Scheffer makes a statement on the situation in Uzbekistan.
15 May 2005	The OSCE CiO calls on Uzbek authorities to resolve the current situation with dialogue instead of use of force.
16 May 2005	UN Secretary General Annan deplores the outbreak of violence in Andijan, Uzbekistan and calls for cooperation with the UNHCR emergency team.
17 May 2005	Peterle, the Personal Representative of the OSCE CiO for Central Asia, meets with the Kyrgyz political leader, Felix Kulov, to discuss issues affecting the upcoming presidential elections, scheduled for 10 July.
17-18 May 2005	NATO Special Representative for the Caucasus and Central Asia Simmons visits the Kyrgyz Republic.
20 May 2005	The Head of the OSCE Centre in Tashkent, Ambassador Miroslav Jenca, appeals to the Uzbek government to allow international involvement in the investigation of the Andijan events.
30 May 2005	Kyrgyzstan's acting president, Kurmanbek Bakiev, addresses a special session of the OSCE Permanent Council in Vienna on May 30.
13 June 2005	The OSCE-facilitated agreement commits Kyrgyz presidential contenders to a fair election campaign.
15 June 2005	The OSCE Representative for Freedom of the Media issues a report on work of the media during the Andijan crisis in Uzbekistan.
16 June 2005	The OSCE CiO, Rupel, welcomes pledges of 670,000 Euro for a police assistance programme in Kyrgyzstan.
16 June 2005	A team from the Office of the United Nations High Commissioner for Human Rights (UNHCR) arrives in Kyrgyzstan to look into events in Andijan, Uzbekistan.
17 June 2005	The OSCE Centre in Bishkek organizes a national forum to draw up a new economic programme for Kyrgyzstan.
20 June 2005	The OSCE CiO repeats calls for an investigation into Andijan events following the OSCE/ODIHR report.
22 June 2005	UN Secretary General Annan expresses his serious concern about the fate of Uzbek asylum seekers in Kyr-

	gyzstan and, in particular, reports on their possible forced deportation to Uzbekistan.
23 June 2005	The special rapporteur of the UN Commission on Human Rights, Manfred Nowak, the chairperson-rapporteur of the working group on arbitrary detention, Leila Zerrouguï, and the Special Representative of the Secretary-General on human rights defenders, Jilani make a statement deploring actions of the Uzbek government in connection with the violent events in Andijan.
23 June 2005	The EU High Representative for the CFSP voices concern for the safety of Uzbek refugees in Kyrgyzstan and expresses his intention to dispatch his Personal Representative for Human Rights, Michael Matthiessen, to Kyrgyzstan to examine the situation of the refugees and hold consultations with the authorities of Kyrgyzstan.
23 June 2005	CIS council of heads of states of the Collective Security Treaty Organization in Moscow
24 June 2005	The OSCE CiO, Rupel, renews an appeal to Kyrgyzstan to protect Uzbek asylum-seekers.
27 June 2005	UN Secretary General Annan asks acting president of Kyrgyzstan, Bakiev, to ensure that no further Uzbek asylum seekers are forcibly returned to Uzbekistan.
28 June 2005	In Brussels UN Secretary General Annan meets with US Secretary of State, Condoleezza Rice, and discusses the situation in Uzbekistan.
1 July 2005	The OSCE CiO, Rupel, expresses concern about the situation in Uzbekistan and the plight of Uzbek refugees in Kyrgyzstan, in talks with the US Secretary of State.
2 July 2005	The OSCE CiO calls for a comprehensive strategy to strengthen democracy and stability in the countries of Central Asia.
4 July 2005	At a news conference in Beijing the Secretary General of the SCO, Zhang Deguang, accuses terrorists of being behind the violent events in Andijan, Uzbekistan.
5 July 2005	At the Astana summit, the member states of the call for the US-led antiterrorist coalition forces to set a fixed deadline for their withdrawal.
11 July 2005	UN Secretary General Annan welcomes Kyrgyzstan's peaceful, credible presidential elections.
19 July 2005	The Cooperation Council between the EU and the republic of Kazakhstan holds its seventh meeting.
28 July 2005	UN Secretary General Annan calls on Kyrgyz authorities to facilitate the evacuation of Uzbek refugees and asylum-seekers.

28 July 2005	The Council of the EU appoints Jan Kubiš as new EU Special Representative for Central Asia.
29 July 2005	The OSCE Secretary General, Marc Perrin de Brichambaut, stresses the need to strengthen the relationship between the Organization and Uzbekistan in talks with president Karimov, and foreign minister Ganiyev.
8 August 2005	Deputy foreign minister of Russia, Dimitry Yakovenko, states the SCO is considering a pipeline project through the territory of Kyrgyzstan.
26 August 2005	Members of the senate of Uzbekistan unanimously vote for the withdrawal of the US military contingent from the country's territory. The senators justify their decision with the fact that the US airbase had been created only for the time of the active phase of the counterterrorism operation in Afghanistan.
27-29 August	CIS-summit where Russia presents a new cooperation agenda. Turkmenistan downgrades the status of its membership in the CIS to "associate member".
9 September 2005	Kubiš, EU special representative for Central Asia, meets with president Karimov in Tashkent. The meeting focuses on trade ties and shared security concerns.
3 October 2005	The Tajik parliament approves a memorandum of understanding between Tajikistan and the OSCE on the proliferation and supervision of small arms and conventional weapons.
3 October 2005	The EU imposes sanctions in reaction of Uzbekistan's refusal to allow an independent international investigation into the violent suppression of an uprising in the city of Andijan. EU resolves to reduce aid, suspends the PCA and imposes an arms embargo.
3 October 2005	NATO's special representative for the Caucasus and Central Asia, Simmons, announces that NATO will expand its use of the Ganci air base in Kyrgyzstan. NATO also plans to deepen its PfP program with Kyrgyzstan by providing technical assistance during the Kyrgyz defence budgetary process and by increasing the scale of training programs for Kyrgyz military personnel.
4 October 2005	NATO appoints Tugay Tuncer as NATO's special representative on communication and cooperation with Central Asian countries. The new NATO liaison will be based in Almaty and will supervise NATO relations with all countries in the region except Uzbekistan.

Contributors

Alisheva, Atyrkul (PhD) is currently the director of the Institute for Regional Studies (IFRS) in Bishkek (Kyrgyzstan). She has conducted field research in Kyrgyzstan focusing particularly on problems of ethnicity and religion, local self-governance bodies, irrigation and poverty. The IFRS is a non-governmental, non-commercial organization. It aims to coordinate the attempts of experts in various fields at more complete and in-depth research on the dynamics of Kyrgyzstan's social and political development, with the purpose of warning about and forecasting conflicts, and supporting education for the development of civil society.

Berg, Andrea is currently a senior researcher at the Institute of Peace Research and Security Policy at the University of Hamburg (Germany). She received her MA in political science at the Free University Berlin in 1997. Her MA thesis was entitled "Local Networks and Public Administration in Uzbekistan". Berg wrote her PhD thesis at the Institute of Oriental Studies at Ruhr-University in Bochum on "Global Concepts Versus Local Reality – A Study on NGOs in Uzbekistan". She has conducted extensive field research in Uzbekistan and has done consultancy work in Kyrgyzstan and Tajikistan in the past several years, focusing particularly on problems of security, democratization, education, gender issues and community development.

Beyer, Judith has studied cultural anthropology, public law and Slavonic studies at the University of Tübingen. During her studies, she focused on Central Asia and developed an interest in theories of transformation, legal anthropology and dispute management. Her master's thesis is entitled "Law in 'Transformation': The Rhetoric of the Constitutional Reform in Kyrgyzstan". Judith Beyer is currently associated with the Max Planck Institute for Social Anthropology in Halle/Saale, Germany, where she is preparing for her upcoming PhD fieldwork focusing on dispute management capacities of the courts of elders in Kyrgyzstan.

Geiss, Paul Georg is lecturer at the Department of Political Science at the University of Vienna and has extensively worked on the problem of political change in Central Asia. He graduated from the London School of Economics in 1996, held a PhD fellowship of the Austrian Academy of Science and previously worked as a research fellow at the German Institute of Middle East Studies in Hamburg. His publications include *Pre-Tsarist and Tsarist Central Asia. Communal Commitment and Political Order in Change (2003)*, *Nationenwerdung in Mittelasien* (Frankfurt 1995) and various articles on social history and politics in Central Asia.

Issenova, Sofiya has been working in international organizations in the field of promoting good governance, anti-corruption and transparent standards in government and business management in Kazakhstan for five years. Her master's thesis (Master in Law) "Economic Bases of Foundation and Development of Civil Society (Constitutional aspect)" was awarded "Best Student Research" in 1999. Issenova was a legal expert and the deputy director of the Anti-corruption Organization in Kazakhstan. She also graduated from the Eurasian Institute of Market with a diploma in "Economical and Legal Analysis of Corruption and Maladministration in Kazakhstan: Mechanisms of Prevention".

Kreikemeyer, Anna is currently a senior researcher at the Centre for OSCE Research (CORE) of the Institute of Peace Research and Security Policy (IFSH) at the University of Hamburg (Germany). She wrote her PhD thesis "Is Russia Capable of Peace? The Transformation of Russia and Its Role in a Pan-European Co-operation and Integration Process" at the Institute for Political Sciences at the University of Hamburg. She also worked in several research projects related to security problems in the former Soviet Union and published books and articles on the role of Russia in armed conflicts in the CIS area, as well as on the compatibility of Islam and security in Central Asia.

Myraunet, John is currently an executive officer at the Permanent Delegation of Norway to the OSCE. He is currently pursuing a masters in comparative politics at the University of Bergen. Myraunet received his *candidatus magisterii* at the University of Bergen in 2003 in comparative politics, European integration and German. He worked as a trainee at the Centre for OSCE Research at the Institute for Peace Research and Security Policy at the University of Hamburg in 2004.

Pikulina, Marina is the director of the S-Monitor Analytical Group in Tashkent (Uzbekistan). She received her MA in oriental sciences in 1984 from Tashkent State University. Since then, she has published extensively on different regional and national problems such as internal and external politics, economics, democracy and political Islam. One of her last reports is entitled "Social networks and decision-making processes in Uzbekistan". Pikulina is the Uzbekistan country coordinator of the FAST project of the Swiss Peace Foundation. Furthermore, she is the country coordinator of the CMCA Working Group in the Partnership for Peace Consortium of the Defence Academy and the Security Studies Institutes.

Satpayev, Dosym is the Director of the Assessment Risks Group (ARG) in Almaty (Kazakhstan). This NGO conducts research on the efficiency of state structures as well as of civil society, and analyses political and economic risks. Satpayev studied political science at the Almaty State University. Since the mid 1990s, he has been working with various organizations, such as IWPR and the Soros Foundation, mainly focusing on political and economic issues in Kazakhstan. He has published extensively on extremism, security and lobbyism in Central Asia.

Šimaitytė, Fausta is currently completing her degree in Political Science und Eastern European Studies at the University of Hamburg. During her studies, she has focused on security issues in Europe and on human rights in Russia, particularly in North Caucasus. Ms Šimaitytė has been working as a student research assistant at the Centre for OSCE Research (CORE) of the Institute of Peace Research and Security Policy (IFSH) at the University of Hamburg (Germany) since 2001.

Tolipov, Farkhod is an associate professor at the University of World Economy and Diplomacy in Tashkent (Uzbekistan), where he received his PhD in Political Science in 1997. His PhD thesis was titled "The Formation of the National Interest Conception of Uzbekistan in the Context of Global Political Development". His current post-doctoral research topic is "Geopolitical and Ideological Problems of the National Security of Uzbekistan in the Context of the New World Order". F. Tolipov is also affiliated with the Institute for Strategic Studies under the President of the Republic of Uzbekistan. He was a Fellow at Harvard University, Georgia University (USA), and the NATO Defense College in Rome, Italy.